Christian Mission in a Diverse British Urban Context

Crossing the Racial Barrier to Reach Communities

Johnson Ambrose Afrane-Twum

© 2024 Johnson Ambrose Afrane-Twum

Published 2024 by Langham Academic
An imprint of Langham Publishing
www.langhampublishing.org

Langham Publishing and its imprints are a ministry of Langham Partnership

Langham Partnership
PO Box 296, Carlisle, Cumbria, CA3 9WZ, UK
www.langham.org

ISBNs:
978-1-83973-875-3 Print
978-1-83973-954-5 ePub
978-1-83973-955-2 PDF

Johnson Ambrose Afrane-Twum has asserted his right under the Copyright, Designs and Patents Act, 1988 to be identified as the Author of this work.

All rights reserved. No part of this publication may be reproduced, stored in a retrieval system or transmitted, in any form or by any means, electronic, mechanical, photocopying, recording or otherwise, without the prior written permission of the publisher or the Copyright Licensing Agency.

Requests to reuse content from Langham Publishing are processed through PLSclear. Please visit www.plsclear.com to complete your request.

Scripture quotations are from the New King James Version (NKJV). Copyright © 1982 by Thomas Nelson, Inc. Used by permission. All rights reserved.

British Library Cataloguing-in-Publication Data
A catalogue record for this book is available from the British Library

ISBN: 978-1-83973-875-3

Cover & Book Design: projectluz.com

Langham Partnership actively supports theological dialogue and an author's right to publish but does not necessarily endorse the views and opinions set forth here or in works referenced within this publication, nor can we guarantee technical and grammatical correctness. Langham Partnership does not accept any responsibility or liability to persons or property as a consequence of the reading, use or interpretation of its published content.

For decades, perhaps even centuries, the British church has been blessed by the gift of diverse peoples sent here by God from around the world. However, to our shame, such Christian siblings have not always been understood, received, and welcomed as that God-given gift. Research on how the church, both locally and institutionally, can engage across cultural and ethnic boundaries in all directions is vital to changing this profoundly unchristian reality. Rev. Dr. Afrane-Twum has done us a great service by presenting his research in this important book which will add real substance to our knowledge and wisdom about how best to be an intercultural church engaging in God's mission in Britain.

Nigel Rooms, PhD
Leader,
Partnership for Missional Church UK, Church Mission Society

African Christianity in British diaspora has come a long way from being on the fringes of society to becoming mainstream. In line with this development has been the plethora of literature on African Christianity and mission written by Africans themselves, therefore developing robust scholarship that offers insights and critique of African mission. This is where the work of Rev. Dr. Johnson Ambrose Afrane-Twum becomes significant, offering us insights on how the African immigrant churches need to develop a model of mission theology that transforms life and the necessity for them to collaborate with white majority churches. In exploring the latter, Rev. Dr. Afrane-Twum develops a form of intercultural ecumenism that could advance the course of the gospel in the UK. I would recommend this textbook to theological faculties and students who are interested in understanding African Christianity in the UK.

Israel Oluwole Olofinjana, PhD
Founding Director, Centre for Missionaries from the Majority World
Director, One People Commission Evangelical Alliance

Contents

Foreword ix

Preface xiii

Acknowledgements xvii

Abbreviations xix

Chapter 1 1
  Introduction
    1.1. Problem Statement 3
    1.2. Purpose of the Study 5
    1.3. Central Theoretical Argument 5
    1.4. Literature Review 6
    1.5. Methodology 9
    1.6. Ethical Considerations 15
    1.7. Classification of Headings/Chapters 16
    1.8. Concept Clarification 17

Chapter 2 19
  The History of the African Immigrant Churches in the UK
    2.1. Introduction 19
    2.2. The Migration Pattern of Immigrants from sub-Saharan
        Africa in the UK 23
    2.3. How the African Immigrant Churches Emerged and
        Gained Landscape in the UK 26
        2.3.1. African Migrants and the Micro-Melting Pots in
              the UK Cities 29
        2.3.2. Finding a Refuge from Discrimination, and
              Discovering a Sense of Identity, Respect, and Belonging 33
    2.4. Summary 35

Chapter 3 39
  Theological Analysis of the African Immigrant Churches in the UK
    3.1. Introduction 39
    3.2. Theology and its Contexts 41
        3.2.1. Black Theology in Context 44
        3.2.2. The Theology of the African Immigrant Churches 49
    3.3. Theologizing within the Multicultural Context of Britain 57

  3.4. Developing a Biblical Theological Basis and Hermeneutics for the African Immigrant Churches in the UK 64
  3.5. Summary 73

Chapter 4 79
 Findings and Implications
  4.1. Introduction 79
  4.2. Case Study Selection 81
  4.3. History, Structure, Vision, and Practices of the Four Case Study Churches 81
   4.3.1. All Nations Church, Wolverhampton 81
   4.3.2. The Ethiopian Church London 84
   4.3.3. The Church of Pentecost of Ghana in UK 86
   4.3.4. The Baptist Church, Harborne, Birmingham 89
  4.4. Vision and Values 93
   4.4.1. Causes of Disagreements among Christ's People 97
   4.4.2. Leadership Style 102
   4.4.3. Worship and Liturgy 108
   4.4.4. The Emphases of the Spirit and Power of the Holy Spirit 112
   4.4.5. The Existential Concerns of the Next Generation 116
  4.5. Summary 119

Chapter 5 125
 The African Immigrant Church and its Implications for Missio Dei
  5.1. Introduction 125
  5.2. The African Immigrant Church as an Instrument for God's Mission to Britain 131
   5.2.1. The Theology of Migration and the African Immigrant Church 133
   5.2.2. Embracing Both Divine and Human Activities Across Cultures 138
  5.3. *Missio Dei* as a Basis for Unity in Diversity 144
  5.4. Summary 149

Chapter 6 153
 Crossing the Racial Boundary to Reach non-Africans
  6.1. Introduction 153
  6.2. Causes of Disagreement among Christians 155
  6.3. Sensitivity to Each Other's Culture 160
  6.4. Mission-Minded Leadership 165

    6.5. The Church of Pentecost's Experience in Cross-Cultural
        Ministry 170
    6.6. Summary 172

Chapter 7 179
   A Model of Christian Mission
    7.1. Introduction 179
    7.2. Creating a Mission Rooted in God's Divine Initiative 180
    7.3. Servant Leadership 183
    7.4. The African Immigrant Churches Regarding the Wider
        Community as Another Stage in their Mission to Britain 188
    7.5. Practical Reflection on a Model of Christian Mission 193
    7.6. Summary 195

Chapter 8 197
   Conclusions and Recommendations
    8.1. Conclusions 197
    8.2. Recommendations 204

Bibliography 207

Foreword

African Christians have become an important part of the religious landscape of the United Kingdom. As a result, whenever we talk about Christians in the UK, (or UK Christians, to be precise), we must also have in mind the many African Christians who have made the UK their home – and "African" here includes those of the first African forced diaspora who have come to the UK from the West Indies. Ever since the late 1940s and 1950s, when the Windrush generations of African Caribbeans came to the UK in large numbers, and the 1960s and 70s, when migration from Africa to the UK began to accelerate, black Majority Churches have become a permanent feature in the UK. African Christians have played a significant role in the shaping of the faith across the country. There is not a major city in the UK that lacks at least a handful of African churches, be they Nigerian, Ghanaian, Zimbabwean, or many other African nationalities. In some cities, Africans are the most visible Christians – they are seen as they attempt to evangelize others on the high street, or in their many churches that have virtually mushroomed across the country since the 1980s or, indeed, in their loud and often in-your-face expression of their faith; their dressing, worship, and prayers. Of course, the list of the largest congregations in the UK is dominated by African megachurches, including Matthew Ashimolowo's Kingsway International Christian Centre (KICC) and Alex Omokudu's Victorious Pentecostal Assembly (VPA). In London, for instance, the city that drew Johnson's attention to the research that informs this book and is home to both KICC and VPA, a majority of the Christians who attend church on any given Sunday are of African or African Caribbean heritage. Without them, London would be a lot more secular than it currently is.

This African imprint on London Christianity is so significant that a riddle is often heard stating that "London's revivals are manufactured in Lagos." Some have said, "as far as Christianity is concerned, as Lagos goes, so does London." Of course, a great deal of London Christianity responds to and follows the trends happening in Lagos, Accra, Nairobi, Kinshasa, Johannesburg, and many other African cities. A young Nigerian man from SPAC Nation in London once interjected in my seminar to say, "Why are you not simply telling it as it is? London Christianity is becoming black!" I would not be so bold as to make that assertion. However there is no denying that African Christians are quite visible and play a significant role in London. Of course, London is not alone in its connection to African Christianity. African Christians have started many churches in all major cities in the West. Thus this growing presence of African Christians in the UK is but a small part of the seismic changes going on in the Christian community worldwide. We are living in a historical moment when the African church is once again rising to shape the course of Christianity. By virtue of the spiritual revival that has happened in the continent in the past 60 years, and due to the fact that Africans are currently the most mobile society in the world, African Christians have taken their faith to all countries. Just like it happened before the rise of Islam, Christians from North Africa (Egypt and the Maghreb) crossed the Mediterranean Sea and shaped a great deal of the history of Christianity and theology, it is today possible that we are seeing the beginning of something significant.

The question that Johnson wrestles with in this book is this: now that African Christians are established here in the UK, how can they partner with local British congregations to be effective in their work of mission and evangelism? Just like any church anywhere in the world, African churches in the diaspora need to do this to engage in mission beyond their own communities. While this may seem a contextually focused question (and as a doctoral research question, it had to be narrow and direct) it has wider implications for our understanding and practice of mission in the UK in the 21st century. The issues he discusses have ramifications beyond the African churches in the UK. The youth riots that were a lightbulb moment for Johnson in 2011 affected more communities than just those of Africans in London, Birmingham, and other cities. Asians, Latin Americans, and all other non-Western migrant Christian communities in the UK face similar issues. He could easily ask,

"How can foreign Christians living in the UK partner with local Christians for the sake of mission?"

To the rest of us, therefore, the implications of Johnson's question are enormous. We learn from him how Africans are trying to make sense of their new context of mission and how they can build cross-cultural relationships that will enable them to reach non-Africans with the gospel. Of course, African Christian leaders have a lot to learn from this book. However the outcomes of his research speak to the wider mission community in the UK, in Europe, and in the West. Missionally speaking Johnson is asking, now that we have cultural diversity in the Christian community, what shall we do with it? This is one of the key questions that we all, as Christians living in the UK, need to reflect upon.

The mission of God in the UK and beyond only will be effective if all Christians in the country, both indigenous and foreign, are enabled to participate. The future of British Christianity depends on this. We pray the message of this book moves us in the right direction.

Harvey C. Kwiyani, PhD
CEO, Global Connections, UK

Preface

There was a youth riot in 2011 in which young people from diverse backgrounds battled with the law enforcement agencies and brought unrest in some UK cities. Having witnessed this civil unrest, I was struck with the realization that all church leaders – regardless of ethnicity – must come together to look for new ways of encouraging their communities to embrace the gospel message which, I believe, has life transforming power.

Today, migration has changed the demography of Britain's urban cities. For example, London, Birmingham, Manchester, and Glasgow have now become multiethnic cities with multicultural identities. The migration of people from different ethnicities and nationalities presents opportunities and challenges to the society and the Christian mission in the UK.

As a result of mass migration into the UK, churches such as the African immigrant churches, amongst others, have emerged and gained a Christian landscape in the country. The migrant churches have created spiritual awakening in their host nation resulting in a tremendous awareness of spirituality spreading through their mission endeavours to revive British Christianity. Some Christian leaders attribute the emergence of migrant churches as divine providence. This is true for the simple reason that British Christianity for the past decades has experienced significant decline in attendance and appear to have lost their God-given vision on their day-to-day Christian endeavours. The migrant churches have enabled their members to discover a sense of identity, respect, and belonging. However, they need to work harder in more creative ways and in partnership with the white majority churches to create a society that models the values of the kingdom of God. Yet it is still not certain how these emerging churches could reach out to the wider community of the United Kingdom.

The first step I believe the emerging church and the professing church should take is to understand that both churches agree on winning souls to Christ, but they are both the subject of cultural change in the country. Hence they must commit themselves to building the spiritual relationship of mutual love and trust, working together as people Christ has called and commissioned for kingdom goals. Understandably, for any meaningful cross-cultural ministry initiative, both sides have to deal with their cultural biases. They have to realize that the need for working together as Christ's people is a call of God. So achieving the highest goals of the kingdom of God should be their goal as people of God with a mission. Just imagine what would happen in the communities of Britain if Christians from diverse backgrounds are empowered and encouraged by their churches to invest themselves fully in propagating the gospel across cultures.

This book therefore explores how the African immigrant churches in the UK could partner with the white majority churches for a more effective sharing of the gospel in the multicultural context of the UK. The study argues that for the African immigrant churches to fulfil their God-given mandate in the UK, they would have to work with the white majority churches. African Christians must consider the wider community as another stage in their mission endeavours to the United Kingdom as they reach out to the communities with an expanded vision of God's whole heart for the uttermost part of the world in line with biblical pattern of Acts 1:8.

However this poses a serious challenge to the African Christian and the host Christian, as it is obvious that there are cultural differences that in a way have kept them apart. This book has explored ways through which both sides could challenge the aspects of their culture and cultural influences on theology, which are not in line with biblical principles, and enter a partnership of mutual respect which could result in creating multi-cultural ministries serving as an alternative to the cultural relativism seen today. This partnership would lead into creating a platform which would be tremendous in sharing the gospel, leading Christ's people, making disciples, and modelling the love of Christ, with a greater impact in British communities. The migrant Christian and the host Christian can come together to play an important role in transforming Britain's communities.

Acknowledgements

I would like to thank all those who have made it possible for me to undertake this study. I am very grateful to my two promoters, and the GST and NWU administration members of staff for their understanding and endless support.

I am extremely grateful to all the church ministers who allowed me unrestricted access into their churches.

Thanks also to my friend, Dr. Harvey Kwiyani, for the encouragement I received from him during the early stages of my work.

Finally, I would like to express my gratitude to my family for their love, support, and encouragement.

Abbreviations

ANC	All Nations Church
COP	Church of Pentecost of Ghana in the UK
HBC	Harborne Baptist Church
ECL	The Ethiopian Church, London
PAUKE	Pentecostal Association of UK and Eire
GCF	Ghana Christian Fellowship
ACF	African Christian Fellowship
PIWC	Pentecost International Worship Centre

CHAPTER 1

Introduction

This study combines my interests in missiology and the study of the "black church" in the UK. It is about the role that African immigrant churches can play in the twenty-first century context of mission in the UK. Frankly, African immigrant churches play a vital role in the everyday lives of black communities across the UK. However, this study argues that these African immigrant churches can also play a very important role in the wider UK community as well, and in so doing, help transform Britain.

There was an influx of migrants from the sub-Saharan countries to the UK in the past few decades. The independence of the sub-Saharan countries like Ghana, Nigeria, Kenya, Zambia, Malawi, and others from the British colonial rule in the 1950s and beyond, led to diplomatic corps, students and refugees migrating to the UK. In a similar fashion, the latter part of the twentieth century and the twenty-first century also saw immigrants from the sub-Saharan countries coming to the UK to fill positions in the UK job sectors. Some immigrants also came as students to further their education.[1] Upon arrival in the UK, most of these migrants first tried to join congregations affiliated with the UK mainline denominations they belonged to in Africa. But they discovered that the UK established churches were unwelcoming.[2]

These factors among many others led to the establishing of the African-led churches in the UK Christian landscape. One of the pioneer churches was the Church of the Lord, popularly known as *Aladura*. This was planted in South London in 1964, by the late Apostle Adejobi, a Nigerian migrant, and many

---

1. Kwiyani, *Sent Forth*, 78.
2. Olofinjana, ed. *Turning the Tables on Mission*, 121.

others followed and arguably, today, there is a proliferation of these churches in the UK Christian landscape.[3]

It is clear that the African immigrant churches are now established in the UK Christian landscape. But the congregations of these churches are mainly black Africans, yet, ideally churches should not seek to be organized primarily in terms of ethnicity as this distracts from the biblical principles of unity in diversity (Gal 3:28). However, there is also the argument that for some categories of people – such as recently arrived immigrants – ethnic churches are necessary to help in their integration into their new communities.[4]

Today, the greatest challenge facing the African immigrant churches is the need to develop a model of Christian mission that inspires and transforms life irrespective of members' background and how they can partner with the mainline UK churches for a more effective delivery of the gospel in the UK.[5] The study has argued that for the African immigrant churches to fulfil their God-given mandate in the UK they will have to work with the white majority churches. However, this poses a serious challenge to the African immigrant churches, as it is obvious that there are cultural differences that in a way have kept them apart. Yet, in partnering with each other, I believe both sides will be able to challenge the aspects of their culture and cultural influences on theology (Matt 15:6) that are not in line with biblical principles.[6]

In this study, therefore, I have sought a new way of how the African immigrant churches could work with the white majority churches to promote the gospel in the UK.

---

3. Olofinjana, *Reverse in Ministry and Mission*, 122.

4. McIntosh and McMahan are of the view that the migration of millions of people around the world is creating great challenges and opportunities and that the migration of people into urban centres and cities could lead to the creating of multi-ethnic churches, yet, they also accept that mono-ethnic churches will continue to be necessary for the recently arrived migrants and people with a high people-consciousness (McIntosh, and McMahan. *Being the Church in a Multi-ethnic Community*, 66–67).

5. After witnessing the 2011 youth riots in which young people from all backgrounds battled with the law enforcement agencies and brought about unrest in some UK communities, I was struck with the realization that all church leaders- regardless of colour-need to come together to look for new ways of encouraging their communities to embrace the gospel which, I believe, has life transforming power.

6. Lingenfelter argues: "it is only as Christians are motivated and inspired by the Holy Spirit and through the Word of God can they relate to one another within the structures of human society to accomplish the purpose of God" (Lingerfelter, *Leading Cross-Culturally: Covenant Relationships for Effective Christian Leadership*, 31).

1.1. Problem Statement

I am of the view that if the Great Commission (Matt 28:19–20), is to be fulfilled effectively in the UK, cultural and ethnic barriers will have to be crossed. Galatians 3:28 gives us a clear picture of being one in Christ. There is a harmonious relationship of give and take among Christ's people when they come together in fellowship, and this prevents the distinctions of race from hindering their fellowship. Christ's kingdom is meant to bring communion and belonging to Christ's people irrespective of their ethnic backgrounds. More so, in Revelation 7:9, the Bible gives us a clear picture of the fulfilment of the Great Commission. In this text, we see the redeemed out of all people groups throughout all human history standing before the Lord. That is not to say, the events in Revelation 7 do suggest that differences will be wiped out completely rather the diversity here reflects God's glory even further, in that God's people from different backgrounds are united in a common act of worship.

The African Christians must consider the wider community as another stage in their missions endeavour to the United Kingdom as they reach out with an expanded vision of God's whole heart for the uttermost parts of the world in line with the biblical pattern of Acts 1:8. In the Book of Acts, the Bible provides us with the understanding that the early Christians began fulfilling the Great Commission when the disciples started reaching out in Jerusalem. It must be noted that Jerusalem was the centre of Judaism. They took another step to reach out in Judea and Galilee, where people of their own kind lived. They then considered their next stage of Christian endeavour in Samaria, where people who were familiar with them lived. Finally, they reached out within the unreached peoples of other parts of the world. The Great Commission calls Christ's people, irrespective of their ethnic background, to measure their lives by this heavenly vision with its universal scope. The scope of this vision comes with an objective which has a specific task of reaching *all nations*. It is therefore right to say that it is the purpose of God that every human being would be reached with the gospel (1 Tim 2:4; 2 Pet 3:9).

The existing relationships between the white majority churches and the African immigrant churches have been cordial in some ways. For example, some white majority denominations such as the Salvation Army, the Methodist Church and the Church of England share the use of their places of worship with some African immigrant churches. Yet, for a more effective collaboration, I am of the view that there is the need for the African immigrant churches and the white majority churches to engage in cross-cultural ministries. Crofton Park Baptist Church in London is one of the few white majority churches that has a history of worshipping with people from all backgrounds;[7] so, there is much to learn from their experience. I am of the view that there is a strong case for further research into churches that are engaged in cross-cultural ministries.

In view of the above evidence, the research question that this study was asking is: How may the African immigrant churches effectively work with the white majority churches for a more effective sharing of the gospel in the UK?

This question is of great importance, as it is my opinion that if the African immigrant churches partner with the white majority churches, this could result in creating multi-ethnic churches.[8] The multi-ethnic congregations would then serve as alternative to the cultural relativism seen today, because of its diversity, hence would lead into creating a platform which would be tremendous in sharing the gospel, leading Christ's people, making disciples and modelling the love of Christ, with a greater impact in the British communities.

Further research questions that have arisen from this problem were:

- Why is it that despite the fact, that African immigrant churches profess and desire to be truly international and integrationist in their vision they, yet do not have many non-Africans among their congregations?
- How can the African immigrant churches, on a small scale, give hope to the wider population in the United Kingdom through offering a model of a transformed, fulfilled, and purposeful approach to living, in an increasingly secular social context?

---

7. Olofinjana ed,, *Turning the Tables on Mission*, 125.

8. The late missiologist Paul Hiebert (cited in McIntosh and McMahan, 27) defined a multi-ethnic church as "a church in which there is an attitude and practice of accepting people of all ethnic, class and national origins as equal and fully participating members and ministers in the fellowship of the church; and the manifestation of this attitude and practice by the involvement of people from different ethnic, social and national communities as members in the church."

1.2. Purpose of the Study

The main aim of this study was to explore how the African immigrant churches could partner with the white majority churches for a more effective sharing of the gospel within the multicultural context of the UK.

The objectives of this study were seen in their relationship with the research questions. My main objectives for writing this book were:

- To attempt to find ways through which the African immigrant churches could become more relevant in the UK landscape and contribute to creating a society that shows forth the kingdom of God.
- To explore ways through which the African immigrant churches could work with the non-African churches in the UK for a more effective sharing of the gospel.
- To attempt to explore ways of developing a model of Christian mission that inspires and transforms life regardless of one's ethnic background.
- To attempt to look for a new way of bringing about unity in diversity among Christ's people which might lead to creating multi-ethnic congregations.
- To make recommendations for the design and implementation of ideas expressed in relation to this work.

1.3. Central Theoretical Argument

The central theoretical argument of this research is that the African immigrant churches in the UK have enabled their members to find a refuge from discrimination and discover a sense of identity, respect and belonging, but they should work harder and in more creative ways in partnership with the white majority churches in the UK to create a society that models the values of the kingdom of God.

1.4. Literature Review

A literature review was carried out for me to place my investigations in the context of previous research. In recent years discussions on the black church in the UK have become of significant interest. Scholars such as Joe Aldred, Keno Ogbo, Anthony Reddie, Chigor Chike, M. and T. Phillips, Mark Sturge, Israel Olofinjana, Afe Adogame, Harvey Kwiyani and more recently Babatunde Adedibu have made major contributions to this field.

Chike documents how Africans have migrated to live in the UK in recent years, which has resulted in a proliferation of churches. Chike states that Africans brought with them a type of Christianity shaped by their own African roots. He makes mention of the fundamental Christian doctrines of these migrant churches; he explains the African Christian's views of doctrines such as "God," "Jesus Christ," and "Salvation" and explains further the meaning of African Christianity in contrast to the predominant expression of it in the Western society.[9] Chike's work is an attempt to explain African Christianity in the West, yet it falls short of how these churches could team up with the indigenous UK churches to influence UK communities.

Phillips and Phillips on the other hand, write about the first wave of immigration of Africans, mainly from the Caribbean to the UK in 1948 to the present. In their book entitled *Windrush*, they inform us of the changes in British social history in the 1950s which came because of the first West Indian immigrants in 1948 and resulted in the British society's categorisation of people into social groups which the country would have to carry forward into the 21st Century.[10] Phillips and Phillips's work provides a distinctive historical insight into what appears to be the first phase of black migrants coming to settle in the UK with their version of the gospel, but the focus of this work is mainly Caribbean hence has a limited scope since it does not address the issues of African originated churches in the UK.

Olofinjana claims in his *Reverse in Ministry* that there has been a shift in global Christianity from North to South and he attributes this to God's providence; he feels that it is God's providential time for Africans who first received the gospel from the West to now bring it back to them.[11] It is clear to say that Olofinjana's contributions to the writings of the black church, though

---

9. Chike, *African Christianity in Britain: Diaspora, Doctrine and Dialogue*, (Bloomington, IN: Author House, 2007).

10. M. Phillips and T. Phillips, *Windrush: The Irresistible Rise of Multiracial Britain*, (London: HarperCollins, 1991).

11. Olofinjana, *Reverse in Ministry and Mission: Africans in the Dark Continent of Europe*, (Milton Keynes, UK: Author House, 2010).

distinctive, yet is limited to the historical aspect of European missions in Africa in the past and the recent emergence of African originated churches in UK and Europe and the contributions of these migrant churches to British Christianity and society in general.

He went further to document in the new book he edited the experiences of contemporary missionaries from the southern part of the globe migrating to the UK for mission endeavours and occupying the UK Christian landscape.[12] In this work, he explores the growing connections and shared values that exist between migrant Christians in the UK and the indigenous British Christians. Olofinjana's work helps us to understand contemporary Christian mission and transcultural endeavours, to some extent.

Reddie adopted a new way in his work. Reddie outlines what appears to be a fresh vision for a new model of Christianity with insights from black theology. Reddie claims that a re-imagined black theology will enable Christianity in general, as well as black Christian faith to influence the world.[13] Reddie's work seeks to offer black people an empowerment through which white people and others may be inspired and act differently. However, it falls short of how Blacks, Whites and others could work together to advance the gospel in the UK.

Sturge has provided a significant contribution to the writings on the black churches by attempting to explore the black Christian faith in the UK.[14] However, in Sturge's work, it appears that not much attention was given to the contributions of the black churches to Christianity in the UK.

There has been a distinctive work done by Aldred and Ogbo. Aldred and Ogbo's work, to some extent, covers the key issues facing the black churches in the UK today and their uncertain future. They also tell us of the current challenges of the black churches and the need for "style and substance."[15] Their work, even though distinctive, still lacks scope and analysis as it is mainly historical and with a Caribbean perspective.

---

12. Olofinjana ed. *Turning the Tables on Mission*.

13. Reddie, *Working Against the Grain: Reimaging Black Theology in the 21st Century*. (London: Equinex, 2008).

14. Sturge, *Look What the Lord Has Done: An Exploration of Black Christian Faith in Britain*, (Milton Keynes, England: Scripture Union, 2005).

15. Aldred and Ogbo eds. *The Black Church in the 21st Century*, (London: Darton, Longman & Todd, 2001).

Adedibu in his recent work, has made a substantial contribution to reshape the black church with mainly a historical approach.[16] Adedibu's thesis and more recently his book present a historiography of black Christianity in the UK. In both works, Adedibu documents the richness and diversity of the mission endeavours of the black churches and explains their impact on British Christianity. He feels that the time is ripe for the black churches to assess themselves in line with their mission endeavours into the UK.[17]

Adedibu's work provides a general overview of the tremendous influence black churches' have in the UK and Western societies, but it has a limited scope as the emphasis is on the history and significance of Africa and African Caribbean Pentecostalism in the UK.

More recently, Kwiyani, in his book *Sent Forth: African Missionary Work in the West* has argued that the growing presence of African Christians in Europe and North America reflects the missionary work of Africans in the early church and in the first five centuries of the church (universal). According to Kwiyani, it would be fair to say that African immigrant Christians in the West signify the rise of the African missionary movement. But he also thinks that this missionary movement, which is in its early days, faces many challenges, the most powerful of which is racism. He suggests that God's preferred future for mission is a multicultural missionary movement, especially in the current context of cultural diversity in the West.[18] Clearly, Kwiyani's work is very distinctive, but lacks an explanation of how the African immigrant churches can partner with the non-African churches in the UK for a more effective delivery of the gospel.

Having reviewed the work of the above mentioned authors, it is clear, at least to me that there was still a gap in this area of study. To date, very little research work has focused specifically on how the African immigrant churches could partner with the non-African churches to bring about the change needed in Britain's communities. This research thus sought to explore how the African immigrant churches could work with the white majority churches,

---

16. Adedibu, "The Urban Explosion of Black Majority Churches: Their Origin, Growth, Distinctives and Contribution to British Christianity and Society", Potchefstroom: NWU (PhD Thesis), 2011.

17. Adedibu, *The Origin, Growth, Distinctives, and Contributions of Black Majority Churches to British Christianity*, (London: Wisdom Summit, 2012).

18. Kwiyani, *Sent Forth*.

to bring about unity in diversity among Christ's people, which might result in creating multi-ethnic congregations, which was the focus of this study.

1.5. Methodology

This study was done from an Evangelical Christian point of view. In writing this book, some of my initial emphasis was both historical and theological investigations into the historical developments of the African immigrant churches and their theological relevance in the UK. However, as time developed my emphasis shifted more clearly to a participant observation in qualitative methodology, in which I chose to investigate four denominations (two denominations with African roots in the UK and two white UK denominations that integrate Blacks). I believed the advantages of an in-depth study of four denominations rather than much wider sampling of denominations or churches was a fairer choice. My main concerns were to make sure that the right participants were chosen. This was the key factor I considered at the initial stages of the fieldwork I carried out in the four case study churches. My choice of the right participants helped to speed up the process of acceptance. It also enabled me to reach the various church leaders and gain valuable insight into the structure and activities of these churches.

The foundation of the methodology of this study was therefore, based on the main research question: "How may the African immigrant churches effectively work with the white majority churches for a more effective sharing of the gospel?" This research question inspired the choice of the general methodological framework for the study. Thus, the dialectics[19] that provide the framework of this study are as follows:

Having observed situations in the African immigrant churches in the UK, that raised questions in relation to the relevance of these churches in the UK landscape, I initially carried out a literature review into this area (see Section 1.2 above) and articulated the views of authors on the black church.

Thus, I started the primary research process with a literature review to learn more about what was already known and what gaps needed to be filled on this subject matter. Research work requires some evidence of reading, and

---

19. The "dialectic" used here means the art or practice of logic discussion as employed in investigating the truth of a theory or opinion (dictionary.reference.com/browse/dialectic).

a literature review provides the researcher with an awareness of the current state of knowledge on the subject matter, according to Driscoll.[20] A literature review, therefore, was carried out for me to place my investigation in the context of previous research and justify how I approached my investigation. I also used secondary data later in this work to provide evidence to help explain the findings of my study.

My reason for using historical investigation and theological analysis in my initial investigations was to engage with the fundamental questions of the historical developments of the African immigrant churches in the UK and to attempt to construct a theological praxis model for the African immigrant churches. In the UK, there was the perception that the black churches have a different theology termed as black theology[21]. Hence, it has become obvious that the African immigrant churches would need to re-define themselves in relation to the UK white churches and would need also to clarify their theology. I therefore explored the key elements of the theology of the African immigrant churches in a broader framework of a biblical theological basis.[22] According to Schreiter theological praxis could also comprise the different theological contexts. These theological contexts usually develop in response to the needs in certain local contexts. He also thinks theology in a local context could be developed from several factors.[23] He mentioned some factors that could influence the development of a theology in the local context as:

(i) situations where the existence of other theologies is already in place.
(ii) events within a particular community that presented themselves and called for a response.

---

20. Driscoll, *Introduction to Primary Research: Observations, Surveys, and Interviews*, 158.

21. Dr. Robert Beckford is one example of the scholars who ascribe theological meaning to 'Black Churches' in the UK. In his book, *Dread and Pentecostal: A Political Theology for Black Church in Britain*, Dr. Beckford asserts the need for black British theology of liberation for the black churches as opposed to what he terms as their black Christian theology which in his words comprises "church life, worship and witness." He also feels that the black churches are different in their theology from the UK mainline churches by their forms of worship and liturgy.

22. Biblical theology is an attempt to articulate the theology that the Bible contains as its writers addressed their particular settings (www.biblestudytools.com/dictionaries/biblical-theology.

23. Schreiter, *Constructing Local Theologies*, 32.

Ukpong asserted the need for Christ's people of all cultural backgrounds to realize that all forms of Christian expression have connections with the cultural context from which they originated.[24] Similarly, Bevans shared the view that there was no such thing as an all-embracing theology for the universal church today, and that theology was the way religion made sense in a particular local or cultural context.[25]

I argued that for the African immigrant churches to become relevant in the UK landscape, they would have to change their theology in line with Scripture, to suit the UK environment in which they operate and adapt to an ecclesiastical style that would be different from those practised in most churches in Africa. Therefore, in my theological construction on what could generally be accepted as a biblical theological basis for the African immigrant churches, I used the tools of biblical criticism and hermeneutics to consider texts particularly favoured by Bible scholars such as Stephen Bevans, Robert Schreiter, David Bosch, and David Hesselgrave. This, I believed would result in at least, a tentative conclusion concerning theology while constructing a model for a theological praxis for the African immigrant churches in the UK.

I continued my investigations by using participant observation in qualitative research as my main methodology for my fieldwork. I carried out investigations into four denominations in the UK: two with African roots, The Ethiopian Church and the Church of Pentecost of Ghana and two white UK denominations that integrate Blacks. Examples of these are Harborne Baptist Church, Birmingham, a congregation in fellowship with the Baptist Union of Great Britain and All Nations Church, Wolverhampton, a congregation in fellowship with the World Assemblies of God Fellowship.

The data of participant observation in qualitative research is most often people's words and actions and so I collected data through face-to-face, in-depth interviews and participant observation of group and leadership meetings, leadership interviews including probing, chatting, and interviewing church members during church activities in the churches mentioned above. According to Maykut and Morehouse[26] this method of gathering data is the

---

24. Ukpong, "Towards a Holistic Approach to Inculturation Theology," 109.

25. Bevans, *Models of Contextual Theology*, 7.

26. Maykut and Morehouse, *Beginning Qualitative Research: A Philosophical and Practical Guide*, 45–46.

most useful way of data collection in participant observation in qualitative research.[27] I carried out my investigations of the participating churches from their own perspective and within the context of their living experience (the churches investigated were in London and the West Midlands region of the United Kingdom). I had the opportunity to talk to the participants, ask questions, while learning from them by observing and participating in their church activities. I also collected observation data in the form of field notes and audiotaped interviews, which were later used in analysing data.

I adopted different approaches in gathering data but relied heavily on the use of in-depth interviewing for collecting data.[28] I believed that this approach of using in-depth interviewing, was the best way of encouraging interviewees to come out whole-heartedly with their views. This approach could be used also to explore interesting areas for further research hence it was fairer than using a questionnaire and a more structured interview.

In interviewing the four denominational leaders (this took place in their various church environments), a checklist was prepared to make sure that all relevant areas were covered in the interviews. Questions on the checklist were covered on how the beliefs, values and practices of the case study churches fell into the outlined aims and objectives of this study. This type of interview was useful in the sense that I could still probe further during the interview by exploring questions deemed useful to the study as these could be done within the boundaries of the aims and objectives of the study.

I also used in-depth interviewing or unstructured interviewing to collect data during activities in the case study churches by engaging participants in chats and asking questions which came from the immediate context; this I believed was useful for exploring other topics for investigations. By conducting in-depth interviewing, in an open situation (as described above), there was the likelihood that new research directions could emerge from the use of techniques such as probing.

---

27. According to DeWalt B. & K this method of gathering data is very useful. But they advised that it is important that the observer develops an attitude of tolerance to poor conditions and unpleasant circumstances and resist impulsiveness, particularly interrupting others (DeWalt B. and DeWalt K., *Participant Observation for Fieldworkers*, 17).

28. J. Manson argues that the use of interviewing people's knowledge, views, understandings, interpretations, and experiences are meaningful properties of the ontological reality that research questions are designed to explore, and that it is an epistemologically valid method of generating data (Manson, *Qualitative Researching*, 63–64).

Because I relied heavily on interviews in gathering data, I first familiarized myself with the interview techniques informed by literature before collecting data. According to Hitchcock and Hughes, the use of "asking questions" through encounters is very important in participant observation in qualitative research. They also stressed the importance of researchers understanding questioning techniques before conducting interviews.[29] I was aware that not all the participants I chose had the same opinion about the topics for investigation. In order, to help determine the differences, I therefore, sought out participants with different points of view. I was of the view that seeking out participants with different points of view, would enable me to fully flesh out the understanding of the case study church environment. De Munck and Sobo share this view.[30]

I used the following questioning techniques that are supported by literature:

- Kvale suggests that clear questions should be asked, and questions should be easy to understand and that it is also important to use words that make sense to the respondents.[31]
- Patton wants one thing or question be asked at a time to ease the unnecessary burden on the respondents.[32] He suggests that asking a truly open-ended question allows room for the interviewees to respond in their own terms.[33] Patton again went on to say that asking behaviour questions before asking questions on opinion, will help the respondents to establish a context to express their opinion.[34]
- According to Patton, the use of probe and follow-up is necessary in gathering data, since it will deepen the response and increase the richness of the data being collected.[35]

---

29. Hitchcock and Hughes, *Research and the Teacher: A Qualitative Introduction to School-Based Research*, 79.

30. De Munck and Sobo eds. *Using Methods in the Field: A Practical Introduction and Casebook*, 165.

31. Kvale, *Interviews: Introduction to Qualitative Research Interviewing*, 130.

32. Patton, *How to Use Qualitative Methods in Evaluation*, 27.

33. Patton, 122.

34. Patton, 115.

35. Patton, 125.

- Kvale suggests that, to avoid misinterpretations, interviewers should clarify and extend the meanings of the respondent's statements and to establish rapport.[36] Kvale would want respondents' opinions to be respected and their responses recognized.[37]

Data collected was analysed and findings interpreted (Action, Data Collection and Data interpretation). The study incorporated findings from the field of missiology and the information gained was integrated into a critical thesis, utilizing methods of comparison, analysis, critique, and evaluation.

The purpose of using qualitative research with a participant observation approach was for me to acquire understanding of the subject matter from a subjective perspective. This enabled me to acquaint myself with the beliefs, practices and values of the churches investigated in this study.[38] Adopting a participatory observation research approach therefore highlighted the observer's experience as an insider. Spradley shares this view.[39] This methodology, which uses the techniques of observing, interviewing, experiencing, and examining has the advantage of enabling the author to acquaint himself with the experience from within.

This methodology allowed me to gain insight into the activities of these churches. My experience as a church minister enabled me to be received with a degree of trust and openness by respondents in the case study churches.[40] According to Swinton and Mowat all field research, to some extent, is carried out in the context of the researcher's own experience and beliefs. This is termed as personal reflexivity.[41] Therefore, the study partly drew upon my experiences and the writings of other authors of the black church in the UK, who are the advocates of the writings popularly known as "reverse mission." I was also aware of how epistemological reflexivity could delineate the way my beliefs, values and interests could influence how the research questions would be framed and investigated. With these in mind, I made sure that this

---

36. Kvale, *Interviews: Introduction to Qualitative Research Interviewing*, 149.
37. Kvale, 128.
38. Taylor and Bogdan, *Introduction to Qualitative Research Methods*, 2.
39. Spradley, *Participant Observation*, 53
40. Jorgensen, *Participant observation: A methodology for human studies*, 70.
41. Swinton and Mowat, *Practical Theology and Qualitative Research*, 60.

research was a disciplined attempt to address the research question through an epistemologically valid method of generating data. Notwithstanding this point, the research question showed a willingness and determination to consider my existing commitments in this area of study and critically reflected on the practical matters that involved the African immigrant churches in the British population, hence my choice of a practical methodological approach.

1.6. Ethical Considerations

There are, unfortunately, cases of unethical research and this makes the field of ethics a complex one. It is therefore important that researchers observe a high standard of conduct to ensure moral practices in research ethics.[42] The strong element of field research in this study required a consideration of research ethics, as such I made sure that all the ethical dimensions of the research work were properly maintained and covered. Adequate information about the study was given to the participants of the research project. Even though it was participant observation for ethical reasons I chose to make it overt. In relation to my role as a participant observer, I suggested that my presence as a researcher be announced to the various congregations of the churches under investigation in my first visits to these churches to avoid any unnecessary appearance of subterfuge. The confidentiality of any representation of data, whether through questionnaires, interviews and otherwise were all protected.[43]

1.7. Classification of Headings/Chapters

The book is structured as follows:
Chapter 1: Introduction This chapter raised the main issues of why I chose this topic. It also gave an outline and overview of the whole topic. This chapter also reviewed the work of previous scholars and key thinkers that supported and provided a context of this study and provided evidence to help explain the findings of my investigation. Here research methods were described, and details provided in order that other researchers and scholars could evaluate

---

42. Banks, *Ethics and Values in Social Work*, 39.
43. McMillan and Weyers, *How to Write Dissertation and Projects*, 85.

this research. The methods for the primary and secondary research were reviewed in this chapter and methods used for analysis were explained.

Chapter 2: This chapter presented the historical investigations into the historical developments of the African immigrant churches in the United Kingdom.

Chapter 3: This chapter undertook the theological analysis of the African immigrant churches in the United Kingdom.

Chapters 4–7: Chapter 4 provided an overview report of the main findings from interviews, documentary, and observer- based analysis. Here, all the main themes that were uncovered in the process of the research were discussed. Chapters 5–7 also presented a systematic analysis of the results of the findings and discussed how the results were related to the research questions stated in the problem statements. Findings were integrated into a critical thesis, utilizing methods of comparison, analysis, critique, and evaluation.

Chapter 8: Conclusions and Recommendations. Having taken results from interviews, documentary, and participant observations I drew conclusions for the study and identified issues for further study.

1.8. Concept Clarification

This section defines some key terms and expressions commonly used within the evangelical circles. The term "African immigrant church" used here means black-led churches in the UK with roots from sub-Saharan Africa. The term "black churches" is also used to mean black majority churches in the diaspora. I also used the term "multicultural" primarily to mean all cultural and ethnic groups in Britain. "Multi-ethnic" is a term used in this work to constitute several ethnic groups in the UK including the indigenous British people. I also used "ethnic minority" to mean people who differ ethnically from the main Indigenous British people, and I have used the expressions "white majority churches" to indicate churches with mainly white congregations and "non-Africans" to mean people who are not of the black race.

"Missiology" is used here to mean an analysis and synthesis of the theological, sociological, anthropological, historical, and practical processes that God uses to bring all peoples to himself.[44]

---

44. McIntosh and McMaha, 2012.

The term "reverse mission," which is commonly used by authors of the black church, is used in this work to mean the conscious missionary strategy by mother churches in Africa to evangelize the diaspora.[45]

---

45. Adogame, "The Rhetoric of Reverse Mission: African Christianity and the Changing Dynamics of Religious Expansion in Europe," http://www.eza.nl/media/upload/files/TheRhetoric of reverse mission-Afe Adogame.pdf.

CHAPTER 2

The History of the African Immigrant Churches in the UK

2.1. Introduction

The emergence of globalization has seen a significant increase of people into Western countries in the past few decades. Other factors such as wars including political and religious persecutions have contributed to the movement of people seeking asylum in Western countries where fundamental freedom is regarded. The United Kingdom has experienced the influx of migrants due to its colonial ties to the countries where these migrants are migrating from. For example, there has been a greater number of migrants coming from its former colonies including Nigeria, Ghana, Kenya, Uganda, Zambia, Pakistan, India, Malawi, as well as others.

The second World War ended with a shortage of employment opportunities throughout mainline Europe, but on the contrary, there were labour shortages in Britain as there were more job openings without the requisite labour force. The British government's policy to fill the job vacancies during this period brought in more than 150,000 Polish workers.[1] However, there were still job vacancies in the transport sector of the economy, so to fill these vacancies, the government recruited labour from the Caribbean Islands from 1948 onwards. Upon arrival in the UK, these Afro-Caribbean immigrants drove public buses.

---

1. Office For National Statistics, 13.

The years when the Caribbean immigrants came to live and work in Britain were termed the *Windrush generation*. This is so called because the ship that the Caribbean immigrants boarded to the UK in 1948 was named 'Empire Windrush.' It is believed that over 120,000 Caribbean immigrants came to Britain within the ten years beginning from the first arrival of the Empire Windrush.[2] Accordingly, this period marked the beginning of mass immigration to the UK, and it also brought with it a significant change to Britain's socio-economic, cultural, religious, and political landscape.[3] For instance, the Caribbean immigrants came to the UK with their own version of the gospel and established churches with an ecclesiology that suited their own worship style; an expression of worship which was unique to their cultural heritage.[4] The first of these churches was the Calvary Church of God in Christ which started in London in 1948. Others, such as The New Testament Church of God and the Church of God in Prophecy started in London in 1953. According to Babatunde Adedibu, it is estimated that by 1962, there were almost 80 congregations representing the Afro-Caribbean Pentecostal churches in the United Kingdom. Today, arguably, there is a proliferation of these churches in the country. This increase in the congregations representing the Afro-Caribbean churches is primarily due to the mass migration of the Caribbean nationals into the UK and partly due to the evangelistic efforts in Caribbean immigrant communities.[5]

Similarly, Joe Aldred highlights that even though the Caribbean migrants came to the UK as economic migrants some discovered their missionary calling not only to their own people, but also to the wider British populace.[6] An example of a Caribbean migrant who came to the UK to work as a missionary was the late Philip Mohabir, who migrated to Britain in 1956 to plant churches. He also founded the African and Caribbean Evangelical Alliance. According to Israel Olofinjana, the African and the Caribbean Evangelical

---

2. Fryer, *Staying Power: The History of Black People in Britain*, 372.

3. Accessed 15.02.17, http://news.bbc.co.uk/hi/english/static/2002/race/short_history of immigration.

4. Adedibu, "The Urban Explosion", 105–106.

5. Adedibu, 1.

6. Aldred, *Respect*, 83–88.

Alliance's main aim was to facilitate relationships between African and Caribbean congregations as well as UK white majority churches.[7]

It is also true to say that some Caribbean migrants were accepted into the mainline and evangelical churches. For example, the congregations associated with the Baptist Union of Great Britain were seen as an acceptable context of a place of worship for some Caribbean migrants who were members of the Caribbean Baptist congregations in their native countries before they migrated to Britain. As such when they arrived in the UK, they joined their local Baptist congregations.[8] But some Bible scholars and Christian authors such as Patel and Grant are of the view that the reason why some of the Afro-Caribbean migrants stayed with the mainline and other UK churches was not that they were in leadership positions of the local churches or fully involved in the church activities of any kind, "but for the fact that they were at best tolerated."[9]

The Baptist 'church' was not the only UK denomination that in a way welcomed the Caribbean migrants, as some migrants also joined other mainline and evangelical churches. However, these migrants soon discovered that British Christianity as demonstrated in the mainline and other UK churches was different from what they accepted as a way of Christian worship and Christian living.[10] For example, some of the mainline denominations and the evangelical churches the migrants upon arrival into the country initially accepted as their places of worship were churches whose liturgy, practices and ecclesiology were different from the ones they were familiar with in the West Indies. Their views of the UK mainline, and the evangelical churches were that of churches with poor attendance, and congregations which appeared to have a form of godliness, yet the power which comes with it has been neglected. More so, they viewed these Christians as Christ's people who have ignored their practical Christian living and adopted the ways of the secular society.[11] In his thesis, D. W. Hall underscored that the first Caribbean post-war migrants

---

7. Olofinjana, ed., *Turning the Tables on Mission*, 193–197.

8. Hiro, *Black British, White British: A History of Race Relations in Britain*, 32.

9. Patel and Grant, *A Time to Speak: Perspectives of Black Christians in Britain, Racial Justice and Black Theology*, 12–13.

10. Hiro, *Black British, White British: A History of Race Relations in Britain*, 33.

11. Edwards, *Lord, Make Us One: But Not All the Same*, 50.

to Britain did not receive the reception they had anticipated before migrating as they were met with a wide range of experience, both positive and negative[12].

Some of the migrants who settled in the white-led mainline and the evangelical churches left these churches. They left these churches out of frustration and started or joined new ones that they thought would be more vibrant and serve their spiritual and emotional needs.[13] The migrants started their own churches and developed a worship environment where they expressed their faith with much emotionalism and enthusiasm.[14] Most importantly, this resulted in the emergence of what was known later as the black majority churches in the UK. The black majority church therefore, came about because of the coming of the Caribbean people to the UK from 1948 onwards.

Similarly, the UK has also welcomed migrants from its former colonies in Africa. After their independence in the 1950s and beyond, many Africans migrated to the UK as diplomatic corps, refugees, skilled workers to fill UK job sectors, and some came to further their education.[15] However, recently, the migration patterns in the UK have changed from people of former British colonies or the Commonwealth, being most incomers, to the European Union members being in the largest group of migrants. This was due to the unrestricted movement of citizens between the European Union member countries.[16] There is a new point-based system introduced by the British government in 2008 which still allows skilled migrants from other parts of the world to enter the UK.[17] Such a huge number of new immigrants still presents challenges and opportunities for churches in the UK and the UK social sector.

The migration of people from Africa in the past few decades, especially from sub-Saharan Africa have witnessed the coming into existence of the African immigrant churches in the UK. According to Harvey Kwiyani, Bible

---

12. Hall, "'But God meant it for Good'. Interpersonal Conflict in an African Caribbean Pentecostal Congregation- a Pastoral Theology," (PhD thesis).

13. Wilkinson, *Church in Black and White: Black Christian Tradition in Mainstream Churches in England- A White Response and Testimony*, 79.

14. Pearson, *Race, Religiosity and Political Activism: Some Observations on West Indian Participation in Britain*, 342.

15. Kwiyani, *Sent Forth*, 48.

16. The trend of migration pattern will surely change because the UK has finally left the EU (31st January 2020). Hence migrants coming from the EU to work in the country will be treated as migrants from other parts of the world.

17. Somerville, "United Kingdom: A Reluctant Country of Immigration." http://www.migration. Information & Organization/Profiles, 5.

scholars and missiologist have not been able to properly distinguish the roles the African immigrant churches and the Caribbean immigrant churches play in the UK Christian landscape. Kwiyani thinks that the African immigrant churches have always been studied by scholars in the shadows of the Caribbean immigrant churches, hence have not received the appropriate level of attention from scholars, researchers, and missiologists.[18] In this connection, Olupona and Gemignani suggested the need for *re-conceptualization*, they assert should be a step further in drawing the desired attention to the type of Christianity African immigrants engage in, in Britain and the West (Western Europe and North America).[19]

2.2. The Migration Pattern of Immigrants from sub-Saharan Africa in the UK

The Black presence in Britain dates back the fifteenth century, and according to Killingray and Edwards the advent of slave trade which was initiated by Europeans resulted in the appearance of black people in Europe in the fifteenth century. However, the era of clear black Christian witness and church presence was not witnessed until the Second World War.[20]

More specifically, the United Kingdom's early post war immigration had been chiefly driven by immigrants coming from their former colonies or the Commonwealth. But in the later years it had reflected worldwide trends whereby new immigrants have been increasingly a cross section of those on the move in Europe and beyond.[21] Even more significant is the fact that until the 1950s the direction of migration involved movement of people from the Western world to areas in the non-Western world where the colonial masters expanded their colonial agenda which has recently changed to mass influx of immigrants from the former British colonies or the Commonwealth to Britain.[22]

---

18. Kwiyani, *Sent Forth*, 106.
19. Olupona and Gemignani, introduction to *African Immigrants Religions in America*, 14.
20. Edwards and Killingray, *Black Voices*, 20.
21. Office For National Statistics, 13.
22. Hanciles, *Beyond Christendom*, 172.

Similarly, David Owen highlights how migration of sub-Sahara Africans to the UK started rather later than that of the Afro-Caribbean people. According to him, until the 1980s, total migration into the UK was around 5,000 a year. But there was a high increase in the number of people migrating in the 1990s as the total reached twenty thousand. At the beginning of the twenty-first century, there was a rapid increase of migrants, and this remained around thirty thousand per year during this decade. Migration from West and Central Africa also increased rapidly. Migration from East Africa increased rapidly in the early 1990s, afterwards falling, but increasing again after the year 2000.[23]

Likewise, migration of people from South Africa was the highest among African immigrants in the year 2000. Before the 1990s, many South Africans had left because of apartheid. After majority rule was established in 1994 and native Africans (the ANC) came to power, the numbers of South African-born persons in the UK continued to rise: it increased 108 per cent from 64,000 in 1991 to 132,000 in 2001. Of the 191,000 South African born people recorded in the 2011 Census, 94,000 stated that they arrived in the UK before 2001; the 71 per cent of the South African born residents recorded in 2001 Census was 132,000.[24] It should be noted that the census of the South Africans who migrated into the UK and those born in the UK covers all South Africans in Britain (Blacks, Whites, and others).

David Owen maintains that between 1960 and 2007, migration for asylum reasons was a major factor underlying Africans migrating into the UK. The reason for this mass influx of asylum seekers from sub-Saharan Africa in the UK was that from 1990 onwards, many countries in sub-Saharan Africa have experienced political unrest including military coups, wars, and civil conflicts. Incidentally, the greater number of these asylum seekers have come from former British colonies or the Commonwealth. David Owen discovered that between 2002 and 2008, migrants from sub-Saharan Africa into the UK migrated for work related reasons and the number of this category of migrants known in the UK as economic migrants far exceeded those who migrated to seek asylum.[25] It is right to say that the reason for this trend of migration may

---

23. Owen, "African Migration to the UK: A Workshop Brought to You by University of Warwick." http://www2warwick.ac.uk/fac/soc/crer/events/African/confp_david_owen.ppt.

24. Office For National Statistics, 1–2.

25. This account focuses on African migrants born abroad; it does not consider, African migrants born abroad, but over the years have become British citizens. The account also does

be partly due to the disruption caused in East Africa by the Uganda crisis,[26] and by disruptions to food supplies as a result of droughts and famines in this period. Understandingly, there was also political repression and ethnic discrimination after Zimbabwe's independence, and this resulted in the wave of Zimbabwean-born migrants arriving after independence in 1991 to seek political asylum.

Additionally, there was a period of political instability experienced in some West African countries. This was due mainly to military take-over of political administrations in these countries which subsequently resulted in economic hardship to the citizens. These countries went through economic hardship because Western countries placed economic sanctions on them. It is also true to say that the economic hardship they experienced was due partly to the economic mismanagements of the military rulers. This may explain the high number of migrants of Ghana-born residents in 1981–1990. Despite this, it should not be ruled out that some Ghanaians came to further their education and others came as economic migrants and not necessarily refugees, in the same period. Nigerian-born immigrants into the UK often came because of educational, economic, and social factors.[27]

More specifically, David Owen discovered that by 2008 Nigeria, Ghana, Somalia, Zimbabwe, Uganda, and Kenya were the countries from which 20,000 (black African) migrants from the sub-Saharan Africa came to Britain. Frankly, the reasons are complex, but may include the restoration of democracy in 1999, civil conflict, the economic opportunities, and educational prospects. There is also a religious reason as some Nigerian and Ghanaian migrant Christian leaders came over to the UK to establish churches that can serve the Nigerian and Ghanaian migrant communities. The influx of migrants

---

not reflect on the second or next generation of children born to African migrants in the UK. But David Owen estimates the black African born population of Britain to be 500,000 in 2008.

26. When the late military dictator, Idi Amin, assumed power in Uganda, he made it as his political agenda to drive away settled Indians from Uganda. Amin accused the Asians of being disloyal and corrupt, and eventually expulsed them with iron hands. Many of these Asians migrated to settle in the UK.

27. There is enormous amount of variation in the numbers of African migrant population in the four nations that form the United Kingdom. However, the greater number of African migrants in the UK are concentrated in England. The figures therefore will not be an indicative of the total number of African migrants in the UK. The statistic here excludes Scotland and Northern Ireland, but it an attempt to get an idea of the number of African migrants coming over to occupy the British landscape.

from diverse background, therefore, poses a big challenge for Britain, which it appears has become a country of immigration.[28]

2.3. How the African Immigrant Churches Emerged and Gained Landscape in the UK

British society uses the term black majority churches with reference to churches formed by people of black African heritage whether coming directly from Africa, the Caribbean, or born in the UK; it can also be used in its general sense to mean all dark-skinned people from any part of the globe.[29] While scholars and missiologists such as Dr. Joe Aldred, Mark Sturge, M. Phillips and T. Phillips, and many others have written about the black majority churches from a Caribbean perspective, not much has been written about the African immigrant churches whose congregations are mainly black Africans from sub-Saharan Africa. This book is therefore about the black Africans from sub-Saharan Africa who have migrated to settle in the UK and the children born to these migrants in the UK.

The establishment of the African immigrant churches in Britain was not a recent phenomenon. It began because of Africans migrating to Britain at the beginning of the last century. There have been some efforts by Africans to plant churches in the UK as far back as 1906, but the mass migration of Africans to the UK in the late 1950s until recently paved the way for the establishing of the African immigrant churches in Britain. The earliest known endeavour was led by a Ghanaian immigrant to Britain, Thomas Kwame Brem-Wilson, who started the Summer Road Chapel (now called Sureway International Ministries), a mainly 'black African' Pentecostal congregation in South London in 1906.[30]

Adedibu attributes the establishment of the Summer Road Chapel to the history of the Azusa Street revival of 1906.[31] In 1931, the African Churches mission was formed. It was a church and mission agency in Liverpool, England, planted by a Nigerian called Daniels Ekarte who was a seaman,

---

28. Owen, 2008.

29. The speech delivered by Dr. Joe Aldred in the EEA3 Conference Forum on Migration held in Sibiu, Romania from 4–9 September 2007.

30. Olofinjana, ed., *Turning the Tables on Mission*, 119.

31. Adedibu, "The Urban Explosion," 19.

migrated from his country of birth, Nigeria, to Britain and lived in Liverpool in 1915. He converted to Christianity in 1922, got married to an English woman and settled in that city, and then established a church there.[32]

There were several other factors that led African immigrants to establish their own churches in the UK. Many of these factors were like the ones that led Caribbean immigrants to establish their own churches. Thus, just as the Caribbean immigrants had done, most African immigrants tried to join congregations affiliated with the mainline denominations they belonged to in Africa, but soon discovered that they were not very welcoming.[33] In other cases, when the Africans realized that the churches they belonged to in Africa were not operating in Britain, they founded new congregations that affiliated to the parent denomination back in Africa. Another reason was the racial exclusion and abuse some Africans experienced in the mainline UK churches, although it must be mentioned that this was not a universal experience of African immigrants as some were welcomed into the mainline churches.[34]

Similarly, Moses Biney attributes African migrants establishing their version of churches to the usual challenges immigrants encounter in their new communities. The African Christian community has become a place of refuge for Africans, especially the newly arrived migrants. Biney observes that the African community in the West, including the African immigrant churches have always enabled Africans to find refuge from discrimination and social injustice. He had this to say:

> Faced with harassment by the government and discrimination by society, the immigrants' community becomes their important source of help and existence. This, is where immigrant congregation comes from.[35]

Harvey Kwiyani shares Biney's views and suggests that the African immigrant churches in the West (Western Europe and North America) operate within African communities and exist in four strands. Dr. Kwiyani states these four strands as follows: the first is the churches with Pentecostal/charismatic

---

32. Olofinjana, *Reverse in Ministry and Mission*, 34.
33. Olofinjana, ed., *Turning the Tables on Mission*, 121.
34. Olofinjana, ed., 131.
35. Biney, *From Africa to America: Relation to Adaptation Among Ghanaian Immigrants in New York*, 27.

traditions followed by those who join the mainline churches; some also join the Roman Catholic churches and lastly the African Independent churches.[36] Naturally, Africans will always congregate because the social, spiritual and other factors motivating them to come together have significant cultural connotations that are shared by most of them as these churches operate in a non-threatening and conducive environment that meets their needs.

In 1964 the late Apostle Adejobi, a Nigerian migrant, planted a church which he named Church of the Lord, popularly known as *Aladura* in South London. According to Israel Olofinjana, the late Apostle Adejobi's church planting effort paved the way for many African-led church plants and the following are some of the initiatives which followed: in 1974, Apostle Omideyi, a Nigerian started the Christ Apostolic Church in London. About the same time, a Ghanaian called Joseph William Egyanka Appiah established an apostolic church called *Musama Disco Christo Church* (translated Army of the Cross of Christ Church) in London. From the late 1990s until today, the church-planting endeavours of Africans who have been establishing churches in the UK have been tremendous because they have experienced rapid numerical growth and are involved in Christian services such as feeding the poor and helping the needy in their communities. Churches such as the New Covenant Church, the Deeper Christian Life Ministries, the Church of Pentecost of Ghana, the Redeemed Christian Church of God, and the Kingsway International Christian Centre have all emerged and occupied a prominent place in the British Christian landscape. There has been

---

36. Dr. Harvey Kwiyani in his book, *Sent Forth: African Missionary Work in the West*, affirms the existence of African Christianity in the West in four streams. He has this to say: "the largest group consists of Pentecostal/charismatic Christians, The Pentecostal/charismatic Christians formed most of the African immigrant congregations in the UK. The second consists of mainline African Christians who have joined mainline Western denominations or formed ethnic-specific congregations within mainline denominations. Most of the Africans in this group usually have strong ties with the African led Pentecostal/charismatic churches and visit them for spirituality in what they called "revival meetings." Actually, many will belong to two congregations at one time: one mainline and another African immigrant or ethnic specific community. The third belongs to the Roman Catholic tradition. These Christians will generally join the nearest Roman Catholic Church. However, even among them, the Roman Catholic influences from Africa often lead them to visit African Pentecostal/charismatic churches. The fourth stream is that of African Independent churches. These are usually exclusive in their approach and outlook. They rarely make missional connections with others around them (Kwiyani, *Sent Forth*, 110–111)."

a proliferation of these churches throughout the United Kingdom in the last 25 years.[37]

Similarly, McIntosh and McMahan support the view that mono-ethnic churches such as the African immigrant churches, will continue to be necessary to serve the needs of recently arrived migrants and people with a "high people-consciousness." For some African migrants, coming together to worship with fellow Africans affords them a sense of community in the church environment where services and events are conducted in line with their cultural beliefs and practices.[38]

Furthermore, Adedibu, argues that the black majority churches are among the fastest growing churches in the UK, hence it is a new phenomenon that has ushered in a distinctive era in British history.[39] He further states that the growth of the black majority churches, which includes the African immigrant churches in Britain have been phenomenal in the past few decades and that they deserve greater recognition from the mainline churches and the UK society in general.[40]

2.3.1. African Migrants and the Micro-Melting Pots in the UK Cities

It is important to highlight that the United Kingdom of today is regarded as a multicultural country because of over five hundred years of integration of people from various ethnic backgrounds and this diversity has made the UK a unique place.[41] However, Asamoah-Gyadu and Ludwig argue that migration is becoming an increasingly complex issue with socio-economic, cultural,

---

37. Olofinjana, *Reverse in Ministry and Mission*, 121.

38. Mcintosh and McMahan, *Being the Church in a Multi-ethnic Community*, 66–67.

39. Dr Adedibu's work generalized all black led churches in the UK and not just the African immigrant churches. He had this to say: "the growth of these churches over time has gradually given most of the churches a global identity, as these denominations or churches are continually exporting their brand of denominationalism into the Western world through their missiological agenda to re-Christianize secularised Europe as they engage in reverse mission." (Adedibu, "The Urban Explosion," 59.)

"Black majority churches are the fastest growing and among the largest churches in the UK, and substantial numbers of these churches are Pentecostals. It is estimated that there are over 4,000 congregations and a membership of one million, most of them in urban cities as result of growth of these churches in the 1980s (Black Majority churches directory, 2008)." (Adedibu, "The Urban Explosion," 59.)

40. Adedibu, 59–60.

41. Adedibu, 79.

political, and religious dimensions. The trend of migration over the past few decades has led to the establishing of new churches, and new forms of religious worship led by African immigrants in this country.[42]

For the most part, what we are seeing today in Britain is the development of micro-melting pots in which the migrant ethnic minority populations have established a presence in the major cities of the UK. It is observed that, migrants upon arrival in the UK, usually settle in the main cities such as London, Birmingham, Liverpool, Manchester, Leeds, Sheffield, Cardiff, Glasgow, and Leicester. The rapid spread of African immigrant churches is found in these cities. Olupona and Gemignani despite the popularity of notions of immigrant identity, agency, and cultural pluralism, argue that the West (Western Europe and North America) has understood African immigrants according to a "melting pot"[43] model of immigration.[44] Mass migration to the UK cities has resulted in different races, cultures and people from wide backgrounds, varied ethnicities and diverse countries coming to live together in the cities and sharing social and economic benefits together. The problems encountered by people from diverse backgrounds trying to "assimilate into a cohesive whole," are shared by John Rex as cited by Solomos, who defines race relations in the following terms:

> Race relations situations and problems have the following characteristics: they refer to situations in which two or more groups with distinct identities and recognizable characteristics are forced by economic and political circumstances to live together in a society. Within this they refer to situations in which there is a high degree of conflict between the groups and in which ascriptive criteria are used to mark out the members of each group in order that one group may pursue one of the numbers of hostile policies against the other. Finally, within this group

---

42. Asamoah-Gyadu and Ludwick eds. *African Christian Presence in the West*, 3.

43. "Melting Pot" is a place (such as a city or country) where different types of people live together and gradually create one community or a place where a variety of races, cultures, or individuals assimilate into a cohesive whole. Available from www.merrian-wester.com/dictionary/melting pot. 'The melting pot model of immigration' is used here to mean a situation whereby people from diverse backgrounds and cultures migrate to the West and contribute aspects of their cultures to create a new, unique Western culture and the result is that the contributions from these diverse cultures become indistinguishable from one another.

44. Olupona and Gemignani, introduction to *African Immigrant Religions in America*, 3.

of situations true race relations may be said to exist when the practices of ascriptive allocation of roles and rights referred to are justified in terms of deterministic theory, whether that theory be of scientific, religious, cultural, historical, ideological, or sociological kind.[45]

John Rex's definition of race relations suggests the problems commonly encountered in race relations through mass migration to the UK and elsewhere. Consequently, mass immigration in the 1950s and beyond brought with it the rise of racial violence and prejudice. Many areas in the UK including cities like London (West London), Birmingham and Nottingham experienced unrest. This unrest was partly caused by the insecurity the white indigenes felt as migrants settled in their communities.[46]

The black Africans in the UK have gained space in the British economy, but they are always caught up in what is perceived as an "entrapment"[47] in British society which undermines their ability to feel at home in their newfound country. On one hand, these migrants have been offered jobs, but on the other hand, many have been experiencing racial prejudice (especially in their places of work) that they had never anticipated. Furthermore, the British government passed legislation in the 1970s which had allowed the UK government to restrict immigration quite significantly, but it had not stopped it altogether as some 83,000 immigrants from the Commonwealth settled in the UK between 1968 and 1975, migrating as economic migrants or obtaining visas to join families.[48]

R. Brown, writing on racism and immigration in Britain observes:

---

45. Solomos, *Race and Racism in Britain*, 19.

46. Casciani, "Why Immigration is Changing Almost Everything." http://www.bbc.co.uk/news/uk-31748423.

47. To entrap is to trick (someone) into committing a crime to secure their prosecution (Concise Oxford English Dictionary, 2009:476). The 2007 report of the Home Affairs Committee on the experiences suffered by young black people living in the country made these comments: "The reality of day to day living of young black people in UK today demonstrates various levels of persecution which is reinforced by negative stereotypes and media portrayals. Unprofessional stop and search practices by the police continue to be high on the list of experiences suffered by black boys and statistics from recent published figures illustrate the scale of the disproportionality." *Great Britain, Parliament, House of Commons Home Affairs Committee, 2007. Young People and the Criminal Justice System Volume 2 (EV.354).* The Stationery Office.

48. Available from: http://news.bbc.co.uk/hi/english/static/in_depth/uk2002/race/short_history_of_immigration.stm.

Whatever the hard facts, the need for immigration controls is widely accepted. The tabloid press is very fond of scare stories about immigrants "fiddling" in benefits systems. The fact that Labour Party and trade union leaders have always supported immigration controls means that racist ideas about immigration can sometimes gain a hearing among workers. Central to much racist ideology about immigration into Britain is the notion that immigration is a very recent phenomenon, which began only with the arrival of black workers from Caribbean and India-subcontinent in the 1950s and 1960s. This view rests on the assumption that the British nation and the "British character" were developed, throughout history, in splendid isolation from the rest of the world, untainted by unwelcome contact or exchange with "foreigners" or "outsiders."[49]

This perception held by some elements of the British public misses the main point. Their view of immigration depends on a deliberate rewriting of history. Homes describes the public view on migration as a version of the past which excludes not only all black people, but most other non-British nationalities from the history of civilisation in what is now called Britain and draws the public's attention to the fact that, the people of what is the United Kingdom today, have always been composed of people from different ethnicities. His examples include the Celts, the Anglo-Saxons and Vikings who migrated to present day Britain as the result of various invasions, making the British the most ethnically diverse of all European peoples.[50]

Britain's immigration policy has had two prongs: the government admits a degree of overlap in the strict controls but has also put in place legislation to protect the rights of ethnic minorities (or migrants). It is rightly maintained by some that the government's two-pronged immigration policy in a way gives conflicting signals on the place of the immigrant communities and the second generation of migrants (children born in the UK to migrants) in UK society.[51]

---

49. Brown, "Racism and Immigration in Britain," 1.

50. Homes, *John Bull's Island: Immigration and British Society*, 3.

51. Available from: http://www.bbc.co.uk/hi/english/static/in_depth/uk/2002/race/short_history_of_immigration.stm.

Consequently, the UK experienced riots in 1981 largely caused by racial tensions. In Brixton, a suburb of London with a majority population of Afro-Caribbean people, youths rioted amid resentment citing the constant police entrapment, as they believed that the white police were targeting increasingly young black men in the belief that it would stop street crime. Some cities in the Midlands and Liverpool also experienced riots in the same period as the Brixton riot. The subsequent Scarman Report ordered by the government discovered in the investigations conducted that "racial disadvantage is a fact of current British Life."[52]

Similarly, Marcia Dixon highlights that some UK major cities again witnessed youth riots in 2011 in which young people from a black background (and others) battled with the law enforcement authorities. Dixon further states that it is widely perceived that a "mix of youth disaffection, poverty, poor parenting, educational underachievement and a lack of godliness and morality" were some of the factors that triggered the public disorder.[53]

The influence of the wider society has caused many, especially children born in the UK to their African immigrant parents (or children born to black parents), to lose faith in God, which frankly, has been the source of strength for black people over the years. The question before the African immigrant churches is how they can meet the existential concerns of the next generation of children born in the UK to African immigrant parents since these children are experiencing a process that is termed *acculturation*. They acknowledge their ethnic heritage but place a greater premium on adapting their lives to the culture and values of the wider population. This is a fundamental problem when an increasing proportion of the wider society does not adhere to the Christian faith.

2.3.2. Finding a Refuge from Discrimination, and Discovering a Sense of Identity, Respect, and Belonging

It is sadly true that the common experience of immigrants from sub-Saharan Africa (and black people from elsewhere) in UK society or in the mainline

---

52. http://www.bbc.co.uk/hi/english/static/in_depth/uk/2002/race/short_history_of_immigration.stm.

53. Dixon, "The Black Church Must Respond to Disaffected Youth." *Voice*. https://archive.voice-online.co.uk/article/black-church-must-respond-disaffected-youth.

churches has been one of racism, exclusion, and struggle. The view taken here by Aldred [54] is that the history of black churches is associated with the history of racism. The point here is that while racism may not be the reason for the existence of black churches, it is a catalyst in their growth and relevance to black immigrants in the UK. Even more significant is the fact that the African immigrant churches serve as places where African immigrants discover their identity. Undoubtedly, these churches have become places for African immigrants to meet in fellowship with fellow black people, share, and socialize with them. In addition, for the newly arrived African migrants, the African immigrant churches help to aid their integration into their new communities.

Equally significant is that, over the years, there has been an improvement in the UK concerning matters of race but the biases against immigrants by some elements of the society have hardly changed. Recently, the rise in asylum seekers arriving and being given social housing and other state benefits has seen a rise in racial tensions. The British National Party,[55] which is a party with a political agenda to stop migration into the UK, won three local council seats in May 2002 and had an electoral breakthrough between 2008 and 2009 that led to the party gaining over 50 seats in the local council elections. The British National Party has since 2014 declined in membership but the rise of the United Kingdom Independence Party, another right-wing populist anti-immigration party, which placed fourth in the number seats won in 2013 local elections and won majority seats in 2014 European elections and had two Members of Parliament (in the last Parliament),[56] cannot be underestimated. Even more significant is the British government's plans for new nationality and immigration legislation that includes a citizenship test as well as a test in the English language which has sparked new controversy.[57]

---

54. Dr. Joe Aldred speaking at EEA3 Conference Forum on Migration in Sibiu, Romania from 4–9 September 2007.

55. Recently, the British National Party has declined in membership and has as in 2014, lost forty-eight of the fifty local council seats. Their leader, Griffin, also lost his MEP seat in 2014 elections.
Available from: www.independent.co.uk/news/ukpolitics/generalelections/general-election-2005-the-bnp-has-almost-vanished-from-british-politics-10176194.htm.

56. Available from: www.bbc.co.uk/news/uk-pilitics-22396689.

57. Available from: www.bbc.co.uk/hi/english/static/in_depth/uk/2002/race/short_history_of_immigration.stm.

Kwiyani, writing for African immigrant churches in the West, observes that the African immigrant churches play an especially significant role in supporting African migrants. He refers to the fact that the African immigrant churches have become places of abode for all categories of African immigrants. Even those who might not have been as involved in church while in Africa, become active members in these churches. Notwithstanding this, Kwiyani declares that there are also many immigrants who have converted to Christianity after the process of immigration.[58]

There is a clear indication that African immigrants are looking for ways to re-define themselves in their newly chosen country, create a distinct identity and express their cultural values. These Africans are very much aware of the need to develop a voice and a presence in their communities. It is fair to say that one of the ways they do this is through their Christian endeavours. Many of the immigrants have found a refuge from discrimination and discovered a sense of identity, respect and belonging in the different churches established by persons of their own ethnic or national origin where they can profoundly assert themselves. This idea was the motivating force behind the African immigrant churches in the UK.

2.4. Summary

The movement of people of African heritage from a wide range of backgrounds into the UK has been influenced by a range of factors including economic conditions, connections through family and cultural tiers and political factors. Both real and perceived influence has led to the migration of people into this country. The English language has become a global language and so the wider use of English globally is one of the factors which have influenced migration into the UK. Hence it is not a surprise to observe that historic and Commonwealth ties may have influenced the migrants' choice of destination country as Africans from the former British colonies make the UK their main choice for migration. Therefore, over the past few decades the migratory pattern, though voluntary, has been influenced by imperialist ties, as most of the migrants were already integrated into the British socio-economic system in the countries of origin through their previous colonial tiers.

---

58. Kwiyani, *Sent Forth*, 109.

Migration in the UK in the last decade is strikingly different because of the surge in net immigration. Following the European Union enlargement the UK government allowed migrants from the Eastern European countries particularly from Poland to take advantage of the job opportunities in Britain. Therefore, since 2004, immigration levels were boosted by waves of migration from some Eastern European countries, whose citizens enjoyed free movement and exemption from UK immigration control to the disadvantage of nationals of other countries, particularly from former British colonies like, Nigeria, Ghana and Kenya which have had access to the UK gradually wear away.[59]

The emergence of mass migration has raised uneasiness among the UK public on immigration matters and clearly, this has been fuelled by media reports. For example, the monthly polling data from the *Ipsos Mori* agency shows that beginning in late 1990s, the British people identified race and immigration as one of the top three most important issues facing the United Kingdom. Other opinion polling data from different sources also show a similar picture, with between two-thirds and four-fifths of the UK public clearly indicating their dislike for mass immigration. In this context of rising numbers and rising anxieties among the British people, the British government have passed legislation and drawn up other policies to manage immigration.[60] Therefore, over 50 years since the start of mass immigration to the UK, questions are still being asked by the British public about whether Britain has truly become a multicultural society at ease with itself as politicians claim, or whether there is still a long road to be travelled.

But for the African immigrant churches, it is obvious that they have found a Christian space in Britain, however, Olupona and Gemignani observe that the factors bringing the African immigrants together in the West are not just spiritual but other factors bringing them together could also include:

> Social identities, transnationalism, migration as a process, civic engagement, political incorporation, and gender relations.[61]

---

59. Sommerville, "United Kingdom: A Reluctant Country."

60. The United Kingdom officially left the European Union on the 31 January 2021, so this date marked the end of mass migration from the EU to the UK and migration from the UK into the EU.

61. Ollupona and Gemignani, introduction to *African Immigrant Religions in America*, 3.

Certainly, these factors are relevant to the African immigrant churches as they serve recently arrived immigrants and migrants with "high people-consciousness." But there is an uncertain future for any church or church movement whose numerical growth or existence depends on the number of immigrants coming into the country. For instance, in the UK, government policies are a major factor in seeking to reduce international migration into this country; hence it is extremely difficult to predict what immigration will look like for example, ten or fifteen years from now.

At this stage in their missionary endeavours in the UK, it is very surprising to say that African immigrant churches have already attributed a theological relevance to this recent phenomenon of establishing black initiated churches in the UK that some African scholars called "reverse mission."[62] But Kwiyani contends that the term reverse mission is a misnomer because African immigrant churches in the West and Britain in particular, are still centred around black African congregations and with very little or no cross-cultural ministries with the wider community (white British).[63]

For the African immigrant churches to regard their mission endeavours in the UK as reverse mission, they would have to consider their next stage of the task of reaching out to the wider UK communities, because the Great Commission (Matt 28:19–20) calls Christ's people to measure their lives by its universal scope of reaching all people groups. Truly, the time has come for the African immigrant churches to re-define their God-given mandate to Britain. They must strategize in such a way that they would become the vanguard of spiritual, emotional, and social liberation to the UK Christian communities and the wider society.

---

62. "Reverse mission" means the conscious missionary strategy by mother churches in Africa of evangelizing the diaspora (Adogame, "The Rhetoric of Reverse Mission").

63. Kwiyani, *Sent Forth*, 75.

CHAPTER 3

Theological Analysis of the African Immigrant Churches in the UK

3.1. Introduction

The previous chapter discussed how in the past few years the UK has opened its doors to migrants from all over the globe, and that today it has become one of the most culturally diverse countries of the world. The previous chapter discussed also how the country's cultural diversity presents both challenges and opportunities to the Christian enterprise. The previous chapter explains that the African immigrant churches have now been established in the UK Christian landscape. But their congregations are mainly black Africans. However, it is right to say that they have attained a measure of success in establishing themselves in Britain. Nonetheless, they are now faced with a choice of reaching out to the British society, something they should regard as another stage in their mission endeavour to the wider UK communities.

It is also important to highlight that immigration which has been the key to opening the door for the African immigrant churches to be established in the UK, has also been their greatest challenge. For example, one of the challenges faced by the African immigrant churches is how they can meet the existential concerns of the next generation of children born in the UK to the African migrant parents since these children are experiencing a process that is termed acculturation.[1]

---

1. The second generation of children born to the African migrant parents acknowledge their ethnic heritage but place a greater premium on adapting their lives and values to the culture and values of the majority population.

Apart from the social and cultural factors that have emerged in the UK because of the migration of people from diverse backgrounds, there have also been ecclesiastical developments within the Christian circles over these past few decades, as such there is the need for a new way of theologizing among the various churches that occupy the UK Christian landscape in line with the current contexts.

This chapter argues that, for the African immigrant churches to expand their base and reach out to the wider communities, they would have to develop a contextual approach to ministry that is suitable to their Western environment. This clearly poses a serious challenge, as it is obvious that there are cultural differences that in a way have kept both the African immigrant churches and the white majority churches apart. Yet there is the possibility that in partnering with each other, both sides will be able to challenge the aspects of their culture and cultural influences on theology that are not in line with biblical principles. For the African immigrant churches and the white majority churches to work together, they would have to share the gospel and minister in a way that is both faithful to the Bible and suitable to their cultural contexts.

On the part of the African immigrant churches, they would have to change their theologies and practices that would be different from those practised in most churches in Africa. However, there is also the risk that their desire to contextualize to be relevant to the host (UK) culture so that they would attract the wider community could leave them vulnerable to the danger that their churches will be shaped more by those (cultural) concerns than by the designs of the Lord. Therefore, to strike the balance, they would have to contextualize the gospel critically, achieving that delicate balance of faithfully communicating the unchanging truths of the gospel in a way that is suitable to their cultural context without compromising the centrality of Scripture.[2]

The perception in the UK that the black churches have a different theology must be cleared. It has now become obvious that African immigrant churches need to re-define themselves in relation to the white majority churches and need also to clarify their theology because their unfamiliar environment would have an influence on their theological emphases. To theologize in this emerging context of multiculturalism in Britain, the multicultural nature of

---

2. Hammett, *Biblical Foundations for Baptist Churches: A Contemporary Ecclesiology*, 11.

the British society should be taken into consideration. This calls for Christ's people from all backgrounds to realise the importance of dialoguing with the diverse cultures that make up the UK Christian communities. There is, therefore, the need for a critical contextual theology, which can ensure the universality of other theologies in the UK, which may in turn result in establishing multi-ethnic churches with a multicultural identity.

Clearly, the time has come for Christ's people in Britain (Blacks, Whites and others) to respond to the new realities that have arisen because of the mass migration of people from different cultural backgrounds into Britain in the past few decades. This book, therefore, believes that for the African immigrant churches to be effective in their outreach to the wider communities, they need to be sensitive to the culture of their new environment and share the gospel in a way that is suitable to their new cultural context without compromising the core message of the Bible.

In this chapter, key elements of theology of the African immigrant churches are also explored. The chapter seeks to examine the theological context that could be accepted as a biblical theological basis for the African immigrant churches by using the tools of critical contextual theology and hermeneutics to consider texts particularly favoured by Bible scholars. Through such an exercise, a comprehensive understanding of theologizing will emerge, but not in its full complexity (the entire work of theologizing for the African immigrant churches is beyond the scope of this study), but at least it will result in a tentative conclusion concerning theology while constructing a model for theological praxis for the African immigrant churches. Hence this chapter will discuss a few key features of theology that will provide a vital means through which the theology of the African immigrant churches can be analyzed.

3.2. Theology and its Contexts

P.G. Hiebert notes that theologies are shaped by the societies and cultures in which Christ's people live. He cited the following quotation as representative of his viewpoint:

> We are assuming here that Scripture is divine revelation given to us by God, not our human search for God. Theology, then,

is our attempt to understand that revelation in our historical and cultural contexts.[3]

Similarly, Boff and Boff also argue that every true theology develops from a spirituality that is from a true meeting or encounter with God in history. Overall, one of the major challenges facing cross-cultural missions and for that matter all contemporary missions are the theological issues involved. The above definitions clearly indicate the importance of theology in the mission endeavours of Christ's people. It is true to say that for Christ's people to reach out effectively, there is a need for a strong biblical grounding and theological understanding of their mission. The issue here is that, for any meaningful breakthroughs in their mission endeavours, Christ's people would need the fundamental truths of God, (clearly, they must have Bible based perspectives and integrity), and divine principles of the Scriptures, which would give them a thorough biblical understanding and missiological bases as well as theological framework for their mission.[4] According to J. J. Davis, the theological framework will boost their knowledge of God and their relationship with him. To this end, Christ's people must be grounded in biblical doctrine and adept at theological thinking, not theology based on creedal statements that do not express with a sufficient degree of adequacy the experiences of believers. But they must understand the Scriptures, its interpretation, and application in their everyday Christian living and mission endeavours.[5]

In the past generation, there have arisen many theologies that have come about because of human suffering and oppression. For example, feminist theology rightly argues for the recognition of the fact that men have dominated Western theology. Hence feminist theology is meant to be a way of establishing a platform for women to have a voice in their society and communities. Liberation theology emerged in the face of oppression under the hierarchical structures within the traditional practices of the Roman Catholic in Latin America, hence human experiences of oppression and injustice were

---

3. Hiebert, *The Gospel in Human Context: Anthropological Explorations for Contemporary Missions*, 38.
4. Boff and Boff, *Introducing Liberation Theology*, 3.
5. Davis, ed., *The Necessity of Systematic Theology*, 23.

the starting points of liberation theology.⁶ Then there is the black theology,⁷ a theological reflection of black people's understanding of God. In addition, there is African theology, which develops in the context of poverty, exploitation, and diseases among many uniquely African social and spiritual issues.⁸

R. J. Schreiter was making the point when he indicated that there are two models of theologizing contextually: First, is the ethnographic model, which he claims emphasizes cultural identity, and secondly, he states that there is the liberation model, which he claims emphasizes social change from oppression and social evils.⁹ Schreiter further states that the gospel of Jesus Christ can come into full realization only in the local church setting, as such without the church, "the incarnation of the gospel will be highly improbable." But according to him, culture is the context in which this interaction occurs. The following quotation is cited as Schreiter's view on the interaction of gospel, church, and culture:

> It represents a way of life for a given time and place, replete with values, symbols, and meanings, reaching out with hopes and dreams, often struggling for a better world. Without sensitivity to the cultural context, a church, and its theology either become a vehicle for outside domination or lapse into Docetism, as though its Lord never became flesh.¹⁰

As has been noted, the values placed on local cultures and the necessities of the situation are the main factors which influence Christ's people to understand and interpret their faith differently, and so contextual way of doing theology in a particular way emerges. For instance, the human experiences of oppression and injustice are the starting points of liberation theology. Liberation theology was developed in reaction to the focus of dominant

---

6. Bosch, *Transforming Mission, Paradigm Shifts in Theology of Mission*, 448–450.

7. "Black theology in the United States arose out of the civil rights and black power movements of the 1950s and the 1960s. However, its historical roots go back to the beginning of African slavery in the United States and the founding of black independent Baptist and Methodist churches in the late 18th and early 19th Centuries . . . As in the United States, the struggle against institutionalised racism, often legitimised by religious beliefs was the source of black theology in South Africa during the Apartheid era." www.encyclopedia.com/topic/liberation_theology.aspx.

8. Bosch, *Transforming Mission*, 449–451.

9. Schreiter, *Constructing Local Theologies*, 13–15.

10. Schreiter, 21.

theology as a response to the issues of oppression within the contexts of individual groups, communities, and societies.[11]

3.2.1. Black Theology in Context

In the UK, there is the perception that the black churches have a different theology termed as black theology. There have been suggestions by some British Bible scholars with Caribbean roots that the Afro-Caribbean churches in Britain should adopt what they called black British theology of liberation. One example of such scholars is Dr. Robert Beckford. Dr. Beckford affirms the need for a black British theology of liberation as opposed to what he terms as their black Christian theology that in his own words comprises "church life, worship and witness."[12] It is probably true to say that Dr. Beckford (with a Caribbean root) speaks out of his cultural context addressing people who are oppressed institutionally and otherwise discriminated against in the British society. In many ways this treatment to them by the wider community has found them excluded in many fronts of the British society. According to Justin Ukpong there is the need for Christ's people of all cultural backgrounds to realize that all forms of Christian expression have connections with the cultural context from which they originated.[13] It is therefore fair to say that Dr. Beckford's perception of theology is meant to address the needs of the Afro-Caribbeans in Britain. However, the form of theology he suggested for the Caribbean people is a theology that comes with political implications.

---

11. Schreiter, 13.

12. Dr. Robert Beckford, speaking for African Caribbean community in the 'Presentations on Black Majority Churches in Britain' (this was a conference chaired by Bishop Joe Aldred in December 1995; organised by the black majority Churches) www.pctii.org/wcc/reports95.html. Dr. Beckford raised a series of issues that have emerged from dialogue with African Caribbean-British church leaders; issues such as Domestic neo-colonialism; he said the Caribbean diaspora in Britain face systems and structures of discrimination and white supremacist thought that has, in some aspects of black life in Britain, been internalised and led to the denial of blackness and use of white colour symbolism in theologising. Speaking in the same conference Reverend Jerisdan Jehu-Appiah of Musama Disco Christo Church in Britain speaking for the African community in Britain among other things said that African churches in diaspora need to re-define themselves, not only in relation to the European churches, but also to the African Caribbean and North American black churches. He went on to say that the Afro-Caribbean church will also have to clarify their theology in terms of systematising it from within the African movements.

13. Ukpong, "Towards a Holistic Approach to Inculturation Theology." 109.

He calls this type of theology, the black British theology of liberation. Dr. Beckford explains this type of theology as follows:

> In order to counter the harmful effects of European thought, people of African descent must construct an alternative way of thinking, believing and doing. In other words, Afrocentricity advocates that the best way of empowering Black people is by developing their own epistemologies for analysis of social and political world.[14]

Certainly, Dr. Beckford's view on black theology is about modelling a form of black British theology; a type of theology which in my view, is socially and politically inclined. It is clear to say that this form of theology is a type of theology that is grounded on a contextual hermeneutic and rooted in a form of spirituality with a purpose for radical social, economic, and political revolution. He understands that for a black theology of liberation to be meaningful for the people of African origin, it must be communal in nature. It should be a theology that places black people firmly within the community of faith by developing a voice which he believes can result in social and political changes within the black community.[15] However, Valentina Alexander asserts that Emancipation Theology in the Caribbean is still in its early stages of formation and implementation.[16]

Similarly, Anthony Reddie, also a theologian with a Caribbean background, highlights a fresh vision for black Christians by challenging the existing frameworks; namely, traditional, missionary Eurocentric, historical, doctrinal Christianity into which he affirms, many black people over the globe have been inducted. When speaking of black theology, Reddie suggests re-interpreting "Christian traditions and practices in the light of liberationists' concepts" that arise out of black experiences. Reddie is of the view that a true emphasis on black theology should be on its commitment to a liberating praxis and social transformation. Reddie further argues that a re-imagined

---

14. Beckford, *Dread and Pentecostal: A Political Theology for Black Church in Britain*, 14.
15. Beckford, 172–174.
16. Alexander, "'Breaking Every Fetter': To What Extent Has the Black Led Church in Britain Developed A Theology of Liberation?," 79.

black theology will enable Christianity in general and particularly a black Christian faith to impact the world.[17]

The Afro-Caribbean churches, especially the Pentecostals, have adopted the idea of creating a contextual theology in response to their experiences of oppression both past and present which L.L. Williams states are the reasons for their "inability to achieve self-actualization." This has resulted in the emergence of a liberation theology that has been influenced by their historical experience of oppression. They believe this type of liberation theology can address their political, cultural, and social matters. But it is worth noting that African immigrants have not experienced the struggles the Afro-Caribbean countries have gone through hence their emphasis on liberation praxis is different.[18]

However, it is also especially important to highlight that it is in South Africa (not all sub-Sahara African countries) where a black theology of Liberation focusing explicitly on issues of contemporary social analysis has developed.[19] Chigor Chike expresses that because of the experiences black South Africans went through during the apartheid[20] era, they have been on a different theological path from the rest of sub-Sahara African countries.[21] Furthermore, Kalemba Mwambazambi highlights that during the liberation struggles from the apartheid era, some black South African theologians created the South African black theology of liberation during the late 1960s and the early 1970s as a "conscious and theological dimension" of the liberation struggle against apartheid.[22] The distinctive theology of apartheid that the black South Africans were rejecting was what is termed the "Afrikaner

---

17. Reddie, *Working Against the Grain: Reimaging Black Theology in the 21st Century*, 14–18.
18. Williams, *Caribbean Theology, Research in Religion and Family: Black Perspectives*, 32.
19. Mbali, *The Churches and Racism*, 4.
20. Saul Dubow in his book, *Apartheid, 1948–1994* underscores the early formulations of the Apartheid ideology which he attributes to the missionary wing of the Dutch Reformed Church. According to Saul Dubow the late 1920s saw the influence of missionary leaders in the Orange Free State in South Africa stressing the need to develop a more communal approach to the Apartheid ideology centred on the premise that it was God's Will that their distinctive identity be protected (Dubow, 17). According to Dubow, 16) Apartheid was developed as a theory of how the native blacks should be treated, even though it was first meant to be a theory of the special nature of the calling and the God-given tasks of the Afrikaners.
21. Chike, *African Christianity in Britain: Diaspora, Doctrine and Dialogue*, 5.
22. Mwambazambi, "A Missiological Glance," 1.

Calvinism."[23] Afrikaner Calvinism is an ideology that developed out of cultural and religious development of Afrikaners that gives the false impression of the Calvinist doctrine by adding a "chosen people syndrome."[24] The black South African theologians rejected the Afrikaner theology and developed the South African black theology of liberation. This type of theology drew inspiration from African American theology and biblical hermeneutics as well as experiences they gained from their struggles with apartheid. While many related questions remain unanswered, it is true to say that the idea of creating this type of theology was to create a new theological paradigm as well as situational and political inclination to liberate black South Africans from apartheid and all perceived foreign domination such as neo-colonialism and other influences.[25] In other words, the South African black theology was a liberation theology aimed at helping to put an end to the then existing socio-political order of South Africa.[26]

In contrast to what has been said about South Africa, other sub-Sahara African countries, even though, they had had struggles with colonialism, they had not gone through the type of struggles experienced by black South Africans. It is therefore fair to say that the South African black theology of liberation is a contextualized theology within the sub-Sahara African context. According to Mwambazambi, during the apartheid era,[27] the Afrikaners viewed themselves as people pioneering civilization in Southern Africa. They saw themselves as a chosen people. They probably thought that they were superior to the black South Africans and the "coloured" people. Therefore, they felt that they were right to segregate them. Consequently, the black theology

---

23. John Calvin's sixteenth century doctrine convinced the Afrikaners that the separation of the people of the world into different races was done deliberately by God and that it was not their responsibilities to bring different races together. They believed also that it was in God's providential plan to create the white race to be his highest image and likeness (Ransford, *Great Trek*, 11–12).

24. Ransford, *Great Trek*, 11.

25. Mwambazambi, "A Missiological Glance," 1.

26. Mbali, *The Churches and Racism*, 4.

27. "The White minority in South Africa consisted of two rival groups: The Afrikaners and the White British immigrants. In 1948, the Afrikaners, who formed most of the White population in South Africa elected to office the National Party to rule the nation based on Apartheid ideology. Apartheid was a political system that depended on extensive police power, and it aggressively entrenched and enforced the existing segregation between White and Black people" (Mwambazambi, "A Missiological Glance," 1).

of liberation, emerged out of the context of the black South Africans' experiences of the brutalities of the apartheid era[28] and according to Mbali it was an attempt to respond to the very material concerns of the oppressed in the South African region in ways which were not considered possible within the Western theological perspective. The black South Africans borrowed much of their black consciousness sentiment from the United States and developed their theology contextually. This theology offered a critique of an oppressive South African society.[29]

Allan Boesak understands black South African theology as a theology within a situational context. He sees this type of theology as an attempt by black South Africans to come to terms theologically with their black situation during apartheid. He further suggested the emphasis of the need for a social analysis to evaluate the main structures of society as well as the individually oppressed components of it so that individuals can interact and live together in harmony. A further factor to consider in the black South African theology of liberation is that this theology seeks to transform the theology black people inherited from Western theologians into a *dialectic medium* of liberation theology, which could advocate a radical transformation of segregation and oppression in the South African society.[30] Frankly, this was theology for the oppressed black people seeking liberation from religious, socio-cultural, economic, and political bondage they found themselves in the apartheid era.

Consequently, South Africans have recently experienced a changeover to majority rule; they have in fact witnessed the end of apartheid as political power is now in the hands of the black majority. But it is still too early to say whether this has had a significant effect on the socio-political and economic transformation of South African society. One thing is certain, it is clear to say that seeing the end of apartheid and initiating black majority rule has not ended what necessitated the birth of black African theology of liberation in the country.

---

28. Mwambazambi, "A Missiological Glance," 1.
29. Mbali, *The Churches and Racism*, 4.
30. Boesak, *Farewell to Innocence. A Socio-ethical Study on Black Theology and Power*, 13.

3.2.2. The Theology of the African Immigrant Churches

Sub-Sahara Africans and the Afro-Caribbean people have different histories and cultures that affect their worldviews. According to Kwiyani the African immigrant churches have always been studied by Bible scholars and missiologists in the shadows of the Afro-Caribbean diaspora churches, hence not received the appropriate level of attention.[31] In this connection, Olupona and Gemignani suggested the need for the *re-conceptualization* of the study of black churches, which they assert should be a step further in drawing the desired attention to the type of Christianity African immigrants participate in, in Britain and the West (Western Europe and North America).[32]

Kathryn Tanner was right to say that every theology is a theology that was developed in a particular context. As such, a given Christian theology is an interpretation of the Christian faith from a particular context, making sense of faith to the realities of that context.[33] For the African immigrant churches, their theological emphasis is on "spiritual freedom."[34] Even though there are similarities between the African immigrant churches and the Afro-Caribbean churches, there are still variations in the cultural context in which these churches operate. In the African theology, the place of the Holy Spirit and his empowerment is incredibly significant. As such, African believers place much emphasis on the power encounters with demonic forces. They believe they are faced up to these unseen evil forces which according to them are overpowered by the power of God.[35] But it is true to say that one of the most striking differences between the African immigrant churches and the white majority churches is the emphasis African immigrant churches place on the spirit and power of the Holy Spirit and their use of Scripture which have been missing in white majority churches, even though very prominent in the Bible.

---

31. Kwiyani, *Sent Forth*, 106.
32. Olupona and Gemignani, introduction to *African Immigrant Religions in America*, 14.
33. Tanner, *Theories of Culture: A New Agenda for Theology*, 19.
34. African churches, both home and abroad, emphasise moving in the gifts of the Holy Spirit, particularly healing and deliverance from demonic powers (Acts 10:35); Africans whose lives are mainly ravaged by poverty, diseases and occult religions are desperate to find freedom, and so the place of their worship is where the depressed, the hurting, "the cultural dropouts," and the destitute can find salvation, hope and acceptance and encouragement to become what they are supposed to become in their Christian lives.
35. Chike, 37.

Recently, there was speculation in the UK that the African immigrant churches have been practising exorcism and witchcraft. In the symposium themed *Christianity or the Occult? Emerging Trends in the African Diaspora*,[36] issues such as the "alleged witchcraft being imported into Britain by migrants" were discussed. Among the people present at this forum was Angus Stickler, the award-winning investigative journalist who covered the original story of "Child B"[37] and ritualistic abuse in Angola for the BBC Today Programme.[38] Stickler was accused by some African Christian leaders for his brand of journalism. He certainly, was not familiar with the culture from which he was reporting hence he generalized and made unfounded allegations. The African leaders told the participants that it was not true that African immigrant churches practise a mix of Christianity and traditional practice as alleged by some members of the British public.[39]

Contrary to this negative report, Pastor Agu Irukwu, who was also at the symposium and who is the senior pastor of the Jesus House for All Nations and chairs more than two hundred Redeemed Christian Church of God congregations, drew to the public's attention the positive impact of the migrant churches within British communities. He gave an example of how most of the African derived churches have grown to affect their communities through social action and today, these churches could be described as vibrant, engaging, and inclusive, contrary to the negative perception presented by a few (white) British individuals.[40]

---

36. This symposium was in London in May 2006 by the Lapido Media.

37. In May 2006, a story emerged in the BBC News Community Affairs about an eight-year-old girl called 'Child B'. The UK authorities adopted 'Child B' as the child's assigned pseudonym to ensure confidentiality. Child B who was brought into the UK from Angola, was mistreated by her aunt and two others who believed she was a witch. The case sparked widespread fears over whether a new form of child abuse centred on "healing and deliverance" customs had arrived in Britain (www.bbc.co.uk/1/hi/magazine/5002054.stm).

38. Stickler had travelled to Angola following the 'Child B' trial, and filmed a boy, who was suspected of being possessed by an evil spirit and was being tortured by a traditional healer who suspected him of being possessed by evil spirits. The boy eventually died. Stickler broke the news in BBC Today linking the 'Child B' case in the UK with the ritualistic child abuse in Angola, making it appear as if this is a general practice among Africans (Taylor, "Rush to Judgement on UK African-Derived Churches 'Inexcusable.'" www.fulcrom-anglican.org.uk/?124).

39. Taylor, "Rush to Judgement on UK African-Derived Churches 'Inexcusable.'" (http://www.fulcrum-anglican.org.uk/?124.)

40. Taylor.

Reports such as this heart-breaking news of exorcism and witchcraft including child abuse among a few African immigrant churches put the migrant churches at the margins of British society. It is a fact that there have been some abuses in some African immigrant churches, but these are just remote cases.[41] Overall, it is fair to understand that the African theology is a theology of liberation, born among people that are struggling with immense poverty, deprivation and diseases who seek to understand God in ways far away from the mind-set of the West (Western Europe and North America).

3.2.2.1. The Ecclesiology of the African Immigrant Churches

It is also important to highlight that culture influences the theological thinking and missiological endeavours of Christ's people. As an example, it is fair to say that, though the African immigrant churches believe that the main objective of the Christian's ministry is not to cast out demons, but to proclaim the good news to the unsaved, yet they believe also that preaching the gospel must be done in the demonstration of the spirit and power of God (1 Cor 2:4). Clearly, the ecclesiological[42] understanding of the African Christian is different from that of the Western Christian. So, it is rather understandable that there is indeed a difference in the way Africans read Scripture. For instance, African Christians understand the church (universal) must have a divinely gifted leadership as suggested by Ralph Mahoney;[43] while Western theology continues a two-thousand-year heritage mediated through science and reason in the Enlightenment and modernity with leadership based only on academic achievement, human calling, and appointment.[44]

Olofinjana observes that African immigrant pastors are very highly respected and this, according to him, reproduces strong leadership. He says:

> The congregation believes in the leadership, and they do not enter debates about issues. The democratic process is not really

---

41. Kwiyani, *Sent Forth*, 108.

42. Ecclesiology is the study of the church and investigates what the Bible teaches about the universal church as well as the local church. "Ecclesiology is important for all Christ's people since it guides them toward a bibical understanding of how Christ's people should relate to God, one another and to unbelievers" (https://www.compellingtruth.org/ecclesiology.htmll).

43. Mahoney, ed. *The Shepherd's Staff*, 219.

44. Kwiyani, *Sent Forth*, 180.

part of the culture; there are principles of democracy in terms of trustees and leadership, but it is not an open debate.[45]

Olofinjana suggests that the top-down system of leadership in the African immigrant churches or for that matter the black majority churches is one of its success stories. The role of church members in the African churches also differ; the African churches model the book of Acts by involving their church members in ministry with less formal requirements (such as formal theological training), and an important level of involvement and commitment in evangelism, including other ministerial responsibilities.[46] To the African Christian, the purpose of the church is what is defined in Acts 2:42–47. The purpose of gathering includes fellowship, teaching, ministry, prayer, and outreach. Kwiyani makes the point when he states that the Christianity of the African migrants is lived in spiritually awakened context.[47] It is true to say that many of these churches model the book of Acts. The book of Acts (Acts 2:1–4) records the coming of the Holy Spirit which empowered people in the early church for the work of the ministry that God commissioned them to do, and this applies to the African immigrant churches too. There is also the renewed interest in personal disciplines like prayer, Bible study, meditation and fasting in the African immigrant congregations.

Since most African immigrant churches in the UK are Pentecostals or charismatics in their faith, they have common rituals and liturgy.[48] For example, the Lord's Super (communion) is observed by all African immigrant churches, even though with different meanings and styles. The praise and worship style of the African immigrant churches is contemporary. The form of worship is using dance (2 Sam 6:14), innovative hymnody, singing in tongues and dancing to the tone of lively joyful music is the type of worship found in the African immigrant churches.[49] They surely want to dance, because it is Scriptural to dance to praise the Lord just as King David did. Similarly, Olofinjana observes that the dynamic style of worship (music) of the African immigrant churches is expressed through *art, dance, and graphic*

---

45. Olofinjana, *Reverse in Ministry and Mission*, 52.
46. Olofinjana, 52.
47. Kwiyani, *Sent Forth*, 182.
48. Liturgy has to do with praise and worship, type of music, prayer, and sacraments.
49. Mahoney, *The Shepherd's Staff*, 12.

design, which according to him, is very appealing to all, especially the young generation.[50] According to Chike, many songs used by the African migrants in Britain are about the power of Jesus Christ.[51] It is true to say that the African Christian's praise and worship is based on Scriptures, and it is all done to glorify the name of the living God who is their great provider in all aspect of their lives.

Mbiti maintains that the African Christian's understanding and use of Scripture liberates them from the ready-made and imported Christianity of the West as they theologize the kind of Christianity that more fully embraces the totality of their existence.[52] That is to say, the African theology models theology and contextualizes it in their African context. Hence the outcome is different from Western theology, which, has problems understanding the spirit world. Chike again notes that the African immigrant churches (like other African Christians elsewhere) undertake regular Bible studies, which they call Sunday School. Chike went on to say that the Bible, clearly is the centre of the life and development of the African Christian and further indicated that most African preachers show this commitment to the Bible by supporting every point in their sermons with biblical references. Chike affirms that the authority of the Bible is respected among African Christians to the extent that even when providing solutions to practical issues they take references from biblical texts.[53]

3.2.2.2. *The Hermeneutics of the African Immigrant Churches*

Unquestionably, most of the African immigrant churches preach the full gospel and are antitheses to values that counter godly living to their own kind and do not have a mix of Christianity and traditional practices in their worship as assumed by some in the UK. They respond contextually to a wide range of Christian experiences and ascribe spiritual factors to all incidents.[54] For example, they believe that sickness entered the world because of the disobedience of Adam and Eve. Therefore, the sin that humankind inherited

---

50. Olofinjana, *Reverse in Ministry and Mission*, 52.
51. Chike, *African Christianity in Britain*, 63.
52. Mbiti, *Bible and Theology in African Christianity*, 32.
53. Chike, *African Christianity in Britain*, 12–14.
54. Kwiyani, *Sent Forth*, 182.

from their first ancestors (Adam and Eve) is the root cause of all sicknesses (Rom 5:12), and that evil spirits can sometimes be the cause of illness and affliction as in Matthew 9:32–33 and Luke 13:11–16.[55] Indeed, some in the West may see this experience strange and may argue that it is unscriptural. But Boff and Boff particularly make the telling point with their holistic argument, which in their own words say: "every true theology springs from a spirituality."[56] It is true to say that the Holy Spirit would work through only those who believe and yield to him as his divine instrument to bring spiritual release (Mark 16:16–18).

According to Chike the African Christian's emphasis on deliverance from evil forces and being blessed materially in this world is their understanding of salvation. What African Christians expect from God in their worship is God's protection, healing, and material blessings.[57] The book of Genesis (chapter 12) reveals how God blessed Abraham in multiple or unusual ways. What was the main reason God decided to bless Abraham? God bestowed his blessings to Abraham because of his obedience to him (God). There is an account in the book of Genesis which makes clear the promised blessings to Abraham. These blessings also included material blessings (Gen 13:1–2). Galatians 3:13–14 is clear about God's promises for Abraham. These promises extend to all Christ's people. In other words, the Lord Jesus became a curse for Christians so that they may receive their salvation. These blessings also include the blessings of Abraham. This, however, begins with the new birth of the believer. The Bible is clear about how the Lord wants his people to prosper spiritually, emotionally, and physically, and materially (3 John 2). The problem here as noted by Chike is that in many cases some African originated churches have presented material blessings as the result of being saved, and this has led to the "prosperity gospel" which clearly relegates the message of salvation to the "promise of material blessings."[58]

The emphasis on the Holy Spirit's empowerment and attribution of material prosperity as a sign of being saved among African Christians has got much to do with their background. But the greatest influence on the emergence

---

55. Mahoney, *The Shepherd's Staff*, 76.
56. Boff and Boff, *Introducing Liberation Theology*, 3.
57. Chike, *African Christianity in Britain*, 77–79.
58. Chike, 90.

of this material prosperity teachings which is described in some circles as 'health and wealth gospel' was the late Oral Roberts.[59] Oral Robert's teachings were embraced by the late Archbishop Benson Idahosa of the Church of God Mission in Nigeria whose ministry influenced several others in sub-Saharan Africa. The teachings of American evangelists such as John Avanzini and Kenneth Copeland have also influenced many Africans on the prosperity gospel.[60] For one thing, the fact that Africans' understanding of salvation is linked to their culture is worrying. D. J. Hesselgrave, when writing about contextualization, stated his concerns about contextualizers re-enforcing several theologies that eventually would give priority to the interests and values of certain cultures and subcultures and warned that in theologizing contextually, it is necessary that the cultural preferences and social concerns that gave birth to these theologies should not relegate the Bible to a secondary position. Hesselgrave cited the following quotation as a representation of his viewpoint:

> It should be made clear that the cultural preferences and social concerns that gave rise to these theologies were for the most part legitimate. Our quarrel is not with the sensitivity of theologizers to those concerns. Rather, it is with a contextualization meaning and method that gives priority to those concerns and relegates the Bible, the Biblical Christ, and Biblical doctrine to a secondary position when theologizing. When that happens, the Bible loses its authority and merely provides an appropriate "reference points" and pertinent paradigms.[61]

Hesselgrave further argues that with the liberation theology, the central biblical paradigm is the Exodus, and that Christ is only portrayed as the 'Liberator par excellence,' in his own words. He goes on to say that liberation theology has proved to be Bible-related, but not Bible based.[62]

It is fair to heed Hesselgrave's warning about liberation theology because his analysis is particularly useful in that it recognises that the central truth

---

59. https://www.lausanne.org/content/the-prosperity-gospel.
60. This was an article written by Femi Adele on "The Prosperity Gospel: A Critique of the Way the Bible is used." (https://www.lausanne.org/content/the- prosperity-gospel.
61. Hesselgrave, *Scripture and Strategy*, 72.
62. Hesselgrave, 72.

of our theologizing should be the person of Jesus. But quite frequently, while approaching theology through an analysis of society, liberation theology, for an example within its Latin American context has been associated with Marxist thought. Consequently, its opponents have made considerable efforts to expose the limitations of this connection. The focus point of the African liberation theology, however, is the active faith and spirituality of the African Christian who though he has gained spiritual freedom believes that God can also deliver him from poverty and diseases.[63] The tools of analysis of the African theology are drawn from the realities of economic and social situation of Africans, but the point of reference to which these tools are responsible are the faith of the African believer and the gospel of liberation as interpreted from the Scriptures.

Another point to consider about the theology of the African immigrant churches is how many of these churches offer practical assistance to their congregations in all aspects of life such as education, career, marriage and family support and function as social hub for the newly arrived immigrants.[64] Some critics call this action a "social gospel," yet ideally, one of the principal concerns of all of liberation theology's expressions is the liberation of the economically poor. As such, their theology has sometimes been described as social gospel. Yet Jesus in his mission on earth did not only teach and practise spiritual things, but also demonstrated practical Christian living. Therefore, Kee suggests that any genuine expression of a theology of liberation should involve deeply held assumptions on human praxis and take into consideration the person of Jesus and the demands of the Christian faith.[65]

Contrary to Hesselgrave's assertion that liberation theology proves to be Bible-related and not Bible based,[66] the African immigrant churches have developed their own epistemology – a liberation theological reflection and expression by African Christians based on their African experiences.[67] However, it is also important to highlight that their theology has the use of the centrality of the Scripture as a foundational tool. Notwithstanding this, there are

---

63. Abraham, *Third World Theologies: Commonalities and Divergences*, 46.
64. Olofinjana, *Reverse in Ministry and Mission*, 52.
65. Kee, *Domination or Liberation: The Place of Religion in Social Conflict*, 5.
66. Hesselgrave, *Scripture and Strategy*, 72.
67. Mbiti, "The Biblical Basis for Present Trends in African Theology," 119.

different African immigrant churches with distinctive styles of ecclesiology, but intimately interconnected in their Christianity beliefs. Yet overall, they combine to form a unique African contextualization of Christianity, which places emphasis on the power of God. This is so because Africans are very much aware of the demonic forces such as evil spirits and witchcraft, hence their absolute trust in the power of the Holy Spirit dealing with these forces on their behalf.

3.3. Theologizing within the Multicultural Context of Britain

Thompson and Keller echo the concerns local people may have about migrant Christians reaching out to them in the West. They offer some very cogent reasons why it is realistic to understand that in today's secularised society, people (the indigenes) will not listen to strangers. They therefore suggest that it is crucial to share the gospel intentionally along existing networks to attract new membership from the wider communities. What Thompson and Keller mean here is that it is strategically important for migrant churches to use the existing network for their mission endeavours to the wider communities. Such a possibility as suggested by Thompson and Keller,[68] however, may not be the only scenario. Nevertheless, it is true to say that the central challenge facing the African immigrant churches is the need to develop a model of Christian mission that inspires and transforms life irrespective of one's background and how they can partner with the white majority churches for a more effective delivery of the gospel in the UK. Therefore, the African immigrant churches would have to re-define themselves in relation to the white majority churches and clarify their theology, if they are truly going to partner with them. This poses a serious challenge to the African immigrant churches, as it is obvious that there are cultural differences that in a way have kept them apart from the white majority churches.

Yet in partnering with each other, there is the likelihood that both sides will be able to challenge the aspects of their culture and cultural influences on theology that are not consistent with biblical principles. Even that which appears strange to their sensitivities coloured as they are by their theological

---

68. Thompson and Keller, *Redeemer Church Planting: Redeemer City to City*, 124–125.

and cultural presuppositions, may be a dynamic and fluid movement on the way to becoming a truly African expression of the Lord Jesus Christ. As such, for the African immigrant churches to become relevant in the UK landscape, they would have to change their theology in line with Scripture, to suit the environment in which they operate (the wider British environment) and adapt to an ecclesiastical style that would be different from those practised in most churches in Africa. Their theology should be a type of theology that is keen to eliminate the harmful effects of an over-spiritualised expression of Christian faith.

Schreiter asks very pertinent questions concerning the relationship between what the Westerners too easily write off as "syncretism" and contextualization:

> If contextualization is about getting to the very heart of the culture, and Christianity is taking place there, will not the Christianity that emerges look very much like a product of that culture? Or (to follow out the "heart of the culture" image) are we going to continue giving cultures the equivalent of an artificial heart-an organ that can do the job the culture needs, but one that will remain forever foreign?[69]

It is fair to say that there is no theology that can be universally accepted for all people perpetually. But theology develops gradually because of the interaction between the gospel and the human cultural context in which the gospel is preached. In other words, theology becomes contextualized because of the human context in which the gospel is ministered. Wilbert Shenk was therefore right to state that one of the key features or definitions of contextualization is that "it is a process whereby the gospel message encounters a particular culture, calling forth faith and leading to the formation of a faith community which is culturally authentic and authentically Christian."[70] When one reflects on this definition the necessity of the process becomes apparent. It is an observable fact that today, the African immigrant churches in the UK find themselves living on the fringes of the environment of the Western cultural context in which they have established their landscape. In a way these churches are already contextualized but only to the minority African

---

69. Schreiter, *Constructing Local Theologies*, 150.
70. Shenk, *Changing Frontier Mission*, 56–57.

communities. Yet ideally churches should not seek to be organized primarily in terms of ethnicity as this distracts from the biblical principles of unity in diversity (Gal 3:28). There is therefore the need for contextualization with respect to the wider British society.

Rooms suggests that human culture and historical context play a part in the construction of the reality in which they live, so the human context influences their understanding of God and the expression of their faith. Rooms cites a situation whereby English Christians' integration of their faith and culture would affect their worldview of live and values.[71] The African immigrant churches have become established in the Western context and so they can work with the white majority churches to promote the gospel in their new context by developing a new way of how being in Christ sees ethnic differences disappear and celebrates God's gift of diversity.[72] Both sides must develop a theology that is truly rooted in a culture and moment of history.

It is true to say that the African immigrant churches and the white majority churches are the subjects of culture and cultural change, as such are seeking to understand the Christian faith in a contemporary context that has developed because of mass migration into Britain in the past few decades which has resulted in creating multicultural communities. Therefore, a type of theology, suitable to the emerging contexts, is to be developed in terms of dialogue between the various cultures.

However, the current context of pluralism and multiculturalism in Britain appears to be problematic to contextualization. The British society is like a 'melting pot' especially in the cities whereby mass migration has resulted in people from diverse cultures living together. In this type of environment there is always a competing interest and so any attempt of contextualization would be susceptible to the negative attitude of competition. Therefore, it is pertinent to ensure that all ethical dimensions are considered in the process of contextualization. The issue here is how the African immigrant churches can contextualize by freeing themselves from identification with Western cultures

---

71. Rooms, *The Faith of the English: Integrating Christ and Culture*, 16–17.

72. I am not suggesting that differences in cultures will be obliterated. What he means is the differences brought about by class and race. The issue here is a situation whereby there is an intentional diminished view of Christ's people from different backgrounds by other Christians having inflated view of themselves. These differences in the author's view, will disappear and give way to the celebration of God's gift of diversity in a true Christian relationship.

and manifesting in their own ministry the universal nature of the church and mission. The African immigrant churches must use critical contextualization without compromising Scripture. Developing an understanding of the principles of hermeneutics to interpret the Bible properly is especially important since this could lead to the establishing of biblical churches and ministries.[73]

Hesselgrave believes that the cultural preferences and social concerns that give rise to contextual theologies are legitimate, but what he is concerned of is "a contextualization meaning and method that gives priority to those concerns and relegates the biblical doctrine to a secondary position."[74] Hesselgrave feels that when that happens, the Bible loses its authority and merely provides appropriate "reference points," and pertinent paradigms.[75] The Apostle Paul in 1 Corinthians 9:19–23 (NKJV) had this to say about winning souls from all backgrounds without compromising biblical morality:

> For though I am free from all men, I have made myself a servant to all, that I might win the more, and to the Jews, I became as a Jew, that I might win Jews . . . Now this I do for the gospel's sake that I may be partaker of it with you.

Paul would go to any length to break cultural barriers to reach out to people from diverse backgrounds. Hiebert also had this to say about contextualization:

> The Bible is seen as containing divine revelation, not simply humanly constructed beliefs. In contextualization, the heart of the Gospel must be kept by encoding it in forms that are understood by the people, without making the Gospel captive to the contexts. This is an ongoing process of embodying the Gospel in an ever-changing world. Here cultures are viewed as both good and evil, not simply as neutral vehicles for understanding the world. No culture is absolute or privileged. We are all revitalized by the Gospel.[76]

---

73. Bosch, *Transforming Mission*, 435–442.
74. Hesselgrave, *Scripture and Strategy*, 71–72.
75. Hesselgrave, 71–72.
76. Hiebert, *The Gospel in Human Context: Anthropological Explorations for Contemporary Missions*, 29.

It is worth noting that Hiebert draws a clear picture between gospel and culture in contextualization. Reaching out to other cultures, would involve understanding such cultures. However, Christ's people must always take heed of Hiebert's advice in drawing the balance between gospel and culture. Where it is noticeable that a particular culture compromises the Bible, the precepts of the Bible must be seen as a barrier that Christ's people should not cross.

Barring the variety of definitions, explanations, and evaluations on the subject matter of contextualization, R. Winter points out that contextualization is a dangerous word.[77] In a similar fashion, he maintains that the problem of contextualization is that it has not been properly defined by its originators. He has this to say:

> But in the case of contextualisation, the definitions supplied by its originators were so biased in the direction of theological liberalism or neo-orthodoxy that some conservatives felt duty-bound to reject it altogether while others went to considerable lengths to redeem and refashion it.[78]

In the past few decades, there have been changes in the nature of the context in the UK due to mass migration into the country. It is right to say that these changes have been accelerated, due to the phenomena of pluralism and multiculturalism. In view of this, it has become necessary for contextual theology to seek new ways of doing theology in a plausible way.[79] According to Tanner every type of theology is a theology of a particular cultural context. Tanner thinks that every human interpretation of theology is done in the cultural context of the interpreter.[80] In other words, a given Christian theology is an interpretation of the Christian faith from a particular context, making faith sensible to the realities of that context. The differences between the theological understandings of various interpreters therefore correspond

---

77. Winter, *Vision for the Nations*, 27.
78. Hesselgrave, *Scripture and Strategy*, 68.
79. Justine George in their thesis, "Intercultural Theology: An Approach to Theologizing in the Context of Pluralism and Globalization" used an analytical process to propose intercultural theology as the right response to the challenges of contextual theology. George says: "the process of intercultural theology with its facilitation of mutuality can balance the particular-universal tension keeping theology relevant and credible and leading the church to a dynamic wholeness." (George, "Intercultural Theology," 2.)
80. Tanner, "Theories of Culture," 19.

to the differences between their cultural contexts. And it is fair to say that culture influences the theological thinking of Christ's people. For example, if one works out of an empirical notion of culture, not only can there be a theology for every culture, but there is also the possibility that other theologies could emerge for every generation of history, and this certainly will lead to proliferation of contextual theologies.

According to Schreiter when pluralism is considered a reality of the human context, the plurality of contexts directly leads to multiple contextual starting points. Considering different social factors, he proposes two models in theologizing: an ethnographic model, which emphasizes cultural change. And a liberation model. This theologizing model places emphasis on social change from oppression and social evils.[81] Bevans on the other hand, identifies four essential realities of context that determine and influence the nature of contextual theology. They are personal or communal experience, culture, social location, and social change.[82] Contextualization in ethnographic and liberation models interacting with the pluralities of the above four realities of context can bring out a proper understanding of numerous contextual theologies. While the ethnographic model takes into consideration the issue of identity and continuity, the liberation model, on the other hand, is concerned about social change and discontinuity.[83]

While many related questions remain unanswered concerning the concept of contextualization, Bevans affirmed that there is no such thing as theology other than contextual theology and suggested that even European (Western) theology was also a contextual theology. The only difference with it was that it was "not confronted by pluralism and was consequently imposed as a universal theology for all contexts."[84]

It is certainly true to say that pluralism creates individuation contexts, hence encourages the development of different contextual theologies. When this happens, there is the tendency that each of these contexts would be influenced by their own cultures. The effect of this cultural influence would be the forging ahead with the type of theology which they believe would be suitable

---

81. Schreiter, *Constructing Local Theologies*, 13–16.
82. Bevans, *Models of Contextual Theology*, 11.
83. Schreiter, *Constructing Local Theologies*, 21.
84. Bevans, *Models of Contextual Theology*, 1–6.

for their cultural contexts (with questionable epistemology). This will result in the proliferation of various kinds of contextual theologies which may be Bible related and not necessarily Bible based.

Bosch observes that when theology was contextualized in the West (Western Europe and North America), and exported to other parts of the world, contextualism then became the universalizing of the Western theological position. Bosch warns that non-Western contextual theologies also have the "same tendency to make a carbon copy of the mistakes of the West and when this happens it will, certainly, lead to new imperialist theology." The emphasis of the contextual theology is on ethnic identity and cultural logic. This in a way counteracts global theological flows, as such the tension of universal versus local continues to exist in contextual theology. In the background of multiculturalism, contextual theology can repeat the same historical mistakes of presenting one contextual theology of a local church, leading to neo-imperialism. There is always the tendency for new imperialism in theology too, which simply replaces the old as has happened with tradition.[85]

Schreiter rightly observes that certain elements of differences are given more prominence while some elements of identity are overlooked.[86] For instance, in the UK there is multiculturalism and multi-belonging, and people in this country live together with attempts to express their unique identities. But in seeking identity and relevance in this multicultural setting, which in a way is *melting pot*, Christ's people are always going to experience tensions between particularity and universality in their current way of doing theology. How do we then theologize to suit the emerging context? There is the suggestion that "an experimental theology in which an ongoing dialogue is taking place between text and context, a theology which, in the nature of the case, should remain 'provisional and hypothetical' should be suitable for any emerging context."[87]

---

85. Bosch, *Transforming Mission*, 437–438.
86. Schreiter, *Constructing Local Theologies*, 26–27.
87. Bosch, *Transforming Mission*, 437.

3.4. Developing a Biblical Theological Basis and Hermeneutics for the African Immigrant Churches in the UK

It is important to highlight that for the African immigrant churches to become relevant in the UK landscape and reach out into the wider communities, they would have to change their theology in line with Scripture to suit the British environment in which they operate; they would have to adopt the type of theology that explores the universal dimension of the Christian faith. Bevans understands that there is no such thing as a comprehensive or all-embracing theology for the universal church today, and that theology is the way religion makes sense in a particular cultural context.[88] The African immigrant churches have become part of the landscape in Britain and are part of the British communities and it is incumbent upon them as Christians to minister to the wider communities. To do this, they need a theology that appeals to their new context. However, they would not necessarily have to adapt a theology that is based on creedal statements and dogmatics as practised in the West, and not the theology which emphasizes spirituality and emotionalism as inherited from their African roots. But rather a theology based on a proper understanding of the eschatological order as demonstrated in the Bible.

Schreiter was making a point about theologizing locally when he argued that for a local theology to be valid, it should be genuinely reflective of the gospel and faithful to the Christian tradition.[89] Schreiter cited the following to support his view on local theology:

> Local theologies are, in many ways, the expressions of popular religions. To develop local theologies, then, one must listen to popular religion in order to find out what is moving in people's lives. Only then can local theologies be developed and the liberating power of the Gospel come to its full flower.[90]

According to Boff and Boff, the human experiences of injustices are the outcomes of theological reflections on liberation and that in its ecclesiology, the church must show that it is an instrument of liberation of the poor. They

---

88. Bevans, *Models of Contextual Theology*, 7–8.
89. Schreiter, *Constructing Local Theologies*, 117.
90. Schreiter, 143.

further argue that, for the church to develop an ecclesiology of liberation that typifies the image of the poor, the church would have to realize its responsibilities for the poor. Similarly, they demonstrated that the Bible should place emphasis on supporting the poor and the oppressed in the society.[91]

Similarly, Schreiter suggests that ecclesiology is going to be one of the key issues in developing local theologies-as prominent as hermeneutics, modes of cultural analysis and Christology.[92] He further states that the struggles of contemporary poor are the most raised moral problem in the gospels.[93] Bosch is also of the view that the theme of justice has been resurrected by the experience of these communities into an awareness of many communities.[94] Likewise, Gutierrez argues that liberation theology must address itself and suggested that the following concerns should be considered: conditions of social, political, and economic oppression, the "need the oppressed have of historical autonomy and the emancipation from sin and the acceptance of new life in Christ." Only when all these conditions are properly taken into consideration in circumstances where the poor are encouraged to vocalise their needs and lead the way through to their liberty, can authentic liberation theology be said to have taken place.[95]

This brings into focus the concerns for a biblical approach to questions of interpretation of the Bible on one hand, and concerns for positive outcomes for churches and missions in other cultures.[96] The response to challenges of pluralism and relativism manifests themselves not only in the way secularist approach questions the truth and goodness. But also, in the way in which Christians from diverse backgrounds approach the Scriptures. These challenges cannot be underestimated.

Hammett was right in his assertion that the pragmatic approach of Christ's people, irrespective of their backgrounds, to church life, their concern to be relevant to their culture, and their desire to see their churches grow leave them vulnerable to the danger that their churches will be shaped more by

---

91. Boff and Boff, *Introducing Liberation Theology*, 44–46.
92. Schreiter, *Constructing Local Theologies*, 38.
93. Schreiter, 34–35.
94. Bosch, *Transforming Mission*, 99–100.
95. Gutierrez, *A Theology of Liberation: History, Politics, and Salvation*, 83–85.
96. Hesselgrave, *Scripture and Strategy*, 60.

those concerns than "by design of the Lord of the church."[97] In the light of these powerful cultural influences, Christian workers desiring to use critical contextualization would find a peaceful anchorage in the Scripture by developing an understanding of the principles of hermeneutics to interpret the Bible properly, irrespective of their backgrounds. It will certainly be useful for them to be equipped and grounded in biblical principles, and adept at theological thinking. For instance, if the African Christians' understanding of salvation, as affirmed by authors such as Chike, is all about being saved and blessed,[98] this will hinder their message to the already rich and those in the wider communities who do not face the social problems which in a way have defined the African theology of salvation.

There is no doubt that African Christians understand salvation in soteriological terms (salvation of individuals from eternal damnation), but the issue here is their over emphasis on material blessings which they claim occurs because of their being saved as well as the spiritual emphasis they place on spiritual warfare. It is true to say that there were several instances in the Bible, especially in the ministry of Christ and the early Apostles where people were said to be afflicted with spirits of infirmity and the only way for them to be healed was to first deal with the evil spirits by casting them out and once the demonic spirits have been cast out such persons received their healing (Matt 8:3; Acts 3:1–6). But the problem here is the too much emphasis many of these migrant churches place on this doctrine.

In contrast to what has been said about leadership of the migrant churches in the UK by some Bible scholars and other authors, that one of the success stories of the migrant churches is their "top down" leadership style,[99] Gibbs and Coffey echo the principle of the lone leader in the top down system, as abnormal and has negative impact on those being led because such a leadership style does not identify the gifts of those being led as their goal is not empowerment, but submission.[100] Similarly, Robinson and Smith were making a crucial point when they said: "we are left to die the death of the

---

97. Hammett, *Biblical Foundations for Baptist Churches*, 11.
98. Chike, *African Christianity in Britain*, 77.
99. Olofinjana, *Reverse in Ministry and Mission*, 52.
100. Gibbs and Coffey, *Church Next*, 87.

strengths and weaknesses of the man at the top."[101] It suggests that Robinson and Smith see this type of church leadership as a kind of leadership that has no knowledge of building a team to get the work done and fails to understand that those who want to be leaders must be servants.

The cult of personality dominates many African-led churches today and this certainly interferes with the development and progress of the ministries because this type of leadership places emphasis on the individual they refer to as "the anointed person of God." The cult of personality, therefore, limits the ministry to that person's vision alone and sadly channels much of the church's resources to the "man at the top" enhancing their image as super pastors.[102] Gibbs suggests that Christian leaders should follow Paul's example of demonstrating the importance of teamwork to get the work done. Corporate leadership expands the church's leadership base, which eventually leads to the diversification of the church's leadership gift and results in a properly developed and balanced manner.[103] Gibbs and Coffey think those Christian leaders who build strong relationships and expand their networks are those who relate well to one another in their congregations, hence command respect and influence within the network.[104]

It is clear to say that any meaningful theologizing would involve interpretation and so doing theology in this emerging context of the UK would involve the human activity of interpretation. According to Tanner, every human interpretation is done in the context of the interpreter.[105] Regarding the African immigrant churches, the factors that informed the development of their African liberation theology are different from the factors that define their present environment. Theologizing would require a proper understanding of the principles of hermeneutics which is important in interpreting the Bible properly as suggested by Tanner. Tanner argues that a given theology is "an interpretation of Christian faith from a particular context." This ensures that faith becomes sensible to the happenings or realities of that context. Tanner further states that the differences between the theological understandings

---

101. Robinson and Smith, *Invading Secular Space*, 126.
102. Brodersen, *Essentials in Ministry*, 7.
103. Gibbs *Leadership Next*, 31.
104. Gibbs and Coffey, *Church Next*, 87.
105. Tanner, *Theories of Culture*, 19.

of various interpreters corresponds to the differences between their cultural contexts.[106] The challenge here is developing the type of epistemology which can make a local theology contextually relevant and comes with a universal acceptance. For them to achieve this there is the need for the African immigrant churches and the UK white majority churches to develop together an intercultural hermeneutics that is for both churches.

W. J. Larkin develops a biblical theology of hermeneutics and culture and sets forth hermeneutical guidelines for interpreting and applying the Bible by providing examples from Western and the majority world cultures. Larkin's work involves four approaches: an overview, analysis, interpretation, and application. Larkin in offering a reflective overview and analysis on how Scripture can be used effectively to communicate the message of the good news to all contemporary contexts suggested some very cogent viewpoint:

> This method of interpretation and application moves back and forth between the part and the whole, the text and the various contexts in which it is to be understood. In overview, interpreters consciously adopt a biblical preunderstanding in viewing the literary and the historical context of the text. They take stock of their own cultural preunderstanding to assess its relation to the message. The next step views the parts through analysis, as interpreters study the grammatical, literary, and historical-cultural factors and what they contribute to the meaning. At this point interpreters return to a concern for context, as they engage in interpretation.[107]

Having considered the above points, interpreters will then put together a coherent understanding of the text in its various literary contexts and relate that understanding to their own cultural context, considering how to propagate the message of the text and how to use it to communicate to the contemporary cultural context and finally, its application, which determines the implementation of the message in the immediate context.[108]

---

106. Tanner, *Theories of Culture*, 19.
107. Larkin, *Culture and Biblical Hermeneutics*, 325–328.
108. Larkin, 325–326.

Theological Analysis of the African Immigrant Churches in the UK

Similarly, Starkloff understands that the propagation of the gospel involves a conversation between the gospel and the cultural context in which the message is delivered.[109] Certainly, in several significant but limited ways, a person can contribute to the contextualization of theology in a cultural context that is not their own. But when they do this, *they must approach the host culture with both humility and honesty.* To reach out to the wider communities, the African immigrant churches must observe that the good news is always propagated through a particular context and that the gospel itself has the power to transform these cultures to fall in line with Scripture. However, a real danger in contextualization is that one could mix Christianity and culture in a way that does not enhance but compromises and betrays Christianity.[110] The fact is that a theology that takes culture seriously can easily become a "culture theology." Geertz has this to say about culture:

> It denotes an historically transmitted pattern of meanings embodied in symbols, a system of inherited conceptions expressed in symbolic forms by means of which (men) communicate, perpetuate, and develop their knowledge about the attitudes towards life.[111]

Rooms also highlights that the meaning a person places on the world, the values he or she holds and the actions that ensue all constitute that person's culture.[112] Newbigin, however, in talking about plurality of human cultures warned:

> From the point of view of a sociologist, religion is part of culture, and no religious belief is without implications for culture. On the other hand, religions may be multicultural, and that is certainly true of Christianity. There are enormous cultural variations between the ways which Christians in Nigeria, India, Samoa, and the USA express their faith. The question of the relation between

---

109. Starkloff, "Inculturation and Cultural Systems," 66–81.
110. Hammett, *Biblical Foundations for Baptist Churches*, 11.
111. Geertz, *The Interpretation of Cultures*, 89.
112. Rooms, *The Faith of the English*, 16.

the Gospel and the different human cultures is a very live one in contemporary missiology.[113]

Newbigin further indicates that McGavran "absolutized culture" and minimised the cultural changes which bring conversion into the believer's life. McGavran, according to Newbigin, affirmed that people who accept the gospel ought to retain their traditional culture. Newbigin went on to say that what McGavran perhaps meant here was such aspect of culture as "music, art, dress, habits of eating and drinking and language" and not elements of culture such as "cannibalism, the death penalty for petty offences, or the ancient Indian concept of sati."[114] All in all, Newbigin maintains that there is no absolute concept of a total relativism in respect of varieties of human culture, but suggests that the most fundamental element in culture is language.[115]

Culture plays a role in missions, but a fear of "syncretism" has been evident from the beginning of the discussions about contextualizing theology. It is worth noting that there is contemporary pluralism in theology and the contextualization of theology is an important contribution factor. Therefore, contextual theologians and Bible scholars deemed it appropriate to look for a more credible way of theologizing when crossing cultural contexts. For example, if theology is grounded in a particular context, it cannot then be found to co-exist with culture that is inimical to human development. The Bible, therefore, must absolutely speak with authority to our different historical and cultural situations.

Rooms describes a given Christian theology as interpretation of Christian faith from that context, making faith sensible to the realities of that context. Rooms further states that any attempt of Christians to integrate their faith and culture will affect the meaning they place on life and values.[116] In other words, any attempt to contextualize the theology of the African immigrant churches to make sense to their new British environment must take into consideration the worldview of the African Christian.

---

113. Newbigin, *The Gospel in a Pluralist Society*, 184–185.

114. Sati is the burning of a man's widow with his body on the funeral pyre (Newbigin, *The Gospel in a Pluralist Society*, 184).

115. Newbigin, *The Gospel in a Pluralist Society*, 184–185.

116. Rooms, *The Faith of the English*, 16.

The gospel, however, is propagated through culture, hence cannot be understood without a particular cultural expression. This calls for inculturation. However, Rooms suggests that the definition of inculturation should go beyond finding correspondences between faith and culture or adapting faith to culture.[117] Magessa argues that:

> The inculturation is a deep experience in the life of an individual and the community that occurs when there is a constant search for identification between Gospel and culture, and where there is mutual correction and adjustment between them.[118]

Rooms noted how implicit inculturation could potentially be inconsistent, but also argues that there could still be a sort of "integration of faith and culture, however, helpful, or unhelpful" (in the UK). He suggested that Christ's people bring the hidden, implicit inculturation to the surface and examine it afresh in the "light of faith, creating a hopefully more helpful, explicit inculturation." [119] There is therefore the need for Christ's people to recognise outreach as a mutual partnership and conversely, dialogue in a particular culture within a biblical perspective. Their mission endeavours should also continue to seek appropriate expressions of the gospel in the cultures that make up the multicultural British communities and reflect inclusivity within these cultures.

According to Starkloff the theological concept of inculturation does not address the interaction between gospel and culture as argued when he said:

> The introduction of the term "inculturation" into theological discourse can be compared to the proverbial stone cast into a pond: it has sent ripples throughout the Christian world. This has happened with such rapidity that inculturation is still often misunderstood in popular conversation, and at times in pastoral workshops and classes. However, I resist attempting to clarify the term further. A summary of existing works on inculturation indicates that it always involves a conversation between two partners-the universal Gospel or fundamental "good news" and

---

117. Rooms, *The Faith of the English*, 18.
118. Magessa, *Anatomy of Inculturation: Transforming The Church in Africa*, 189.
119. Rooms, *The Faith of the English*,18.

the cultural uniqueness of each context in which that message is heard.[120]

In the light of these contrasting backgrounds, it is clear that "inculturation" does not consider a more complex reality of the interaction between the corporate Christian culture in which the gospel is propagated and the various levels of meanings that other cultures manifest. Bosch affirms that the philosophy that "anything goes as long as it seems to make sense" can be catastrophic. There are many cultures in the world and even within one country there could be different tribes and cultures.[121] The challenge here is the value system diverse cultures attach to similar issues and how these issues are addressed in the local cultures. For example, diverse cultures have different meanings to matters such as illness, death, prosperity, spiritual warfare, sin and forgiveness and many others. The African Christian places emphasis on spiritual warfare, divine protection, healing, and prosperity while in the Europe and North America where guilt is an issue, the emphasis is on sin and forgiveness.[122] It is true to say that the concept of inculturation overlooks serious issues such as the interaction between the Christian culture in which the good news is being propagated and the other meanings manifested in other cultures within the same society.

Bosch affirms that the concept of inculturation still remains unsettled, but it is a continuing process not just because cultures are sporadic, but the likelihood that the church (universal) may discover new truth of the Christian faith. Bosch states that there is no eternal theology, no *theologia perennis* that exercises influence over other theologies. Bosch went on to say that "in the past, Western theology arrogated to itself the right to be such an arbitrator in respect to Third-World theologies. It implicitly viewed itself as fully indigenized, inculturated, a finished product." Conversely, Bosch suggests that all theologies, and that includes the Western theologies, need one another because they influence, challenge, and inspire one another,[123] and clearly this can in a way liberate the Western theologies, from what he describes

---

120. Starkloff, "Inculturation and Cultural Systems," 69.
121. Bosch, *Transforming Mission*, 466.
122. Chike, *African Christianity in Britain*, 79.
123. Bosch, *Transforming Mission*, 466–467.

in his own words as "Babylonian captivity" which they have been held for many centuries.

In relation to this, Bosch understands that what the Christian world participates in is not just inculturation but what he terms "interculturation"[124] which he argues is an appropriate way of theologizing in the emerging context of pluralism, multiculturalism, and globalisation.[125] In this novel approach the African immigrant churches and the white majority churches could have shared common ground to do theology in the process of a mutual understanding of give and take and this will initiate a change in basic assumptions in their understanding of ecclesiology.

It is widespread practice that Christ's people usually pay much attention to the role of culture in interpreting the Bible. However, interpreting Scripture and communicating its meaning and its message to the nations is different from attention to the mission itself. Proper communication of the word of God should lead Christians to unravel God's great plan to include all humankind in his eternal family, and to his desire to use Christ's people in the fulfilment of that plan.

3.5. Summary

For the African immigrant churches to work with the white majority churches, there is the need for contextualization. However, the issue here is how they can contextualize the gospel critically in a way that will be appropriate to their adherents, by achieving the delicate balance of their various cultural contexts without compromising the truth of the Scriptures. There is therefore

---

124. Interculturation assumes that local incarnations of the faith should not be too local. On the other hand, "homogeneous unit" church can become so ingrown that it finds it impossible to communicate with other churches and believes that its perspective on the gospel is the only legitimate one. The church must be a place to feel at home; but if only we feel at home in our particular church, and all others are either excluded or made unwelcome or feel themselves completely alienated, something has gone wrong (Bosch, 2014:467). Intercultural theology is the scholarly theological discipline that operates within a particular cultural framework without absolutizing it. It will select its methods appropriately. Western academic theology is not automatically privileged over others. They also have the responsibility to search for alternative forms of doing theology. All theologies must be measured for their capacity for bridge building between diverse groups (Jongneel, *Pentecost, Mission, and Ecumenism* 11–12).

125. Bosch, *Transforming Mission*, 467.

the need for the emergence of new paradigms of theologizing that are compatible to Scripture.

In the UK, it is observed that contextual theology may be appropriate for theologizing in the emerging context of globalisation and pluralism, because the UK is a multicultural country. The UK cities comprise people from different ethnic and cultural backgrounds. Contextual theology, therefore, gives significance to the various Christian communities and their ways. However, it has its downside of competitive behaviour which may in some cases lead to competitive culture. The reasons being that multiplicity of contextual theologies results in mutual exclusivism, relativism, and absolutism, and this in most cases have been some of the challenges of pluralism in the process of contextualization. There is therefore the need for a proper methodological framework that can help balance the particularities and universalities. This in a way will maintain identity and relevance while doing theology contextually.

A critical contextualization would ensure that it is not simply the interaction between gospel and culture as if they represent two monolithic meanings, but rather between multiple cultural orientations.[126] All Christ's people are shaped by the culture in which they are nurtured, and their culture influences their theological thinking and missiological endeavours. Overall, Christ's people remain unaware of their cultural biases until someone from another culture is sufficiently frank to confront them with the issues.

It is true to say that waves of immigration have influenced the shape of the white majority churches in the UK, particularly in the cities, from the grass-roots level up. African immigrant churches preach the gospel and are the antithesis to values that counter godly living among their own kind. They have a strong 'spiritual worldview.' The white majority churches have strong organizational skills. These are examples of some of the values that can be extended to the wider UK church communities through partnering.

However, theologizing in multicultural Britain comes with challenges. For instance, the nature of the context undergoes changes due to emerging scenarios of pluralism and so for contextual theology to be relevant there should be the need for Christ's people to study the Scriptures to understand and to bear witness to the gospel. However, studying Scriptures alone does not help to see their sociocultural biases and so Christ's people need to study

---

126. Bosch, 437–444.

also human cultural contexts to understand themselves and others and to communicate effectively.[127] Christ's people need to study divine revelation and communicate that revelation in ways that remain true to it and yet are understood by people from all cultures. Failure to do so leads to syncretism in which the truth of the gospel is faded away and Christ's people go astray. Church leaders, therefore, have a greater responsibility in nurturing their congregations to become mission-minded with the understanding that all Christ's people are together in the mission of God, irrespective of their backgrounds or ethnicity. Non-Western churches such as the African immigrant churches have emerged in the UK with their own local theologies, but they are caught between two cultures: they have discovered that they are no longer in Africa, but they are not yet at home in the host culture. They could therefore play a role by creating space for particularities and universalities as admitted by Wijsen and Nissen.[128]

Arguably, dialoguing between the African immigrant churches and the white majority churches has always been problematic but possible. The superiority complex of some white British Christians and the suspicions of the African migrants make dialogue exceedingly difficult as rightly highlighted by Kwiyani who argues that issues of race, among other things, is the main factor hindering dialoguing. Kwiyani mentioned that the pain of discrimination some Africans face in the white majority churches make them resolve to go to the African-led churches "where they do not have to apologise for being African."[129] It is fair to say that, in most cases, migrants in the white majority churches have been made to feel like outsiders despite having all learned to speak English fluently and some of them possessing British passports.

Conversely, Wijsen and Nissen suggest that theology should be used to tackle the issues of race in a way that Christ's people could see their racial differences as diversity.[130] This perception could bring about unity within the body of Christ. The use of effective dialoguing is especially important in bringing about unity. But this can only be achieved in the environment where

---

127. Tanner, *Theories of Culture*, 18–19.

128. Wijsen and Nissen, eds. *Mission is a Must: Intercultural Theology and the Mission of the Church*, 221–222.

129. Kwiyani, *Sent Forth*, 110.

130. Wijsen and Nissen, 222–223.

Christ's people from the diverse cultures can come together to theologize with mutual respect.

Anthony Reddie affirmed that for black Christians in Britain to say they do not see colour as a factor in their hermeneutical engagement with the Christian faith is shortsighted. Reddie affirms that there are racial differences but maintains that the differences should not bring a disunity into the body of Christ. He feels that it is not the physical differences that are the problem but our value system. That is to say, the meanings we attribute to notions of race and ethnicity have always divided people from different racial backgrounds. Reddie cites the experience in Pentecost (Acts 2) to bolster his claims. He had this to say: "In the Pentecost narrative, we see the difference itself is not a problem. The believers at the epoch-making event in Jerusalem are united in faith and adherence to God and not through a sublimation of their material differences."[131]

There have been some suggestions by Bible scholars such as Kwame Bediako that Africans should have their own version of the Christian faith that responds to their context and that "this would affirm their humanity and enable them to be more genuinely Christians because they would be practising Christianity that rings true within."[132] In contrast to the assertion of Bediako, which to some degree can apply to the Christian faith in Africa, the African immigrant churches in the UK find themselves in a diverse cultural context. Ideally, they must regard the whole British society as another stage in their mission endeavours. However, if they are truly going to reach out to the wider communities, their theology would have to reflect their present environment. It should be a theology with universal scope.

There is, therefore, the need for a contextualization of the African immigrant churches,[133] and contextualization, if managed critically, can result in free interaction and involvement of people from diverse backgrounds without ignoring their individualities but recognising their differences as a gift to the

---

131. Reddie, *Working Against the Grain: Reimaging Black Theology in the 21st Century*, 18–20.

132. Bediako, *Theology and Identity: The Impact of Culture upon Christian Thought in the Second Century and in Modern Africa*, 237.

133. The African immigrant churches have now gained their landscape in the Britain and are now part of the fabric of the British society. If they really want to reach out to the wider communities, they would need a theology which reflects the culture of their new environment.

body of Christ. Creating an atmosphere of sensitivity to each other's culture will result in *intercultural* relationship, which will bring about a reciprocal interaction of the diverse cultures that make up the British communities. This can result in reconciled unity, which will reject the false belief that one culture is the best and that all others must follow their ways.[134]

In general, it is true to say that one of the challenges facing cross-cultural missions is the theology. However, theologizing in the emerging context alone will not bring about the desired unity. Christ's people, irrespective of their backgrounds, must take biblical inerrancy and authority seriously. They must also use valid principles of interpretation and application. A common theological approach in part can prevail in the diversity between the white majority churches and the African immigrant churches as this may increase their conversation which will create awareness and move the dialogue forward, even though, uniformity is not to be sought.

---

134. Bosch, *Transforming Mission*, 466–468.

CHAPTER 4

Findings and Implications

4.1. Introduction

I did a historical development and theological analysis into the mission of the African immigrant churches in the UK in the last two previous chapters (chapters 2 and 3). The initial investigations in chapter 2 were to engage with the fundamental questions of the historical developments of the African immigrant churches in the UK; how diversity brought by international migration has resulted in a rich ethnic blend in Britain's urban communities that naturally finds its way into churches. The theological analysis of the African immigrant churches (chapter 3) was undertaken to determine the theological relevance of these migrant churches in the UK Christian landscape. It was discovered in chapter 2 that through the mission endeavours of the African immigrant churches, many migrants have found a refuge from discrimination and discovered a sense of identity, respect and belonging in the different churches established by persons of their own ethnic or national origin where they can profoundly assert themselves. Undoubtedly, the African immigrant churches have found a Christian space in Britain and it is true to say that the factors bringing them together are not just spiritual but also other factors include "social identities, transnationalism, migration as a process, civic engagement and political incorporation, and gender relations" as observed by Olupona and Gemignani.[1] Certainly, these factors will remain with the

---

1. See Olupona and Gemignani, introduction to *African immigrant Religions in America*, 3.

African immigrant churches and frankly, they are good for the recently arrived immigrants and migrants with a high people consciousness. Yet ideally, churches should not seek to be organized primarily in terms of ethnicities as this distracts from the biblical principles of unity in diversity (Gal 3:24).

More so, there is an uncertain future for any church or church movement whose numerical growth or existence depends on the number of immigrants coming into the country. How then can the African immigrant churches redefine their God-given mandate to Britain and work cross culturally with the white majority churches? In addition, how can they strategize in such a way that they would become the vanguard of spiritual, emotional, and social liberation to the UK Christian communities and the wider society?

In general, it is true to say that one of the challenges facing cross-cultural missions is the theology. However, this study proved in chapter 3 that theologizing in the emerging context alone would not bring about the desired result. Even though, a common theological approach in part can prevail in the diversity between the white majority churches and the African immigrant churches, as this may increase their conversation and thereby create awareness and move the dialogue forward, yet, in this case uniformity is not to be sought. There is, therefore, the need to learn from other churches and denominations that have African roots and white majority churches that integrate blacks, on how their visions, values and practices can bring about the desired aim of this study. This chapter therefore focuses on investigations into four denominations in the UK: two with African roots, the Church of Pentecost of Ghana in UK and the Ethiopian Church London and two white UK denominations that integrate black people, the All Nations Church (ANC) and the Baptist Union of Great Britain. It is fair to say that any attempt to investigate all the four denominations would take several years so I decided to study a single local church taken from each of the denominations.

The primary sources of information used in this chapter include research findings obtained from observation, interview, field notes and documentation. I gathered the themes, insights and patterns that emerged from the research fieldwork and integrated them into a critical thesis, utilizing methods of comparison, analysis, critique, and evaluation in the next chapters (chapters 5–7).

4.2. Case Study Selection

The ANC was chosen because it is a white majority church that incorporates people from diverse backgrounds, hence it has the potential to suit the description of a multi-ethnic church with a multicultural identity. The Harborne Baptist Church (HBC) was chosen because it is a welcoming church which has integrated people from nineteen diverse backgrounds; the Church of Pentecost (COP) was chosen because it is a migrant church which has tried to work with a white majority church in the UK; it also offers a strong cross-current debate of what African Christian scholars termed as reverse mission. The Ethiopian Church London (ECL), on the other hand, was chosen because it is an African immigrant church that has become part of the Christian landscape in Britain, and now has many branches in different parts of the country. I made initial contacts with the leadership of all the four churches by writing to ask their permission to carry out this research fieldwork. I was assigned a minister by the leadership of each of the four churches to act as the main "gatekeeper." I received the full co-operation of all the four pastors and their congregations. A high degree of access and intensive participant observation were carried out as listed below: The fieldwork was carried out during five Sunday visits to each of the four churches and during some of their week activities. This lasted for a period of 24 months starting from April 2015 to April 2017. There were also follow-up visits during and after the fieldwork.

4.3. History, Structure, Vision, and Practices of the Four Case Study Churches

The following are the history, structure, vision, and practices of the four denominations that were researched:

4.3.1. All Nations Church, Wolverhampton

The ANC was initially called Temple Street Pentecostal Church. It is situated in the geographical centre of Wolverhampton, near Birmingham in the West Midlands in the UK. ANC is missional, charismatic, and compassionate. It was planted by two young sisters in 1941 from Lancashire. Initially, the vision was to reach out to the needy in the poorest communities. In other words, the aim was to make it a place where the hurting, the depressed, the frustrated and destitute could find salvation, hope, forgiveness, restoration, acceptance, and love as well as help and encouragement to become what they were supposed to become in their Christian lives. There was a major shift in ministry practice when Pastor Steve Uppal became the senior minister in 2001. Even though, the church still maintains the vision of the founders in ministering to the needy in the community, and welcoming people from diverse backgrounds, when Pastor Uppal became the senior minister, he and his team of ministers changed the church's name to the ANC as they believe the new name is what reflects the vision of the church. They believe also that it is a prophetic name and suits the diverse nature of the Wolverhampton communities as well as the multicultural identity of their ministry.[2]

4.3.1.1. Vision and Values

The church's vision is for all people, irrespective of their backgrounds, to glorify God through knowing Christ after receiving salvation and becoming, sanctified, spirit filled Christians. These born-again Christians would in turn make Christ known to others through evangelism and by their practical Christian living. The values of the church are written on their website and during the interview with the leadership, they mentioned these values with much emphasis.[3] "Building a healthy culture that attracts the presence of the Holy Spirit" among Christ's people is the church's main goal and they believe they can achieve this by practising the following values:

- The centrality of Christ is their core values. They believe that Jesus Christ is supreme in all things and is central and the example in all things.
- They believe in an authentic community, valuing relationships above gift and function as they think that the greatest commandment is relational.
- They are of the view that all Christ's people must have audacious faith, insurmountable hope, and extravagant love since they believe that these three are supernatural powers for all Christ's people.
- They believe that spiritual disciplines such as prayer and fasting should be practised by their leadership and congregants.

---

2. Copied from the All Nations Church website: www.allnations.org.uk/about/values.
3. All Nations Church website.

- Another value is living a life of humility and sacrifice since they believe that God esteems humility and sacrifice and that believers must follow the example of Jesus.
- They are committed to extending the kingdom of God by proclaiming the good news to the poor, bringing deliverance and new life to all. This, they think is the Great Commission which requires urgent full obedience as the whole world is their mission field.[4]

4.3.1.2. Sunday Worship and Ecclesiastical Style

During my fieldtrips, I observed that there were three main Sunday services: the first service starts at 9.30 am. It is a multi-ethnic service officiated in the English language; the second service starts from 12.00 pm and it is officiated in the Chinese language; the last service is the Asian service ministered in Punjabi. This service starts at 3.30 pm. The Sunday morning services are contemporary, with lively band-led worship and an informal feel. They have recently built a large, modernized church auditorium with modern facilities which has created a conducive environment for their church activities.

4.3.1.3. Other Groups

I discovered during my fieldtrips to the ANC that the church is involved in a variety of ministry activities including preaching, teaching, pastoral care, and prayer meetings. Besides, the Sunday services, there are other regular groups for different ages which meet during the weekdays. For example, the Friday Night's Frontline Youth service, which is a fellowship of 11- 18-year-olds. They meet on Fridays from 6.30 pm to 9.00 pm. They also have home groups, 319 Café and other citywide activities.

4.3.1.4. Church Leadership and Structure

The ANC is intentional about raising leaders. They equip Christ's people to maximize their potential through practical hands-on experience, discipleship, and leadership development. Currently, their leadership team comprises two Asians and two white British pastors and their wives. The team's role is to work together to support the Senior Pastor to develop and communicate the

---

4. All Nations Church website.

vision of the church, oversee, and facilitate the work of the ministry. As well as meeting for church business, they also meet as a Life Group because, according to them, authentic community matters. There is also a pastoral team who helps to disciple and care for the various ethnic communities of believers. The pastoral team's primary function is to help provide care and discipleship to the ANC family through overseeing, supporting, and developing "Area Leaders and Life group leaders." They also step in to help with pastoral needs, although the senior minister is clearly, the main leader of the church, yet, the role of guiding and directing is delegated to a wider leadership structure and in some cases along the ethnic church. For example, there is a Zimbabwe-born minister in charge of ministering to the Zimbabweans in the church. Clearly, the responsibilities of leadership are not the sole responsibility of the senior pastor as it is structured for the benefit of the wider community of believers from a diverse background. The ANC also enjoys good working relationship with other churches especially churches and fellowships within the Wolverhampton municipality.

4.3.2. The Ethiopian Church London

The ECL is in Kings Cross in London.[5] It started in London in 1979 as a home fellowship with a handful of migrant Christians whose main aim was to come together to worship God in their local language. Even though, the ECL started home fellowships in 1979, it was not until 1994 that they started a full church service. Two factors influenced the growth of ECL over the years. The first factor was mainly the arrival of Ethiopian migrants, most of whom were evangelical Christians who came into the country as refugees. The second factor was through evangelism as the church started reaching out to Ethiopians and Eritreans living in the UK.

4.3.2.1. Vision and Values

The broader vision of ECL is to reach out to all people irrespective of their ethnicities, but their emphasis is on the Ethiopian and Eritrean communities in the UK. Their ultimate desire is to equip their adherents to know and experience the love and power of Jesus Christ in its fullness. It is their desire to praise and worship God and to enjoy his fellowship; they strive to

---

5. Copied from the Ethiopian Church London's website: www.ecfcuk.org.

achieve this by living holy, sanctified and spirit filled lives that they believe, may be pleasing to God. The church's vision has developed over the past few years and has become more outward looking in their outreach to the lost. The emphasis has now shifted from winning only Ethiopians and Eritreans to a broader vision of reaching out to the wider community. It is their firm and unequivocal belief that it is the responsibility of all their adherents to evangelize and win the lost to Christ. It is also the role and responsibility of the leaders to equip and mobilize the church to accomplish her mission as evangelism is the primary purpose for their existence as a church. They believe that evangelism is a God-given task for Christ's people to deliver the gospel to the unsaved, as such they have created a department for evangelism. They absolutely believe that Christ's commission to the Christian is to preach the gospel and make disciples of people. Moreover, to ensure that the gospel is preached among Ethiopians and Eritreans and for that matter all others, the church in its vision statement expects each member to win a minimum of three souls to Christ every year. The department of evangelism explores every possible way of equipping, encouraging, and organizing its members to the task. By engaging the church in prayers for the lost, adherents are encouraged to have a list of people they could pray for as they lead them to Christ. They believe in the local church as the "'pipeline' of the Gospel to all people." The purpose of their department of evangelism, therefore, is to bring glory to God by making disciples of his Son Jesus Christ.[6]

4.3.2.2. Sunday Worship and Ecclesiastical Style

It was observed during my field trips that the ECL meets at Pentonville Road, Kings Cross, London for their Sunday service from 10.00 am to 12.00 pm. There is also an afternoon Sunday service held at the Lillie Road, Fulham, South-West London, from 2.00 pm to 4.00 pm. This service is conducted in the Amharic language, which is the Ethiopian national language, and widely spoken by Eritreans. The ecclesiastical style is grounded in their understanding of Scripture, but it is also contextualized within the Ethiopian culture as the music, the dance and the liturgy are all based on their Ethiopian cultural and religious practice.

---

6. Ethiopian Church London's website site.

4.3.2.3. Other Group

I observed during my field trips that there is a small group in ECL called the Kingdom Youth Ministry that is open to all high school pupils aged between 11 and 18 years. During meetings, they study the Bible and its application to their lives. This programme helps the youth to understand that "Christ is more than just a person from history and that the Bible is more than just a book." There have also been events such as sporting activities for boys and girls, and this has in a way created a conducive atmosphere for the youth who are mainly the second or even third generation, to socialize and understand their roots as well as the culture of their newly found country.

4.3.2.4. Church Leadership and Structure

The ECL maintains a simple leadership structure. They believe that the church (universal) is a divinely ordained organism rather than a man-made organization such as a club or association. A such their leadership ministry is not based solely on academic achievement but by also the calling of God. They have pastoral staff as well as deacons and elders. These men and women must always possess certain personal qualifications (see 1 Tim 3). They think that Christian leadership should be supernaturally chosen and ordained by God and that these should be gifted leaders, which Christ has provided for the church. As part of a wider spectrum their ministry practices are not evident only in their leadership structure and tenets of faith, but more often in the unwritten theological belief system informed by their cultural beliefs, which they often claim is epistemologically valid as they believe that it is consistent with Scripture.

4.3.3. The Church of Pentecost of Ghana in UK

The COP is a worldwide Pentecostal church with its headquarters in Accra, Ghana. The beginning of the COP was linked to the missionary efforts of Pastor James McKeown, an Irish missionary who in 1937 was sent by the Apostolic Church in Bradford, UK, to the then Gold Coast which became Ghana after independence in 1957. In the 1980s, many African migrants in London joined Christian associations such as PAUKE, GCF and ACF[7] recognized the Kensington Temple (Elim Pentecostal Church) and other

---

7. See full names in the Abbreviation's page.

Elim churches in London as their established places of worship. The idea of starting a COP Britain was devised by some Ghanaians who were members of the above-mentioned associations and worshipping in Elim churches in the 1980s. Even though, these Ghanaians were welcomed into the Elim churches, they still thought that to have "a unique Ghanaian/African identity in worship" in the UK, they would need a separate fellowship based on the Ghanaian culture. Hence, in 1986 they gathered at three houses across North London for fellowship. By 1989 these home fellowships had developed into a Sunday service. The COP headquarters in Ghana heard about the progress of these endeavours, and arranged for a minister from Ghana to migrate to the UK to take care of the newly planted church.[8]

4.3.3.1. Vision and Values

The vision of COP is to establish a global Pentecostal church that is holistic in ministry, vibrant in evangelism, church planting and discipleship. They do this by spreading the word of God, transforming lives, and bringing the world to the saving knowledge of the Lord Jesus Christ. Their mission statement states that: "the COP exists to establish responsible and self-sustaining churches filled with committed, Spirit-filled Christians of character, who will impact their communities."[9] The COP believes that reasons for its continued existence are their involvement in missions because mission is the heartbeat of God. Therefore, at COP, they see missions as a great responsibility of making significant contributions to global mission. They think that their success in this direction will depend on their ability to rise and meet the challenges of the contemporary world. Therefore, at the COP, evangelism is the responsibility of every member. They believe in "power evangelism" and think that members have a duty to share their faith after conversion. They maintain high standard of excellence in all ministries by seeking to honour God who gave humankind the Saviour. They believe in the presence and leadings of the Holy Spirit in worship and in their daily lives. They think that the new birth is the work of the Holy Spirit and that the baptism in the Holy Spirit is for power to do God's work. In addition, the gifts of the Spirit, are for the building of the body of Christ and the fruits of the Spirit, to them,

---

8. See the Church of Pentecost's website: www.copuk.org/history.
9. See: https://thecophq.org/mission-vision/.

help Christians to develop Christ-like characters. Their distinctiveness is in their "self-supporting attitude, faithfulness and integrity, prayer life, church discipline, liberality, mutual respect and respect for authority," and the sense of belonging for all members without discrimination. In their discipleship training, they emphasize "holiness, righteousness, faithfulness, honesty, sincerity, humility, prayer life and a disciplined and responsible life." Some of their core practices are regular prayer for the baptism in the Holy Spirit with initial evidence of speaking in tongues but emphasis is placed on the believer bearing the fruits of the spirit and the gifts of the Holy Spirit. Their leadership development is based on the apostolic foundation, hence their appointment and calling into ministry are also based on the character and charisma, and the directions of the Holy Spirit. Clergy and lay ministries are equally encouraged. Faithfulness in all forms of contributing to the church is welcomed and there is much emphasis on members giving offering and paying tithes (one tenth of their incomes) to the church.[10]

The COP believes in communal living with members supporting one another, participating in communal work. The church, in some cases helps the entire community by providing social needs such as health services, schools and agriculture as well as donating to the needy in society. There is an elaboration on providing sacrifices to the church without expecting pecuniary reward. They teach their adherents to abstain from alcohol, tobacco and other hard drugs and monogamous marriage is enforced as well as chastity before marriage.[11]

4.3.3.2. Sunday Worship and Ecclesiastical Style

The COP local assemblies conduct their services mainly in the Ghanaian Akan language with their ecclesiastical style modelled on the Ghanaian culture, but recently there has been the establishment of PIWCs that run concurrently with the Akan services. The PIWCs provides a well-organized, cross-cultural church, primarily for people of non-Ghanaian cultural background who want a place of worship. This is also open to all Christ's people, especially

---

10. The distinctives referred to above can be found on the Church of Pentecost UK website: https://copuk.org/core-values/.

11. See the Church of Pentecost Vision 2018, Five-Year Vision, Covering the period 2013–2018.

the second-generation members of Ghanaians in the UK and elsewhere, who want to worship in the English language or in a multicultural setting. Praise and worship in the PIWCs are contemporary.[12]

4.3.3.3. Other Groups

There are other groups such as children's ministry, Youth ministry, Women's and Men's fellowship and prayer groups in the COP local assemblies. Some of these groups meet on Sundays while others meet during the weekdays.

4.3.3.4. Church Leadership and Structure

The General Council at the COP headquarters in Ghana is the highest governing body of the COP and while the planting of new COP branches in the UK by individuals is not centrally controlled from the headquarters in Ghana, the international headquarters plays a supervisory role and intervenes in matters where appropriate. The headquarters serves as a centre of excellence in COP's administration. It sharpens its effectiveness by offering periodic and relevant training for the staff. Recently, it has acquired the Birmingham Christian College premises in Selly Oak, Birmingham for the training of its leaders in Europe as it sees ministerial training and development partly as the answer to the challenges Christ's people go through in the ever-changing dynamic and trends of the contemporary environment. These challenges, to them, call for a constant upgrading and increasing of knowledge and skills for all ministers.[13]

4.3.4. The Baptist Church, Harborne, Birmingham

The HBC is an evangelical church located in Harborne, a suburb of Birmingham. It is within walking distance of the University of Birmingham campus. It is an old Baptist church, a member of the Baptist Union of Great Britain, hence operates within its tenets and principles. It was once housed in an old building, but its transformation came in 2012 when, by the generosity of some of its members the old building was renovated and transformed into

---

12. This was observed during my fieldtrips to the Church of Pentecost branch in Birmingham.

13. See the Church of Pentecost Vision 2018, Five-Year Vision, Covering the period 2013–2018.

a new building. This has made it an attractive place of worship. This transformation of their worship place, according to them, would allow those passing by the location of the church to have a clear view into the church building so they can see their transparent worship and be challenged to see how they are proud of God in their worship. The front of the church has become a beautiful glass atrium, topped by a simple cross, which was purposefully designed to attract the world to share their love of Jesus Christ.

4.3.4.1. Vision and Values

The HBC has a vision to be a community of believers who seek to use their gifts to propagate the gospel of Christ. The vision statement is "we desire to be a family, rooted in the word of God, whose love for Christ and for one another overflows in joyful sharing of the good news of Jesus with all, irrespective of background or status." Their mission statement is "we are learning to live with God and to love like Christ." Their mission is clearly to glorify God with the worship of their lives as they believe that he has called them to the following priorities in this time: community, teaching and learning, prayer, evangelism and mission, students, and internationals ministries. HBC is a community of Christ's people who are committed to the following: they believe that a right relationship with God is possible only through him. They also believe that God's written word, the Bible, is an unerring word and shows them the way to know God and live for him.

They can be described as what we term "evangelical and Baptist." Their mission, therefore, arises both from these convictions and from their understanding of the time and place in which they live. They believe that as their church grows spiritually so it grows in mission, reaching the wider community with the gospel of Jesus Christ that is shaping lives together. They also think that in a diverse city like Birmingham, more so, being located near a university campus with its international students, there is the need to create a community where, as the Bible says: "there is neither Jew nor Greek, male nor female, slave nor free, but all are one in Christ Jesus." (Galatians 3:28 NKJV) The HBC believes that all Christ's people have a duty to share their faith with the unsaved and they recognize that mission is "not just evangelism, but includes, promoting justice, social welfare, healing, education, and peace in the world."[14] They think that religious freedom should be for all people and this generally, has always been a keystone of Baptist understanding. Acceptance of differences of outlook and diversity of practice is encouraged within the HBC and in the Christian community as well as in the wider world.[15]

4.3.4.2. Sunday Worship and Ecclesiastical Style

The HBC's approach to ecclesiology begins with Scripture. Their preaching is mainly expositional even though, in some cases they do topical preaching. They interpret the Bible as teaching Baptist positions on the traditional ecclesiological questions.[16] HBC understands the church as a community of believers gathered in the name of Jesus Christ for worship, witness, and service. There is no set liturgy. As a local church of the Baptist Union of Great Britain, HBC is free to determine its own pattern. Prayer and praise, listening and reflecting on Scripture, and sharing Holy Communion have always been central to their worship. Their praise and worship are mainly hymnal in a typical Sunday service but in some cases, they use contemporary worship especially in the days that they give the youth the opportunity to conduct service. There is moderation in their worship.

4.3.4.3. Other Groups

There are many groups in the HBC. One such group is Christianity Explored.[17] The congregation is deeply involved in this group because of the inspiration they receive from it. They also think that it meets their spiritual needs. It is a Bible study structured for those who would like to investigate Christianity or just brush up on the basics. Its duration is seven weekly sessions; it examines who Jesus was, what his aims were, and what it means to follow him today. There is also the Southlink Charter Centre, which is next door to the church. This centre has over the years proved very useful not only to the congregation but also to the secular community. The centre is opened seven days a week; it is a welcoming environment. It functions as a place of support and friendship

---

14. From an interview with the senior pastor of Harborne Baptist Church.

15. See the Harborne Baptist Church's website: https://www.harbornebaptistchurch.org/Groups/295363/What_Is_Christianity.aspx. Also confirmed in a recorded interview with the senior pastor.

16. Hammett, *Biblical Foundations for Baptist Churches*, 20.

17. Copied from the Harborne Baptist Church's website: www.harbornebaptistchurch.org.

for adults who have experienced mental health problems of any kind. The Charter Centre can also provide information on welfare and mental health issues and link service users to stakeholders. It is equipped with a kitchenette, a pool table and a television and offers recreational activities, day trips and coffee mornings. It provides a conducive environment for people to relax and feel accepted. There is also a *Discipleship Explored* course. This course is intended as a 'follow-on' course from Christianity Explored but can also be attended as a stand-alone course for Christ's people who want to go on to the next level in their Christian development or a little bit deeper. it is an informal 8-week course for those who wish to make the most of their Christian lives. There is also a dedicated team of children's church leaders in charge of their children's ministry. This ministry is very important to the church because they want to create a conducive environment to make sure that all children in their church feel safe, loved, and supported and that these children will have the chance to grow up learning about God and his love for them.

They have a café called International Café which is run by a group of Christians who live locally in the Harborne vicinity. This café is hosted at HBC for international students living in the Harborne area. It is opened on Thursdays between 8.00 pm and 9.30 pm; coffee and tea with light refreshments are served free. Added to this is the Coffee Stop, which opens on Tuesdays from 11.00 am until 2.30 pm. It serves as Harborne latest coffee and cake venue. Homemade soup, baked potatoes, sandwiches, and toasties, including various teas and coffees are served to the community.

4.3.4.4. Church Leadership and Structure

The HBC practices congregational church government. In this type of church government, the congregations exercise the ultimate authority in the local church, but they assume to do this under the divine authority of Christ hence they do not recognize the positions of, for example, bishop, general overseer, and many others over their local church. They believe that everyone who attends the HBC has a role to play and can use their God-given skills and talents for the good of the church and the community. These gifts include teaching, evangelism, social action, pastoral care, prayer, and healing, taking part in worship, administration, or hospitality. At HBC when a person is baptized (through immersion), they normally become a church member. Church members are called to discern prayerfully God's will for their shared life.

Final authority does not rest with the ministers, deacons or any other local, national, or international body, but with the members meeting together under God's guidance. Church members, during church meetings make significant appointments including ministers, and agree financial policy and mission. Clearly, HBC is outwards focused as it is linked regionally, nationally, and internationally with other churches for support and fellowship.[18]

4.4. Vision and Values

Even though these four churches differ in their ecclesiastical styles, their visions and values are similar. The four case study churches have different backgrounds and doctrinal emphases, but they share similar visions, which in a sense is to glorify God through the evangelization of their area and city for the transformation of lives and communities. They also ascribe high value to team working and team building. Their compassion is expressed by showing the practical love of Christ through social actions within their churches and wider communities. They are aware that the youth are the 'life wire' of their ministries, hence are keen to develop further their young people's initiatives, which they believe are key for the future of their churches. They encourage their adherents to develop confidence in their faith in God concerning their personal spiritual lives and the ministries the Lord has commissioned them to undertake. There is therefore an encouragement in the areas of participating in small groups, a culture of invitation, and having fun together as they deepen their commitment to Jesus. The ANC and the HBC, which have a multi-ethnic membership, rejoice in the great diversity of their membership and the rich variety of their social context. They value the unique contributions and ideas that every member of their community of believers brings, including their cultures and ministry activities.

The four church leaders did not wish to be tied down by specific vision statements (even though they have these statements in their churches' websites and the COP has a vision statement for 2013 to 2018) as they believe in the leadings of the Holy Spirit in all matters pertaining to ministry. In my observation, four fundamental values came to the fore at the heart of church life of all the four case study churches. It is my opinion that the following

---

18. Copied from the Harborne Baptist Church's website: www.harbornebaptistchurch.org.

values were born out of the genuine spirituality of these churches resulting from the depth of their relationship with God:

(i) A very important place was given to the preaching and teaching of the word of God; the Bible to them is inerrant, clearly respected as the supreme authority on all matters of faith and practice and as the main source of revelation.

(ii) A central value was placed on worshipping (music) which was corporately expressed primarily as praising and worshipping God by singing and in some cases dancing to the tune of the music. The worship is mainly contemporary but in some cases hymnal (as in the case of HBC), yet they are all focused on God and done to his glory hence, worship time is a moment of expectancy for these congregations as they release their faith to "receive spiritual inspiration from God."

(iii) The supernatural attributes of God were heightened in the ANC, ECFC and the COP with the expectation that the church (universal) could reach out for more manifestations of the supernatural in its regular life and in the lives of their adherents corporately and personally. Their goal was to express the manifestation of the spirit and power of the Holy Spirit in their congregations and their members' daily lives to bring personal as well as community transformation.

(iv) The expression of church as a living and growing community of believers cannot be overemphasized in these churches. They do not just see the church as a place where only spiritual matters should be addressed but they also see it as a place to belong and make friends centred upon the love of Christ.

The Christian journey, as presented in these churches appears to be an exciting adventure. Their leadership has caught the vision of "equipping Christ's people for the work of the ministry." They do not only equip their members, but they also prepare them to get practically involved in ministry and missions. Hence their adherents seem to be naturally committed to advancing the vision of their churches, especially in the areas of evangelism and other meetings without been cajoled into doing so. It was observed that the COP believes in equipping its members for the work of the ministry, hence spends a considerable amount of time and resources in shaping a shared vision that captures the aspirations of its adherents. This vision, supported by good biblical preaching and teaching which is stated in their document detailing the activities of the church, is kept before their congregation worldwide as a reminder of the main goals that the COP shares together within a particular period. For example, they currently have the COP Vision 2018 document and this in a sense, was their vision for a five-year period starting from 2013 to 2018. They believe that God's vision requires their obedience, so they first wait on the Lord to be clear of the leadings of the Holy Spirit, obey by taking the necessary steps, and then share the vision with their adherents by inviting them to come together to pray. At the COP, following Christ is the priority of their members and this would mean that one must become a born-again Christian and become a committed member before he or she can consider a calling to lead. They believe that they began by the Holy Spirit and think that God will go to tremendous lengths to make certain that his chosen leaders rely on his Spirit and not on their own understanding:

> The Church of Pentecost was begun by the work of the Holy Spirit, and we believe that every church movement which is born of the Holy Spirit must also remain in the Spirit. We don't want to be hot today and then get cold tomorrow. Yet, church history will tell you that some church movements which were born in the Spirit ended up in the flesh. This, we have observed, continues to be a cycle in the history of the church (universal). There are some movements that were once alive and moving in the spirit and power of the Holy Spirit but have now become dead and entered ritualism. So here, it is our practice to constantly renew our spiritual lives. We do this by respecting the Word of God in our daily prayer lives, showing the practical love of Christ to all people we come across and, in some cases, we seek the face of God in fasting.[19]

At the COP, proper care is taken in order not to adopt the ways of the world and all its entrapments (as they called it) as such they try to avoid taking on in their ministry, the complexity of human wisdom by not trying to be an

---

19. In a recorded interview with a COP pastor.

attraction church by merely using carnal techniques. They have simple faith in God, and they absolutely believe in the Bible and what it says. They seek the face of God in prayers and fasting concerning important ministry decisions. Obviously, this and many other good practices inform their ministry practices today. The HBC is a place where the hurting, the depressed and the destitute can find salvation, hope, forgiveness, restoration, and love to enable them to become what they are supposed to become in their Christian lives. As the senior pastor puts it regarding their openness to people from all walks of life:

> At the Harborne Baptist Church, we seek to minister to the lost and hurting souls. It is our desire and ministry responsibility to see them repented from their sins and completely restored, back on their feet, functioning as sanctified Christians. Our goal is winning souls and restoring souls that have backslidden. As such we have it in mind that repentance is necessary in all cases. We are always all delighted to see a life that has been bruised or gone astray become fruitful again for the kingdom of God. We are deeply sensitive to the people we lead to Christ hence it is our desire to see them mature in their relationship with Christ so that they can also become part of the work of ministry to reach their communities and in some cases the world with the gospel.[20]

In my field trip encounters to the case study churches, I observed that the HBC and the ANC emphasize character qualities. Their focus is on the Christian's efforts, work values, and ethics. They place emphasis on reliability, humility, and commitments. The HBC gives a higher priority to the formation of a community of believers where there is trust rather than giving priority to attaining vision and meeting goals. The COP and the ECL on the other hand, emphasize spiritual and social values. They want to work with born-again Christians who manifest the calling of God, sanctified for the work of God, filled with the Holy Spirit, and showing love for fellow Christians and the unsaved. They also think that true Christians should be compassionate and generous to all people. But all the four churches are congregations that take the inerrant and inspired word of God seriously and believe in the workings of the Holy Spirit. They may have different ways of expressing their mission,

---

20. In a recorded interview with the senior pastor of the Harborne Baptist Church.

vision, and values but they all have a mission to make whole-life disciples of Jesus Christ wherever they have the opportunity, and their vision is to grow spiritually, cultivating the fruits of the Holy Spirit and growing their local churches numerically for the sake of the kingdom of God. They all share values that embody the teachings and character of Jesus Christ as revealed in the Scriptures.

In essence, all the four churches see their mission as people of God who have been given a new identity in Christ with a calling to the mission of God, hence they have no intention of looking down on people but value equally individuals of all ethnic identities. They are all welcoming churches and respect all people irrespective of their ethnic backgrounds or positions in the society. The key element, for example of the ANC is simplicity. A conducive atmosphere is created in their services. Their church services are very informal, conducted in a non-threatening environment and are intentionally programmed to attract people from all walks of life. For the ANC, diversity is not about acknowledging that all human beings are the same; they accept the differences in the people from a diverse background who fellowship with them, but they also think that they can embrace those differences as they strongly believe that people from different ethnicities make a stronger and healthier community of believers.

4.4.1. Causes of Disagreements among Christ's People

All the four pastors accept that disunity among Christ's people is a negative reflection on the character of God. However, they believe also that the life and teaching of Jesus gives Christians the spiritual resources essential to meet the challenges of interpersonal conflicts and misunderstandings. They think that there is the likelihood that interpersonal conflicts and misunderstandings could rise among Christ's people when they find themselves with conflicting views. But they also believe that the message of the gospel, when embraced by Christians could be a way of resolving differences.

The pastors believe that the witness of the church (universal) over the years, has been ruined many times for the lack of Christ's people's expression of love for one another. They also think that often, Christ's people have been lukewarm in dealing with conflicts and issues among fellow Christians. Consequently, this has resulted in creating divisions and factions within the body of Christ. These divisions and factions, which are mainly over petty issues of what is regarded as "secondary doctrines" have caused so much havoc to the evangelization of the world and the work of the ministry. Yet in most cases, these are matters which should not in any way bring divisions. All the pastors share the view that when Christ's people disagree about deeper values and essential doctrines such as those regarding one's relationship to God, for example, the virgin birth of Christ, the death and resurrection of Christ, they think that at this point the gulf of mistrust may become so wide that working together will surely be impossible. They think also that when Christ's people are working together as a multicultural team, they will, nonetheless, experience disagreements about core values which emerges because of their cultural differences. For example, they all accepted the fact that there is a vast difference between what Africans regard as values in terms of their culture and what the white British people accept as their cultural values. There is much evidence to suggest that the British (Whites) are more task-oriented while most Africans value relationships, hence place more emphasis on maintaining relationship than fulfilling a particular task no matter how valuable these tasks may be. Three of the pastors had the following to say to support their viewpoints:

> The All Nations is a culturally diverse church. We receive people from different countries and ethnicities. Frankly, there are a lot of cultural differences in the people who make up our congregation but then we also realize that when culturally diverse people try to work towards mutual goals, their assumptions about structure and working relationships may create serious issues of conflict and disagreement. This is natural because there is always going to be the difficulty of identifying and maintaining coherence and unity within a congregation which comprises of people from diverse backgrounds. This obviously means that there will be a time when there will be tension. Hence leaders will be faced with the challenge of listening and taking into consideration diverse views. What Christians have to understand is that there are no perfect cultures and that all Christ's people, in spite of their ethnic and cultural background, come to the church with some sort of cultural bias but we understand that

when we mature in God's word and are filled with the Holy Spirit, we will be able to overcome these biases.[21]

There are many good and spirit filled Christians who teach and practise misguided doctrines especially in areas of church leadership. Some of their teachings seems right but in the long run destroys their vision and ministry. We, at the Church of Pentecost, do not believe that effective cross-cultural ministry can happen unless God's people are willing to learn about and accept the views of the other Christians they are partnering with. For instance, how can you think that the African-led churches can work with the white majority churches when there are obvious cultural differences including disagreements over legitimate forms of our behaviour and action especially when it comes to matters of holiness and sanctification? I think for us to come together in any form, we first must listen carefully to one another with an attitude of respect and acceptance.[22]

In the UK, your fellow Christian can use their cultural values to criticize the way you act or approach issues. I believe that disunity among Christians happen when our own Christian brothers and sisters, who are not like us use their cultural values to criticize people like us who cannot speak with their accent and think that we fail to live up to their values. However, I believe that if we are truly born-again Christians, we will all follow God's ways despite our backgrounds. Our focus should be directed towards loving one another as Christ commands us to do.[23]

All the pastors believe that there are theological and cultural issues that need to be addressed if Christians from a diverse background desire to work together to impact their communities. For example, there are still liturgical and ministerial differences, but the pastors believe that these should not divide the body of Christ. However, they also think that the issue of concern here is a situation whereby there is a clear difference in the fundamental doctrines

---

21. The All Nations Church pastor in a recorded interview.
22. The Church of Pentecost pastor in a recorded interview.
23. The Ethiopian Church London pastor in a recorded interview.

such as the one triune God, the deity of the Lord Jesus Christ, the salvation of humankind and many others but few to mention. The pastors think if these differing views (in the fundamental doctrines) exist in any Christian relationship, it will bring genuine divisions based on their biblical teachings hence it cannot be regarded as a healthy diversity of expression.

They accept that unity among Christ's people would be proved too challenging to be realized when for example, both the African immigrant churches and the white majority churches do exactly what they think is good in their various cultures instead of learning about each other's culture. They admit that there is a perceived arrogance among some of the white people that reflects in their Christian relationships with others who are not like them. They think that some of these white people approach cross-cultural relationships with only their culture to interpret a given situation, and this approach, according to them always results in doubts and a weakening of the relationship. They also accept that it will be more appropriate if Christ's people from all backgrounds can at least agree on matters of the greatest importance, which according to them should be issues that can deepen their relationship with fellow Christians and result in unity. However, they believe also that unity in itself does not necessarily depend on sharing similar views and expecting a situation where all differences will be obliterated, because unity is not uniformity, yet it can lead to diversity if handled appropriately:

> There are many different cultures in our churches, be they white or African-led but we should not forget that what the Bible teaches should be the final judge of all kinds of cultures be they Western cultures, African or otherwise. I think the white British people must acknowledge that they do not have exclusive insight into rights and wrongs and that the Spirit of God works among all people despite their background. I think the people here (Whites) need to humble themselves so that they can understand people from other cultures. After all, we all have something to offer to the body of Christ no matter where we come from.[24]

> Obviously, there are cultural differences between us (Whites) and lots of people in our church so what we have learnt to do

---

24. A respondent from the Church of Pentecost in a recorded interview.

is that we encourage our members to acknowledge our differences, but we do not stop there; we work on those differences with all humility. We do not look down on people because they are not like us or they do not speak like us, instead we try to respect all people despite their background and by so doing we have been able to build bridges across the various cultures that make up our church.[25]

Obviously, Christ's people have the opportunity of building bridges across the diverse cultures that make up the UK urban communities, but the way to do this involves commitments; Christ's people must have the intention of dealing with their own shortcomings, first. For instance, believers despite their backgrounds should first deal with their cultural biases and realize that working together to achieve the highest goals of the kingdom is their goal as Christ's people.

It was also observed that it is the desire of the ANC and the HBC not to divide Christ's people over non-essential (secondary) doctrines. On other issues they try to recognize the Scriptural validity of both sides of a debate and avoid excluding or favouring those with differing views over the other.

They show this kind of inclusiveness for example, in their approach to debatable issues concerning the baptism, gifts and ministry of the Holy Spirit. The philosophy of ministry here is to create an environment whereby they will be able to minister to as broad a group of Christians as possible. However, in the fundamental doctrines they take a firm stance. In other words, they accept that fellow Christians may differ in the secondary doctrines and think that the differences in the secondary doctrines should not divide the body of Christ. As one pastor put it:

> At the All Nations Church, we worship with people from a diverse background, and this comes with its challenges. For example, one of the challenges is how we the leadership can help our multi-ethnic members whom we think are called to ministry in our church, to draw their identities from being an

---

25. The All Nations Church pastor in a recorded interview.

English, Ghanaian, Nigerians, Chinese or Punjabi to being first and foremost Christians.[26]

Asked what they think could be the solution to disagreement, all the pastors suggested that Christ's people should follow what Christ said in John 13:35, that his disciples would be identified by their love for one another. The HBC pastor went further to state that if love can cover a multitude of sins (1 Pet 4:8); it certainly should cover disagreement of Christ's people. The HBC pastor remarked:

> In some cases, I may not necessarily agree with certain ministry practices or Christian doctrines as practised in some churches, but I don't think I will speak out negatively against Christians who have differing viewpoints. Also, I may not agree with certain theological views, but I am convinced that there are many good Christians who hold different theological views. Frankly, it is only when the love of Christ is no longer the driving force of Christ's people that they find themselves in unnecessary theological arguments and misunderstandings.[27]

Overall, they believe that it is possible for them to agree to disagree and still maintain a spirit of unity and love and that Christ's people can always resolve their cultural differences, but only when they have committed themselves to building the spiritual relationships of mutual love and trust necessary to working together. Therefore, they accept that disagreement between Christ's people becomes a problem in situations where Christians refuse to use their God-given abilities to listen, without being biased by taking sides in matters. They are therefore, supposed to be accurate in assessing information from both sides of any argument in relation to Scripture.

4.4.2. Leadership Style

The task of creating a leadership structure that mirrors all the decision-making and leadership styles of the various ethnicities is a complex one. This task, in my view, is so complex that perhaps only a few Christian ministries can master it. All four pastors believe that leading people is much more than

---

26. All Nations pastor in a recorded interview.
27. The Harborne Baptist Church senior pastor in a recorded interview.

having people follow you. They accept that leading Christ's people is about mentoring them in such a way that they can be equipped, empowered, and released to go forward and fulfil the responsibility of continuing to do the same thing on their own that their leaders have done for them. As one pastor put it regarding relational leadership:

> My understanding of ministry as a Church of Pentecost pastor is that I, as a Christian leader, must be prepared to value and practise the essential lessons of ministry taught to us by the Lord Jesus Christ. I see this as my priority. The next thing is that I must be willing to practise the Bible. In my day-to-day ministration, the early church becomes my example. We read in the book of Acts that the early church was dependent upon the leadings of the Holy Spirit, so should all Christians, in my view. And finally, as a leader I must be serious with my daily devotion which includes my prayer life, Bible reading and meditation. I try to maintain my personal relationship with Jesus Christ through my daily devotion and other Christian practices because I believe that having a good relationship with Christ is the source of power and inspiration for all Christians and Christian leaders.[28]

Frankly, obedience to do his will is the basis of Christians and Christian leaders' ability to fulfil their God-given tasks. When we as Christians have fully lived up to God's expectations as leaders, then we can lead others to also follow. It is the opinion of the COP that Jesus Christ is the head of their church. They believe their church, like any other living church, is his and that he (Jesus) is the one in charge of their ministry and all their endeavours. As pastors, they think they need to be leading the church in such a way that Christ's people will know that the Lord Jesus is the one in control. They do not want to draw attention to themselves as seen in some circles, where we always hear invitations to the public which say, "come over to see an anointed man of God." They think that people coming to their church must have their focus on the Lord Jesus and not the so called anointed man of God. They also have the elders, the deacons and other church workers who are there to

---

28. In a recorded interview with Church of Pentecost pastor.

support the pastors in different ways including praying and supporting them in seeking the face of the Lord concerning what he is doing in his church. The COP realizes the hard facts that leading is a very difficult thing to do, and that the challenges of leadership usually result in something less than the success which leaders anticipate. In view of these challenges, they have learned to depend on God through prayers and the leadings of the Holy Spirit, especially when they are considering taking very sensitive decisions as leaders. The COP leadership style reveals the importance of having godly men and women who recognize that God has called and ordained their senior ministers usually called "apostles" as the ones to lead their church movement.[29] These are people who work diligently with the ministers in the local churches and support those things that God is directing them to do in their local assemblies. The leadership believes that a good board is one of the greatest assets that they can muster in this worldwide movement as such there is much trust in their leadership board. Besides, the pastoral staff in the local assemblies, they have the elders who, they believe are people committed to their churchs's task and yielded to the Holy Spirit and have had ministry experience. They serve as a real protection for the ministers and their local assemblies. They also have an additional responsibility of taking part in pioneering roles. They play an important role in settling matters brought before the church leadership by acting between the ministers and the congregation. When the congregation brings any problem, they (the elders) find the best solutions to them and lead the local assemblies in the absence of their local ministers.

The ANC also believe that God's model is that the senior pastor is ruled by the Lord Jesus Christ and aided by assistant pastors and elders who are placed in the ministry to discover God's purpose for his church. The senior pastor is regarded by the congregation as God's anointed instrument to lead the church, with the board guiding and directing. Complementing this is the role of the pastoral staff which is there to minister to the spiritual and emotional needs of the congregation. It is worth noting that they ascribe high value to team working and team building, having a leadership which fully affirms men and women equally in ministry. They strongly encourage

---

29. The senior ministers are recognized as "Apostles" and their leader is designated "Chairman". There are many such apostles in the church's leadership but one of them is selected to the position of a chairman to lead the entire movement for a period of five years and could be renewed for further five years.

vocations, lay and ordained. They celebrate and take pride in their diversity. Their numerical growth was due partly to their diversity, which has become a tremendous resource for evangelism. They have clearly presented an alternative to the cultural relativism seen today in some circles. As a diverse church, they value the unique contributions and ideas that every member of their community of faith brings because of who they are and what they do. They think that diversity recognizes that God gave his children different skills, abilities and gifts for a good reason and that God's church should exist to train, equip, and release all within the body for the work of the ministry as one pastor illustrated:

> At the All Nations, we recognize the complexity of leading our church cross-culturally lies in the challenge of building a church community of faith with trust among Christ's people who come from different cultures, different nationalities, and a diverse background. These people, because of their diverse backgrounds come to us with different cultural identities, traditions, and diverse worldviews. But we believe that what the Lord is looking for is a church which is united in fellowship and diverse in ministry, a church which is multi-ethnic with a multicultural identity. So, here at the All Nations, our goal therefore, is to create a congregation with a multicultural identity and this is given all serious attention in everything we do as a church: in our worship service, teachings, preaching, discipleship ministries, and leadership structure.[30]

The model of leadership of the ANC is ideal as they seek to engage members that reflect the multiple background of people from different ethnicities in their leadership. Natural and gifted leaders from diverse backgrounds have emerged in the church and these leaders have credibility and respect from their relationship's networks. For example, there are ethnic minority leaders who oversee different nationalities and ethnicities such as Zimbabweans and Punjabis. They believe also that churches will have to find a balance between the unity of the gospel and how God calls Christians as people with different identities. They present the gospel as something that holds for people from

---

30. In a recorded interview with All Nations Church pastor.

diverse backgrounds hence their multicultural identity is manifested in all their gatherings, especially during their Sunday morning worship. They want their members to develop confidence in their faith and to be enabled to participate in every-member ministry. Central to this are their small groups, strong pastoral relationships, a culture of invitation and having fun together as they deepen their commitment to Jesus. They believe that the secret to a diverse mission strategy is to ensure that they identify and understand the needs and aspirations of their communities and then seek to engage them in all areas of their lives.

The ECL leadership is very simple. Because their congregation values open sharing of all available resources, their emphasis is on mutual, rather than superior relationship. The leadership is committed to relational goals and relational activities as one respondent explained:

> At the Ethiopian Church, we have a leadership style which identifies with our mono-ethnic membership. Our type of leadership is spiritually, culturally, and socially relevant to the needs of our church members. After all, we are here to serve our people, most of whom have language barriers and prefer to worship in the Ethiopian language. Anyone visiting our church will discover the strong bond of relationship between us and our church members.[31]

The ECL believes that wise planning rather than too many goals will reap a good result in ministry. First, they think that it is necessary for them to know where they are going and what their prime objective is. The next thing is to prioritize every activity and resource quickly and properly. They then allocate resources to each need according to its importance. They think that it is wise for leaders to avoid the mistake of doing tasks that others can do. They, therefore, delegate the less sensitive tasks to others within their congregation.

The HBC leadership style is on the premise that leadership activity should align their members by translating their vision and values into understandable and attainable acts. They understand the challenges in leadership and believe that the godly leader should be concerned about how power can easily be abused so it is their practice to use power biblically. It is their opinion that

---

31. In a recorded interview with a respondent from the Ethiopian Church London.

Christ's people should reflect on their thoughts, words, and actions in the areas of diversity. Rather than denying that in some cases, Christ's people intentionally or unintentionally stereotype people based on ethnicity, or subtly seek to disassociate themselves from people of other ethnicities, Christians need to take positive and practical steps to appreciate the wonderful diversity that is in the body of Christ as one respondent enthused:

> At the Harborne Baptist Church, we don't spend time figuring out and coming out with programmes that will grow our ministry, but greater priority is given to building trust relationships essential for leadership in our fellowship which is very diverse. We make sure that the way we do things here does not offend others from different backgrounds.[32]

The HBC realizes that they cannot accomplish the work of the kingdom of God unless they are willing to work together in the fellowship of a loving community hence, they welcome Christ's people from different backgrounds who seek to fellowship with them. They have practically expressed their compassion across all contexts through initiatives such as their International Student Café and service at Field House and other community initiatives such as ministering to the elderly. They believe that having people from a diverse background brings with it stronger and more creative ideas. This, in their view, produces more imaginative solutions, and ultimately, solving problems that are likely to result from the best efforts of just one ethnicity.

The COP, the ECL and the ANC don't see formal theological training as the only prerequisite for ministry, because they believe that by imposing educational standards on Christ's people, they could possibly keep out many gifted people from fulfilling God's true calling upon their lives. Therefore, intentionally, they encourage both the laity and clergy to exercise their ministries in the congregation and wider community. The leaders of the four churches are all mission-minded pastors hence are equipped to shape the culture and the identity of their congregations by reminding their congregations of God's purposes concerning them as Christians and communicating to them the core values of Christianity which give definition to the vision and purposes of their various churches.

---

32. In a recorded interview with the Harborne Baptist Church senior pastor.

4.4.3. Worship and Liturgy

The four case study churches have common rituals and liturgy. For example, they practise believer's baptism by immersion only; they also observe the Lord's Supper, even though with different meanings and styles. They, however, differ in their praise and worship styles. The ANC has contemporary worship style, and the HBC uses innovative hymnody and, in some cases, contemporary worship style. Hymns provide great themes to inspire the HBC fellowship and furnish it with anthems of praise; while the COP and ECL's form of worship is dancing to the tone of lively joyful music. They all believe that singing praises to God is a sign of gladness and contentment. It is also a sign of joy, indicating a satisfaction with the believer's general situation in life. It is a healthy expression of effervescence that ministers strength in the total being of Christ's people. All the respondents in this interview thought that worship and liturgy were very important in their choice of church. They all felt that the church they attend should be a welcoming church and besides it should be vibrant and serve their spiritual and emotional needs. Moreover, the worship environment should be a place where they can express their faith freely.

The following interviewee, for example, joined the HBC on his arrival from Jamaica:

> In my native country (Jamaica) all my extended family members starting from my dad's grandparents were members of the Baptist Church. This is the church I have been attending from my infancy and as such when I arrived in Britain, I joined the local Baptist congregation in my community.[33]

Baptist churches are known to be welcoming churches. The HBC, being a welcoming church is a view shared by the senior pastor:

> Baptist communities have biblical commitment and response to embrace and celebrate differences as well as respecting the uniqueness of their diversity. At the Harborne Baptist Church, our congregation comprises people from 19 diverse backgrounds. We worship harmoniously with these people because

---

33. A recorded interview with a respondent from the Harborne Baptist Church.

we see their presence as an expression of God's purpose for his children.[34]

The local churches associated with the Baptist Union of Great Britain are seen in the eyes of some migrants as welcoming and are regarded as an acceptable place of worship for migrants who were members of the Baptist congregations in their native countries before migrating to Britain. The reception into the mainline churches that these migrants experienced was not the norm. Most migrants did feel very welcome at Baptist churches because in their native countries some of these migrants had attended a church belonging to the same Baptist denomination. The HBC is a multi-ethnic church with a multicultural identity. It, nonetheless, has a mono-cultural approach in its worship style and ministry expression, yet migrants fit so easily into this mode of worship because the Baptist denomination, is a denomination with an international dimension. Hence most of their migrant members were members of the church in their countries of origin and as such were integrated into this system in their countries before migrating to Britain.

For the most part, Bible exposition is one of the hallmarks of the HBC. They preach and teach the Bible as if the very life of their church depends on the word of God because they believe it has the power to save lives, change lives and give life. This does not mean that on some occasions they do not address a particular topic or give topical messages. They are not saying that topical messages are wrong, but they think that by expositional preaching they are delivering to their congregation the whole counsel of God as they believe in the supremacy of the Bible.

Another experience of a respondent (migrant) who joined the ANC was:

> When I arrived in Britain, I first joined an orthodox church, but I soon discovered that the type of Christianity as demonstrated in this church was different from those practised in Africa, so I joined the All Nations Church, which in my view is a welcoming church and has a contemporary worship style.[35]

---

34. In a recorded interview with the senior pastor of the Harborne Baptist Church.
35. In a recorded interview with a respondent from the All Nations Church.

Another respondent regarding his place of worship:

> When you come to the All Nations Church, you will experience a very strong family relationship; we are one family in Christ and no matter who you are, your nationality or your ethnicity, we receive you equally, for "God is no respecter of persons." Our church is a vibrant church; we have a vibrant worship, and the word of God is taught in the power of the Holy Spirit. The power of God is present in our church and where the spirit of the Lord is there is liberty. It is a church where all feels being loved. In fact, it is like a community where members are concerned about one another's welfare.[36]

To describe the ANC as a community of faith for believers from diverse backgrounds is not to suggest that church discord, which is normal in churches, is obliterated. What it does suggest, however, is that it is a place where people from diverse backgrounds meet in a relaxed atmosphere where they expect to encounter God. God's word is relevant for them today as it was the day it was written. Members are encouraged to learn and memorize Scripture and ministers preach and teach the full Bible. They firmly believe that corporate worship should involve the coming together of peoples from diverse backgrounds in terms of ethnicity, class, age or otherwise, to glorify God and to help one another to follow him. They think that such gatherings require sacrifices in terms of preferred styles of singing and preaching, yet there will be other occasions where differences are recognized.

It is not only spiritual matters that bring the ANC together in worship; they are structured in such a way that communication and support are always extended to all members, especially those from the minority backgrounds. Through the week, small groups comprising people from diverse backgrounds gather in home fellowships, youth club meetings and the café 316 is opened to the public. They are at a different level of development. For example, they are involved in other projects, such as putting up a new church auditorium, which is at various stages of development. The ANC encourages its members in both spiritual and social matters. It is a welcoming community, and a sense of community is a major identity that it offers its congregation. When asked

---

36. In a recorded interview with a respondent from the All Nations Church.

the reasons for having a multi-ethnic congregation instead of mono-ethnic church, one respondent argued that he viewed the Wolverhampton city as a diverse community, hence it would be wrong for their church not to reflect the people in their community. He remarked:

> The Wolverhampton community where our church is located is a multicultural community. It is also a university city; in this case we come across a lot of international students and for us to ignore them just because they are different from us, is not the way we understand Christianity. Therefore, we believe that to fail to address the needs of our surrounding community is not a simply cultural issue but a theological issue of failing to live up to our biblical responsibility.[37]

The ANC has the desire intentionally to celebrate the diversity that is in their congregation. They have a common multi-ethnic worship service, but also language specific worship services. They clearly have a multicultural identity in their worship attendance as their congregation represents a wide diversity of ethnicities, but the culture of their Sunday morning service is decidedly mono-cultural. They could also go a step further by intentionally weaving various cultural traditions into a single service instead of mono-ethnic groups, such as the Punjabi and Chinese, by ensuring that bringing these groups together in worship would not result in their giving up their identity. But in modifying their worship styles, the ANC, though quite intentional about blending the cultures at some levels, often use a combination of multi-ethnic gatherings and mono-ethnic groupings in their worship. They serve the diversity of the congregation by adopting separate worship services based on languages. For example, there is Chinese and Punjabi services ministered in their various languages.

Praise and worship are regarded very much at the COP, where believers sing songs based on the Scriptures which is done to glorify the name of the living God whom they see as their great provider in all aspect of lives. As one of their pastors explained:

> At the Church of Pentecost, we think that our contemporary expression of our faith should resemble the body of Christ and

---

37. In a Recorded interview with a respondent from the All Nations Church.

our practices should also resemble the ministry of Jesus. As a body of Christ, we must truly display Jesus in our worship and so here, we worship God in the spirit and in truth and we believe that worshipping him this way results in the visitation of the Holy Spirit in our gatherings.[38]

The COP is of the view that as Jesus boldly declared his mission in Luke 4:18–19 as the Messiah, a proper evaluation of the church (universal) all these centuries later, must certainly bring recognition of the ministry of Jesus in churches and mission endeavours. All churches must replicate the mission of Christ in their worship.

The four churches have different worship styles, but they have all created faith communities that take worship seriously and have made it (music) an intentional part of the experience of their adherents to share in their communities of faith. Their worship focus is on God as the source of all that they are as Christians.

4.4.4. The Emphases of the Spirit and Power of the Holy Spirit

Even though, all the four churches believe in the work of the Holy Spirit in their ministry, yet the emphases of the Spirit and power of the Holy Spirit differ from one church (denomination) to another. For example, it was discovered during the fieldwork that the COP places much emphasis on the Holy Spirit in all areas of their ministration. It was observed that they acknowledge the importance of the Holy Spirit in the work of evangelism and church life and they do not emphasize philosophy instead of the Bible. They teach their members to prepare for a spiritual battle with Satan and his demons. They also teach their members how to heal the sick, cast out demons and preach the gospel with miracles confirming the ministry of the word. They have a Bible College where they prepare their members for the work of the ministry, but in their Bible College, instead of merely turning out students with degrees which they do, their emphasis, however, is to raise up God's people who are aflame with the Holy Spirit. These they believe could dispel the demonic

---

38. In a recorded interview with a Church of Pentecost pastor.

influence spread over the United Kingdom and elsewhere (Acts 8:6–7). They emphasize the role of the Holy Spirit as one of their core values:

> We believe in the manifestation of the Holy Spirit and that the Christian life can be led only by being born again and receiving the grace gifts from the Lord. We believe in the new birth as the work of the Holy Spirit, and then the baptism in the Holy Spirit for power to serve and the gifts of the Spirit for building the body of Christ. The Holy Spirit helps the born-again Christian to develop a Christ-like character which is manifested through the bearing of the fruit of the Holy Spirit. The leading of the Holy Spirit in all aspects of the believer's life and all spheres of activity in the church is paramount.[39]

The emphasis of the Holy Spirit in the work of the ministry was evident repeatedly in a variety of forms throughout the fieldwork with COP:

> In my experience as a Christian leader, I have come to understand that some Christian leaders possess great intellect and powers of speech. They can appeal to the emotions of their followers. But their messages are mainly philosophical. These people because of their oratory can impress the minds of people but I don't think that kind of preaching can penetrate the heart of people as they mainly appeal to the emotions. As a church, our understanding of preaching is that the Bible should be ministered in prophetic power. It is the demonstration of the Spirit and power of the Holy Spirit and not an exercise of human wisdom and ability as described by the Apostle Paul in 1 Corinthians chapter 2.[40]

Another member of the church had this to say:

> The church is supposed to be a place where people sense God's presence and hear his voice. The spirit filled preacher's voice should be the medium through which the Lord can speak

---

39. A respondent from the Church of Pentecost in a recorded interview.
40. Church of Pentecost pastor in a recorded interview.

to his people. Our pastors are people who pray and seek the face of God.

These views were shared by a respondent from the ANC:

> As Christian leaders, we spend time in prayers preparing for ministration of the word. As we do this, we make sure that we regard the sensitivity of the Holy Spirit and preach the word. The book of Acts tells us that the early church was under the directions of the Holy Spirit. Sadly, what we see in some circles today is human work rather than Holy Spirit directed work, but the early Apostles were dependent on the leadings of the Holy Spirit as such Christ's people can emulate the example of the early church.[41]

It was observed in the fieldwork that the COP shares the need for baptism in the Holy Spirit and then gives opportunity for those who would like to receive the baptism to be prayed for. If people are sick or suffering, they are being encouraged to be prayed for. Believers lay hands on them and pray for them. Those praying are encouraged to share a word or revelation they receive from the Holy Spirit for the person they are praying for. The COP's concept of church is that a church should be a place where people not only learn about God but also experience his presence. Therefore, the place of the Holy Spirit and his empowerment is very significant in their worship as they place much emphasis on the power encounters with demonic forces that are confronted and overpowered by the power of the Holy Spirit. The ANC believe in the gifts and ministry of the Holy Spirit, but they also have a strong emphasis on biblical teaching and look to the Scriptures to guide their experiences with what the Holy Spirit reveals to them. At the ANC, one finds the teachings of the Bible and there is also an open heart for the work of the Holy Spirit, which makes the ANC distinct and unique. The COP, the ECL and the ANC do not think that their churches can properly accomplish their God-given task without the gifts of the Holy Spirit. To these churches, the baptism in the Holy Spirit was not optional for the first century church, neither should it be optional for the twenty-first century church. They believe that the Lord wants to empower believers for ministry and the gifts of

---

41. Church of Pentecost pastor in a recorded interview.

the Spirit are to empower Christ's people for the work of the ministry. They, therefore, encourage the exercise of these gifts and give their congregations the opportunity to use them.

In the ministry of the Holy Spirit, one characteristic of the HBC is their relaxed casual style. They do not get involved in spiritual hype and emotionalism because they do not want to motivate their congregation carnally. They simply trust in Jesus Christ and the Holy Spirit, and they teach the Bible, deeply trust, and absolutely rely on the Scriptures. They believe in the validity of the gifts of the Spirit, and that the gifts can be expressed today. What they do not believe in is the excesses and the emotions that so often accompany the use of these gifts of the Spirit. For example, they encourage members who want to speak in tongues to do so in a private devotional setting such as prayer meetings but not necessarily in their public services like, for example, the Sunday worship service. They are of the belief that Christ's people should have a spirituality based on an intimacy with the Heavenly Father and an involvement in the lives of fellow believers as well as people of the world.

They have the realization that their fellowship is the Lord's church, and this relieves them from the burden of being pressured to grow their church by using all sort of carnal means. Because they refuse to put themselves under pressure for results, they have learned not to create schemes and manipulate people. They believe that it is the Lord's church and if it is the Lord's church then the Lord will take care of his church and build it in his own time (Matt 16:18). It is the Lord's responsibility to add to the church and to build his church (John 21:16). But it is also the responsibility of pastors to love the congregation, equip them for the work of ministry and trust the Lord to use them to build his church by adding those that should be saved:

> Our emphasis is on the Scriptures, and we believe that this ministers to the spirit of our congregation as our Bible-based ministration is not to appeal to emotions, and it does not come from the wisdom of the world but the guidance and wisdom that comes prophetically from the Holy Spirit.[42]

The HBC realizes that there are some Christians who place a heavy emphasis on speaking in tongues and other manifestations of the Spirit and

---

42. In a recorded interview with the Harborne Baptist Church pastor.

power of God. These people look on speaking in tongues as the primary evidence of the infilling or baptism in the Holy Spirit, but they (the HBC) think this gift in the believer's life may not evidence anything if there is no love. They understand that God's supreme desire for his people is that they will experience his love and share that love with others. That love needs to be demonstrated by Christ's people in actions, attitudes, and life. When asked during the in-depth interview with the pastor (the HBC pastor) about how the gifts of the Holy Spirit are ministered in his congregation, he admitted that they do not allow speaking in tongues during Sunday services and other public services, but members are encouraged to use the gifts in their own personal devotional life:

> We don't allow public utterances in tongues as practised in some Pentecostal churches but there are a group of believers in this church who gather for prayers and exercise the gifts of the Holy Spirit. In as much as it's done in their own personal devotion and not in our public service, I don't think there is any problem with it.[43]

It was observed that the ANC, the COP and the ECL emphasize tongues as the primary manifestation of the baptism in the Holy Spirit, while the HBC looks for emphasis on love as the fruit of the Spirit.

4.4.5. The Existential Concerns of the Next Generation

All the four churches have active children and youth ministries and see the growth of these ministries as a vital part of their vision as a church. The HBC is a missional and forward-thinking church helping young people to grow to a strong and mature faith so that they would take responsibilities not just in their local church and communities but also worldwide. They commission and guide their young people in adventurous, outgoing, and pioneering ministries. For example, during an observation, the Sunday worship service was devoted to some of the youth (18–23 years) who just returned from their missionary trip to Uganda. In their message to the congregation, they shared their missional experiences and the motivations they had received from their mission endeavours in Africa. The ANC has developed programmes that help

---

43. In a recorded interview with the Harborne Baptist Church pastor.

to shape the church's engagement with young people in some exciting and challenging contexts. Their youth development is focused on providing mentorship and support. It is about growing leaders for Christian ministry. Their programmes are organized by implementing fellowships, worship, biblical teaching, discipleship, and evangelism as well as ministry and mission. The youth are equipped and empowered to take responsibilities in the church, such as leading praise and worship, prayer meetings, youth evangelism and developing strategies to reach and meet specific needs of their community. The leadership prioritizes the exploration of vocational leadership among the youth. Here, they see it as the pastors' responsibilities to instil in the next generation of believers, absolute confidence in the authority of the Bible and an absolute dependence on it for their understanding of the Christian life and ministry.

My notebook reveals the information I gathered during a conversation with some of the second-generation youth during my fieldwork at the COP. The conversation showed the tension the youth have towards the liturgy and ecclesiology. These second-generation immigrants who have been assimilated into the dominant culture in the British system want their church to embrace a contemporary worship style aligned with the host culture. During a casual conversation with a couple of them, I observed that the second-generation remains in the church's fellowship but not without stress. The leadership does not appear to have a deep understanding of the needs of the youth who complain about the type of ecclesiology used in their church setting. But in their effort to please their parents, these young people remain in the fellowship, however, with a negative attitude and some of them become disengaged and eventually leave as one respondent explained:

> Everything we do in worship here is as if we are still in Ghana. We can't invite our (white) friends here. The way our people organise worship here is difficult for young people like us to understand. We want our worship songs to be contemporary worship, and these are twentieth century songs. If not because of the respect I have for my parents, I would have left this church a long time ago.[44]

---

44. A recorded interview with a respondent from the Church of Pentecost.

The specificity of the above response led me to ask in the in-depth interview with the COP pastor, how as a church, they could address the existential concerns of their next generation in areas of worship (music). The pastor responsed as follows:

> The issue of the second generation is a complex one. We encourage those who don't want to worship in the Akan way to join our multicultural service where service is conducted in the English language and the praise and worship is contemporary. We are aware of the challenges they face as they are caught between two cultures. We are very prayerful about addressing these issues.[45]

This issue about the existential concerns of the second-generation youth of the COP was made evident in numerous responses during the fieldwork. It is evident that there is a misunderstanding between the second-generation and the first-generation in the areas of theology and ecclesiastical style. The COP is aware that the future of their diaspora church depends on the young generation catching the vision of the first-generation migrants. Therefore, several measures have been initiated to mentor the youth to know Christ in a personal way and to know the distinctiveness of the church. COP allows the youth to ask questions on issues they do not understand, and the youth are encouraged to bring forth their ideas for discussion on how to move the church forward. The leadership identifies the giftedness of the youth, trains, and encourages them to preach during services on weekdays, as well as some Sunday services. COP local churches are encouraged to establish youth centres where counselling, recreation and reading facilities will be provided for the youth. These youth centres should also provide career counselling and guidance as well as mentoring.

The practices of the ECL on the other hand, help their second-generation to replicate their cultural heritage and maintain their identity. Their ecclesiology is designed to replicate their Ethiopian/Eritrean cultural identity to the next generation. It is for this reason that many of the Ethiopian/Eritrean youth interviewed, expressed a strong preference for an Ethiopian/Eritrean pastor whom they think could lead them to replicate their cultural heritage and maintain identity. They also think that having a pastor from the same

---

45. In a recorded interview with Church of Pentecost pastor.

background would mean the desire to empathize with their spiritual, emotional, and material needs. Because the ECL offers its members a sense of community, their youth and most of them, British citizens, still think they are Ethiopians and Eritreans, first, before being British. In other words, they identify themselves as British but retain the lifestyle of their parents. They demonstrate allegiance to their cultural identity and this in part has been encouraged by their first generation. Their sense of community is not necessarily meant to ignore people from the wider community, but it is meant to discover their identity and respect and belonging.

4.5. Summary

All the four ministers believe that God's vision clearly takes diversity seriously. They also believe that God does not obliterate the differences, but they think that the differences exist to create room for diversity, which is God's nature. They all think that bringing hope to the world, and in so doing demonstrating Christ's love for it must be the priority of all Christ's people. Therefore, the African immigrant churches and the white majority churches must see themselves as players in bringing about God's kingdom to the communities in the United Kingdom. Apart from their normal Sunday worship services, all the four churches have weekday programmes such as small groups, youth club, prayer meetings, men and women fellowships and other programmes that encourage interaction among their congregations. A sense of community and belonging is developed during these weekday services because of their informal nature and then also these meetings are conducted in a non-threatening environment. Hence as a result supports in different forms are extended to members for their developments and to meet their emotional, spiritual, and physical needs.

The COP and the ECL were established as a worship place where their African members can discover a sense of identity, respect and belonging. This sense of need has immensely contributed to the development of a healthy prayer and devotional lives of their adherents. Racism may not necessarily be the reasons for the existence of these churches. But it could be the catalyst in their growth and relevance to the African community as these churches serve as places where African migrants meet with fellow Africans, worship, share and socialize with them. The sense of identity that is so important among these churches does not mean that they ignore people from other cultures or the wider community. However, it is worth noting that the primary concern of most migrants is not with integration; faced with immigration matters and other social issues, migrants are first concerned with how they will survive in their newly found country, and this is where the African immigrant churches come in. Frankly, the roles played by the COP and the ECL in assisting their congregations have facilitated the role of their churches as both social and spiritual liberation for their adherents. This role is action is rare in the traditional white majority churches. It is not so much of the fact that the traditional churches are consciously deciding that they will never change; it is just the fact that some Christians tend to get comfortable with the way things are.

It was noted in this research that disunity among Christians occurs mostly when there are doctrinal differences. For example, when churches take a dogmatic position on issues such as being Arminian or Calvinist, in the view of all the four pastors, this in some way brings division. But this should not bring division as Scripture teaches both the sovereignty of God and the responsibility of God's people. The disunity among Christ's people becomes imminent when they take their strong positions on these doctrines to an extreme. But the Bible clearly reveals much about the two positions. So, what God's people must realize is that there is much theological argument for and against both doctrines. As it is properly explained by the Apostle Paul in his epistles, both sides of the argument were taken into consideration by him. Hence the fact that Christ's people can present strong point of view in the interpretation of this matter demonstrates that there are two sides of the argument. Therefore, issues of being 'Arminian or Calvinist' should not divide the body of Christ. The pastors, therefore, feel that it would be appropriate to accept people they come across, who in some cases have different doctrines (secondary doctrines). However, they also think that unity should not be at the expense of the biblical truth as much as they all agree in the fundamental doctrines, secondary doctrines should not divide the body of Christ. For this reason, Christ people must realize in all their interactions with other Christians that, all Christ's people form his body (the body of Christ) and are called together to express and continue his ministry of reconciliation by representing his words and deeds to all humankind. Therefore, the metaphor of the body of Christ ministering to itself in love should be the example in all Christian endeavours if they share the same beliefs in the fundamental doctrines. It is true to say that the fundamental doctrines shape the view of Christ's church and determines how Christ's people live out their mission and this view is respected by all the pastors.

The study shows that the four churches have different emphases regarding the Spirit and power of the Holy Spirit. The COP, the ECL and the ANC have similar understanding of the gifts of the Spirit. The HBC, however, shares different views as they believe in the Holy Spirit, but not in the charismatic sense. The other three pastors argue that the New Testament states that Christ gave to the church (universal) apostles, prophets, evangelists, pastors, and teachers (Eph 4:11) to enable God's people to fulfil their ministries, hence they all think that it is difficult for them to believe the type of theology which says that spiritual gifts including apostles and prophets died out with the early Apostles. They remarked that such thinking is not true to Scripture, to history or experience and that today, there are apostles who are pioneers, church builders and there are prophets too who bring clarity, vision, and perspectives to the church (universal). All the pastors, including the HBC pastor, agree that there are evangelists, pastors, and teachers but the view held by the other three pastors is that all the five leading ministry gifts in Ephesians 4:11 are essential if the body of Christ is to function properly. According to them, Christ gave these gifts to the church (universal) for the equipping of Christ's people and for the work of the ministry.

Equally significant, is the fact that the absence of spiritual hunger is a real problem for the indigenous British (white) Christians. The fact is they recognize this thirst for spirituality but the structures (leadership) in their places of worship stand in their way of satisfying this thirst for spirituality. It was also noted that any attempt of the ECL to assimilate into the British culture of contemporary worship would often encounter stiff resistance from its first-generation migrants and this may result in the members withdrawing and moving into places of worship that they are familiar with. In such cases the ECL pastors and in some cases, pastors of other black-led churches have the responsibility of helping their congregations to emphasize their new identity in Christ and help lead them in a process of commitment to Christ and to one another to be the people of God on a mission together with the wider community in Britain. The ECL leadership is involved in cross-cultural initiatives that bring Christians from diverse backgrounds together by building bridges and outreaches to communities. They have gone a step further by allowing the Church of England in the Kings Cross area of London to share the use of their church building. However, the gathering of ECL is typically mono-ethnic, yet, not out of hatred towards others, rather those who attend the ECL are desperate to preserve their roots in a foreign land. The ECL will remain a mono-ethnic church for the foreseeable future because it is observed that the issue of identity for the Ethiopian/Eritrean believer is one in which their Christian faith and cultural loyalty is connected.

The ANC and the HBC are churches modelling diversity. As they find ways of creating, building, and connecting truly diverse communities rather than mirroring a society divided by race and other negative factors, they are announcing the kingdom of God here on earth. Clearly, the demography of Britain is diverse as there are people from different backgrounds, varied ethnicities, and diverse countries and so churches must take this into consideration in their mission endeavours. The goal of the pastoral staff in both mono-ethnic and multi-ethnic churches should be to recognize where people are in their journey to becoming more culturally, inclusive, and to serve them in a way that is appropriate to what God is doing in their hearts and lives. It is understandable that the need for unity in diversity is about Christian unity; the idea of unity here does not mean the promotion of religious pluralism or bringing all Christian churches under one umbrella. In other words, the need for unity in diversity does not mean that all religions must come together in unity. The gospel, unlike other religions is about what the Apostle Paul clearly described in 1 Corinthians 15:1–4.

It was also observed that there are existential concerns about the second-generation migrants who themselves are valuable assets for reaching out to the wider community because they naturally negotiate between their parents' cultures and the host (UK) culture. It is with these next generation migrants that new cross-cultural ministries can be constructed. The challenge, however, is how these second-generation immigrants can maintain the identity of family, culture, and their Christian beliefs, while at the same time adapting to the culture of the host country. For example, it was observed that the COP's youth are the generation to establish a multi-ethnic church because they understand the culture of their first-generation parents and are also comfortable with white British culture. The COP leadership has put in place measures to encourage their second-generation and some of these measures are the 'open forum' given them to operate in the church to identify with them in matters of concern to them (the youth) and opportunities to teach and preach when necessary.

None of the four churches had a leadership team that reflected the diverse backgrounds of their congregation. Most of the leaders of the COP were Ghanaians and the ECL also has its leaders from Ethiopian /Eritrean communities. The ANC's leaders come from diverse backgrounds. Notwithstanding this, there are still some disparities. The HBC, on the other hand, is in a process of building a multicultural team. All four pastors understand that the factor that informs selecting or choosing leaders, is making sure that one chooses the type of leaders who will broaden the experience of the existing team and that they make sure that the types of leaders they choose listen to their congregations.

The study has shown that changes happen when people move to new places. In the new communities, one can find people (like recently arrived migrants) who have experienced a great deal of change and are open to new relationships. Mono-ethnic churches offer migrants, who may not fit the conforming expectations of many traditional churches, a place to grow spiritually and relationally, a place to call home as they worship with people of their own kind. Ideally, all churches must be biblically inclusive, seeking to grow in love and respect for people who are different from most of their congregations. However, these outward-looking qualities are generally perceived as lacking within many white majority churches. Hence there is the need for some of these churches to learn to be welcoming churches, seeking to overcome the cultural barriers that separate them from people "who are not like them." Clearly, they have a responsibility as Christ's people, to be concerned about the wellbeing of the minorities who share the same faith and worship with them. But getting involved in the lives of people from other backgrounds is a difficult task hence the need for mission-minded pastors who will equip the existing members of their white majority churches to understand the reality of the ethnic changes going on around them in their communities. They should see the people they meet in their communities as people who could also be part of the kingdom.

The study shows that churches do not necessarily have to be multi-ethnic before they become faithful to God's vision. However, due to the multicultural nature of the UK's urban communities, the multi-ethnic church has a role in these communities. Nonetheless, there is also a place for mono-ethnic churches in the communities. In most situations, mono-ethnic churches are best for reaching first generation migrants because in the mono-ethnic churches there are not many cultural issues to be addressed while the migrants adjust to a new life. There will always be people who prefer not to cross-cultural barriers to understand, accept, and practise the gospel. This is where the ECL and the COP come in. They offer their congregations a sense of community, identity and belonging. They are also involved in finding solutions to the economic situations of church members. They have therefore created a conducive environment to enable members to share their economic, educational, and other social needs with the church.

Certainly, this study makes us to understand that there will always be communities in places (towns and villages) where there is only one ethnic group and there will always be people with a common identity (like the Ethiopian/Eritrean community in Britain) or with a language barrier. In these cases, mono-ethnic churches would be ideal. Leaders, whether from a multi-ethnic or mono-ethnic background, must therefore be mission-minded and passionate about their church and communicate a great deal to their congregations about their church's values whether mono-ethnic or multi-ethnic.

The themes, insights and patterns that have emerged from the research fieldwork has been integrated into a critical thesis, utilizing methods of comparison, analysis, critique, and evaluation in the next chapters (chapters 5–7).

CHAPTER 5

The African Immigrant Church and its Implications for *Missio Dei*

5.1. Introduction

God is a relational God and as such, he expects Christ's people from all backgrounds to express their theology and communicate his love relationally to all people irrespective of their backgrounds. Therefore, the framework of any meaningful partnering between the African immigrant churches and the white majority churches should be based on the formulation of a meaningful understanding of mission based on theological reflection and not anthropological underpinning. Verstraelen, Camps, Hoedemaker and Spindler shared this view when they emphasized the impossibility of formulating an overall perspective on mission from one perspective, which in their view, has always been the Western perspective.[1] In conducting an empirical study using four

---

1. Verstraelen, Camps, Hoedemaker and Spindler had this to say: "the theological undergirding of the church's mission has often been intertwined with a legitimation of the superiority of Western Christianity. That is, the undergirding of missions often served to justify views and actions that in retrospect betray a denial of and contempt for contextual diversity. Therefore, it is no longer possible to formulate an overall perspective on "mission" naively from one perspective, and certainly not from a Western perspective. It will only be possible to formulate such an understanding of "mission" based on theological reflection on the unity that arises in, behind, and above contextual diversity. This unity will then have to be defined "missionarily": It will have to be defined on the basis of understanding of the journey of Christianity in the world as a journey with a starting point of reference (the kingdom of God). And it will have to be defined in terms of the "real presence" of that starting point and the focus on the common point of reference becoming visible in all the (contextual) ramifications

churches, all the four pastors who were interviewed shared a similar view on mission. They all accepted that mission is God's mission, and that God has called the church (universal) to participate in his mission. They believe also that God can do everything in the world through people and nations to establish his kingdom here on earth – within the church and beyond the church – but salvation is only through God's son Jesus Christ. Therefore Christ's people, irrespective, of their backgrounds, are privileged to be called to participate in God's mission wherever they happen to be in the world.

It is obvious that the church (universal) does have a special role, sent by God to continue in his (God's) mission of salvation of humankind. Christ's people, regardless of their background, must deeply take to heart the Great Commission (Matt 28:16–28) which calls for all Christians to measure their lives by this heavenly vision of reaching all nations. In view of this, it will be fair to say that the African immigrant churches must regard the whole British society as another stage in their mission endeavours to the United Kingdom as they reach out with God's whole heart for the uttermost part of the world in line with the biblical pattern of Acts 1:8. Evidently, the African immigrant churches have a mandate in Britain in what some African Bible scholars called "reverse mission."[2] These African Christians believe that they have a God-given mandate for the discovery of Christianity in Britain, which in a sense was once the centre of support for Christianity to other countries. Britain has now become a mission field and it appears that the professing church is short of ideas on how to move to the next level in their Christian endeavours. The assertion of Wan supports the migrants' claims of having a God-given mandate in their newly found land, when he stated that "international migration could be interpreted as a God-given opportunity to

---

of the journey." (Verstraelen, Camps, Hoedemaker and Spindler, *Missiology, An Ecumenical Introduction: Texts and Contexts of Global Christianity*, 120.

2. Adogame, had this to say about reverse mission: "Nineteenth-century Britain was a golden age for Christian missionaries who took the word of God around the globe to countries in which that religion remains and is now thriving. In a reverse of those great missionary journeys, idealistic modern-day missionaries travel to Britain to discover the historical roots of their faith and try to pursue their own missionary agenda in the 21st Century Britain, trying to breathe new life into churches with declining attendance" (Adogame, *The African Christian Diaspora: New Currents and Emerging Trends in World Christianity*, 172).

spread the Gospel as the golden age of the mission endeavours of Western missionaries appears to have come to a halt."[3]

It is clear to say that Western Christianity and for that matter Christianity in Britain, is declining and many people are very pessimistic in Western Europe and North America today. This reinforces the reason why the African Christians and the British Christians must discern the divine providence in their partnering together with a missional intention. Clearly, it is obvious that the influx of migrant Christians into the UK is a providential means for reaching out to the host in post-Christian British society. However, it is also amazing to note that many churches in Britain do not come to this same place of faith.

It is obvious that the African immigrant churches have a God-given mission to reach out to UK communities. But what immediately comes to mind is whether these churches have the theological framework that could unpack itself through their missiology, which in a way can shape their ecclesiology.[4] To reach out to the wider community, it is necessary for the African Christians to change their theology and practices so that they can consistently address the crucial areas of people's lives across cultures. In their missionary effort, Adogame was right to suggest that the African Christians must shape their theological thinking and must have a drive for ecclesiastical liberation from the "paternalistic apron strings of Western mission bodies."[5]

If God has a mission in Britain and the African immigrant churches are participants of God's mission in this country, what then is the mission? The four pastors interviewed in this work, have a similar understanding of the mission of God as Karl Barth who believes that the mission of the church (universal) is the mission of God, because God is the originator of mission, and the church is the respondent to what God is doing in his mission.[6] The

---

3. Wan, ed., *Diaspora Missiology: Theory, Methodology, and Practice*, 275.

4. Chalke, *Intelligent Church: A Journey Towards Christ-Centred Community*, 13.

5. Adogame, *The African Christian Diaspora, New Currents and Emerging Trends in World Christianity*, 177.

6. The idea that the mission of the Church (universal) is the mission of God, and that God is the originator of mission, and the Church is the respondent to what God is doing in his mission has its origins in the thought of Karl Barth. Barth's argument that God is the originator of mission, and that mission must be understood as an activity of God was first proposed in a paper given at the Brandenburg Missionary Conference in 1932. However, the full concept of the mission of God was articulated in 1952 at the Willingen Conference of the International Missionary Council. It is worth noting that the expression *missio Dei* was not used during the

history of *missio Dei* can be traced back to Augustine and has over the years emerged as a theological concept. However, its origin and historical concept is not my main concern in this work. I will in this chapter concern myself more about its implications for the mission endeavours of the African immigrant churches in the UK.

I am of the view that salvation is the aim of *missio Dei*. But the aim of *missio Dei* also includes vertical relationship or communion of Christ's people with God and the horizontal dimension of human relationships (how Christians relate to one another). I support the view of Bosch who argues that mission derives from the very nature of God and that the church (universal) is viewed as an instrument for that mission, a ministry in which the church is privileged to participate. He had also this to say:

> To participate in mission is to participate in God's love towards people, since God is a fountain of sending love . . . Since God's concern is for the entire world this should also be for the scope of missio Dei[7]

This chapter seeks to understand the concept of *missio Dei* that God has always been on a mission to seek, save and redeem. The mission of God dominated the life and teachings of Jesus and calls all Christ's people, regardless of their backgrounds and no matter what part of the world they find themselves, to embrace this very lifestyle of Christ. Christ's people are asked to live by the same rule that governed his time here on earth. However, there must be adaptations to his approach to ministry to suit the situational context in

---

conference, but it featured in the report of the Wurttemburg by Karl Hartenstein, the former director of Basle Mission. He created the term *missio Dei* to state in a nutshell, the outcome of the conference's closing statement which said: *"The missionary movement, of which we are a part has its source in the Triune God Himself. Out of the depths of His love for us, the Father has sent forth His own beloved Son to reconcile all things to Himself, that we and all men might, through the Spirit, be made one in Him with the Father in that perfect love which is the very nature of God . . . We who have been chosen in Christ . . . are by these very facts committed to full participation in His redeeming mission. There is no participation in Christ without participation in His mission to the world. That by which the Church receives its existence is that by which it is also given its world-Mission"* (Richebacher, "Missio Dei", 589). Mission was understood to derive from Trinitarian nature of God: The Father sends the Son; the Father and the Son send the Spirit; and the Trinitarian God sends the church (universal) into the world as an embodiment of divine love towards God's creatorship. In this case, 'mission' is no longer seen merely as the practical extension of the Church; it has to be understood fundamentally as a representative of the Triune God (See: https://www.postost.net/2011/01/missio-dei-historical-perspectives-part-1).

7. Bosch, *Transforming Mission*, 400–401.

which they find themselves. For example, the strategy Christ adopted in the Mediterranean culture over two thousand years ago would not be the same techniques he would use today. Yet the core message would remain the same. Coleman thinks that "methods are variable, conditioned by the time and circumstances, which are constantly changing." However, the principles inherent in Christ's way of life would never change.[8] These principles, Coleman believes provide guidelines for making disciples in every society and every age. How then do Christ's people seek to understand the Christian faith in a contemporary context, which has developed because of mass migration into Britain in the past few decades?

This chapter indicates that the essence of missional theology is relationships. The triune God, the ultimate relational being, expects Christ's people from all backgrounds to express their theology and communicate his love relationally. In Britain, 'mission' is still perceived by some people (white British) as the initiative of the church and more specifically with the perception of missionaries migrating from the West to foreign lands. They portray mission as taking the gospel from Western developed countries (Western Europe and North America) to the unreached parts of the world. In the context where the professing church has for several hundreds of years accepted that it has the authority for mission, how can the professing church respond to the new realities that have arisen because of mass migration of people from diverse cultural backgrounds who have joined their Christian landscape in Britain in recent years?

What then is the existing relationship between the African immigrant churches and the white majority churches? As Christ's people, called to be light and salt of the world, are they striving to invest God's resources at their disposal where it makes the most impact? The new covenant in Christ calls Christ's people to covenant with God by participating in his mission, by being a light and salt to the nations while proclaiming the gospel of Christ. The *missio Dei*, therefore, calls all Christ's people to redefine their local context. Where they work, play and live is a mission field and that is where their ministry begins. In other words, due to the multicultural nature of the UK urban communities, cultural and ethnic barriers would have to be crossed if the Great Commission is to be fulfilled effectively. How can Christ's people

---

8. Coleman, *The Great Commission Lifestyle*, 54.

from all backgrounds share the gospel in a way that is suitable to their new cultural context without compromising the core message of the Bible?

This chapter seeks to understand that the ways the African immigrant churches relate to their new communities should be missional and that they should not only seek to minister to their own kind but should also focus on the wider community. Frankly, how the white majority churches seek to understand the Christian faith in a contemporary context that has developed because of mass migration is particularly important because their mission endeavours must indicate action on the part of God, who calls for a response from his church (universal), be they white majority or black led.

It is true to say that there is much talk in the evangelical circles in Britain that identify the problems that are encountered in the African immigrant churches partnering with the white majority churches, but it is more important to produce solutions now. For example, Steve Clifford, the General Director of Evangelical Alliance,[9] stated that their One People Commission was working to see the type of unity for the purpose expressed in Jesus's prayer of John 17:21, reflected in their mission endeavours to Britain.[10] However, Christ's people are yet to see the implementation of this fresh expression of unity among Christians from diverse backgrounds. Finding solutions to the identified problems, therefore, is the essence of this book.

Christian mission in a diverse British urban context requires an understanding of the culture that informs the local mission. Local church pastors must, therefore, be mission-minded equipping their congregations to understand that the African immigrant churches and the white majority churches, both agree on winning souls to Christ. Just imagine what might happen in the communities of Britain if believers from all backgrounds are empowered and encouraged by their churches to invest themselves fully in propagating the gospel across cultures!

---

9. As at the time of going to the press, Dr. Israel Olofinjana has become the new Director of the Evangelical Alliance. This gives hope for new outcomes of the alliance since his writings have proved that he is capable of leading the organisation in the right direction.

10. Olofinjana, ed., *Turning the Tables on Mission*, 8.

5.2. The African Immigrant Church as an Instrument for God's Mission to Britain

The African immigrant churches in the UK are established in the Christian landscape in their host country. They have clearly enabled their members to find refuge from discrimination and discover a sense of identity, respect and belonging. But they need to work harder in more creative ways and in partnership with the white majority churches to create a society that models the values of the kingdom of God. They must therefore regard the whole British society as another stage in their mission endeavours to the United Kingdom as they reach out with an expanded vision of God's whole heart for the uttermost part of the world in line with the biblical pattern of Acts 1:8.

It is certain that reaching out to the wider UK communities would mean a situation where the African immigrant churches develop a contextual approach to ministry (ideally ministering in Britain should mean doing ministry in the British context). But this poses a big challenge as it is obvious that there are cultural differences that would need to be addressed. For example, the perception in the UK that the "African originated" churches have a different theology must be cleared (see chapter 3).

The African immigrant churches preach and teach the whole concept of the Bible, but their inability to reach out to the wider community is worrying. Adogame also raised concerns about the inability of the African-led churches reaching out to the wider community when he stated that at this stage of their mission endeavours to the West, and for that matter to Britain, what the African immigrant churches are involved in, is to engage in developing a sort of "structure and practices" to enable their African migrant members to maintain and reproduce their cultural identities. He had this to say:

> The African-led churches' communities represent pivots of attraction to their African congregations and the reasons for this is that most of these churches replicate the cultural and religious sensibilities of their home context, in a way that creates a comfort zone for many African immigrants. Despite targeting both Africans and non-Africans in their membership drives,

their social-ethnic composition is still dominated largely by the former with White converts forming a negligible percentage.[11]

Adogame understands that African Christians would have to rework language, and would also need a good approach, and move away from their present theological understanding if they really want to do cross-cultural ministries in their newly found country. They also need to present in a new way, their context and make it more welcoming to their new geographical and cultural environment.[12]

Edward, Joel (cited by Adogame) shares similar view:

> African and Caribbean Christian communities often suffer from an acute case of "cultural dissonance," "contextual abstinence" and a "crisis of self-preservation." It is one thing to talk about black churches influencing British Christian faith, but it is quite another to recognise the number of black Christians seeking cultural refuge in White-led churches. African congregations replicate Africa on Sunday and co-exist with the culture for the rest of the week. They have a crisis of self-preservation which threatens to castrate the mission enterprise. In this sense, sometimes remaining and being African or Caribbean is the mission.[13]

The above comments from Joel Edward, (as cited by Adogame) indicate that the African communities iIn the UK are not inclusive in their orientation. For these churches to become relevant within the multicultural context of the UK, they would have to explore ways of changing their theologies and practices to become churches that can strategize to be the vanguard of spiritual, emotional, economic, and social liberation by consistently addressing the important needs of people's lives and focusing their resources to transforming lives. These churches would have to negotiate between adapting and changing their religious cultures to fit into their new UK cultural context.

Duane Elmer underscores that there are sound theological reasons for understanding other cultures and appreciating them because making that commitment according to him, "will unfold for us new and wonderful

---

11. Adogame, *The African Christian Diaspora*, 202–203.
12. Adogame, 205.
13. Adogame, 208.

dimensions of God's character, for our God can be properly revealed only through diversity."[14] It is true to say that there are cultural differences between the African immigrant churches and the white majority churches, but by partnering with each other and understanding each other's cultures as suggested by Duane Elmer, both sides will be able to challenge the aspects of their culture and cultural influences on theology that are not in line with biblical principles. Christ's people from both backgrounds would have to grow in a knowledge of and appreciation for what God has been doing in the migration of people into the UK over the past few decades. They would need to combat the mission ignorance and apathy that has over the years affected the work of the ministry in the country.

5.2.1. The Theology of Migration and the African Immigrant Church

The migration of God's people to where God has ordained for mission endeavours for his providence dates to the book of Genesis. From chapter 1 to chapter 11 of Genesis, the Bible makes us to understand the goodness and beauty of God's creation, the fall of humankind and the resulting satanic dominion over God's creatorship. Chapter 12 describes God's plan of salvation for all people regardless of their backgrounds, that is, every tribe, tongue, and nation. In other words, the purpose of God's plan of restoration of humankind was as though his kingdom was to strike back against Satan. In its most specific sense, this was fulfilled when the Lord Jesus Christ was crucified, and subsequently trampled Satan at the Cross of Calvary. But in its wider sense, all Christ's people have victory over Satan and his works of darkness through Christ's redemption work. This reversal of the evil world by the coming of God's kingdom is indicated from Genesis 12 to the book of Revelation. That is to say, the theme of the Bible from Genesis 12 to the book of Revelation is about bringing forth restoration, reconciliation, and God's righteousness into every people, tribe, tongue, and nation. According to Ralph Winter, the reason God sent Abraham to Canaan was because of its geographical position in the world. It was centrally located in the largest land mass of the planet. It was also a popular trade route. It served as a key to the centres of trade and

---

14. Cited Elmec, *Cross-Cultural Conflict, Building Relationships for Effective Ministry*, 12–13.

communication.[15] The mandate given to Abraham was to lead to the blessing to all the nations. These promises and mandate are clearly continued in the New Testament. Galatians 3:6–9 describes God's call and covenant with Abraham as the theme of the Bible, hence the marching orders of all Christ's people. According to Galatians, Christ's people are heirs of the same covenant God had with Abraham as well. Just as Abraham left the comfort of his home, God's people everywhere may voluntarily or involuntarily move away from their familiar surroundings to get a fresh perspective on missions.[16] Christ's people from all backgrounds are all part of the cause of completing the Great Commission wherever they find themselves.

Certainly, God's unchanging purpose throughout the Scriptures is that all peoples would be blessed through those who know him, and that missions is the basis of the Bible. As such there is only one cause, the mandate of completing the Great Commission. Christ's people have been called to be part of it irrespective of their backgrounds and no matter where they find themselves. This assertion is brought out clearly by the Apostle Paul in Acts 17:26–28 NKJV as he spoke to the people of Athens:

> And he has made from one blood every nation dwell on all the face of the earth, and has determined preappointed times and the boundaries of their dwellings, so that they should seek the Lord, in the hope that they might grope for him and find him, though he is not far from each one of us; for in him we live and move and have our being, as also some of your own poets have said, 'for we are also his offsprings.'

It is clear from the above quotation that migration is in the will of God and that all Christ's people are the offspring of God. Hence all people, regardless of their background, are equal before him in worth and all have an equal right to respect. If all people are equal in his sight and he uses migration of his people to advance his kingdom, it will be appropriate if God's people in Britain and elsewhere understand the role of migrants in their communities. During my interviews with the members of the four churches I mentioned earlier on this writing, it was revealed that these Christians were all eager

---

15. Winter, ed., *Vision for the Nations*, 2–3.
16. Winter, ed., 2–3.

to share fellowship, and partner with people who are not like themselves but the reasons they gave for partnering together were anthropological and sociological. This is overly concerning as these opinions prove to be more complicated. It is fair to say that the church members' opinion only gives Christ's people humanistic explanations and not a proper missiological understanding through the concept of *missio Dei*.

Ideally, it will be appropriate, among other things, if Christ's people from all walks of life in the UK could seek his face in prayer concerning what he is doing in the twenty-first century context of mission in Britain. Payne warns Christ's people not to look at the trend of migration from sociological and anthropological point of view but suggests that the focus of Christ's people should be that God is working out his will in the universe and that migration of people is not, in his own words, "serendipitous."[17] The professing church in Britain still carries forward the inherited deficiency of an anthropocentric approach to ministry. But for the African immigrant churches and the white majority churches to work together there is the need for formulating an understanding of mission based on theological reflection. Hanciles understands that if Christ's people are to accept that the biblical God is a God of mission, then they also must accept that he makes himself accessible through experiences like migration of people.[18]

Understandably, the waves of immigration have influenced the shape of the white majority churches, particularly in the urban areas, from the grassroots level up. For example, there have been priests, pastors, and missionaries, who themselves were African ministers in the Anglican Church, the Roman Catholic Church, the Assemblies of God, Methodist and other orthodox and evangelical churches in Africa coming over from sub-Saharan Africa to fill ministry positions in the UK, at the request of their British denominations. In addition, there are also independent churches from Africa extending their mission endeavours to Britain. Some African theologians and Bible scholars apply theological relevance to these efforts of African Christians reaching out in the diaspora in what they termed as "reverse mission." However, Adogame feels that this reverse mission initiative cannot be claimed to be a peculiar

---

17. Payne, *Strangers Next Door, Immigration, Migration and Mission*, 30.

18. Hanciles, *Beyond Christendom: Globalization, African Migration and the Transformation of the West*, 140.

feature of African Christian communities, nonetheless, he thinks that the Africans have tried to spread their type of Christianity beyond their immediate geo-ethnic context.[19]

At this stage of the mission endeavours of the African immigrant churches, Kwiyani thinks that the term "reverse mission" is a misnomer because according to him, the African immigrants' Christianity in Britain is limited to only their own kind. And that there is just a limited cross-cultural ministry effort with the wider community.[20]

I am of the view that "reverse mission," is a major shift in understanding of the migrants' mission endeavours to Britain which once brought the gospel to their African colonies. However, at this stage in their missionary efforts, the African Christians' claims of fulfilling their mission to the UK is obscured. It is true to say that the Great Commission, and for that matter their mission in Britain should not be limited to people of their own kind. Yet evidentially, the African Christians have not been able to have breakthroughs in the wider community. Frankly, their inability to have much impact on the wider community is evidenced by the homogeneous complexion of the people who worship in these churches. It is, therefore, obvious that any talks of "reverse mission" in terms of missions remain a concept for now.

In like manner, priests, pastors, and missionaries coming over to the UK from their denominations in Africa[21] to work in their "mother" denominations in the UK, for example, the Anglican Communion, cannot be regarded as "reverse mission." However, the missional content of this effort cannot be downplayed. This type of mission encounter is more of a "Macedonia call"[22]

---

19. Adogame understates: "the rationale for reverse mission is often anchored on claims to divine commission to spread the gospel . . . It is so far unclear whether 'reverse mission' is simply operating as mere rhetoric, and/or what shape, structure and dynamic will emerge through the process in the long run. Nevertheless, 'reverse mission' as a rhetoric or an evolving process is of crucial religious, social, political, economic and missiological import for the West and World Christianity, as the non-Western world were hitherto at the receiving end of missions till the late twentieth century." (Adogame, *The African Christian Diaspora*, 169–170).

20. Kwiyani, *Sent Forth*, 75.

21. This type of migration is not limited to African Christians alone as there are other Christian leaders coming over to the UK from Eastern European countries and elsewhere to fill positions in the mainline and evangelical churches.

22. a vision appeared to Paul in the night. A man of Macedonia stood and pleaded with him saying, "come over to Macedonia and help us." Now after he had seen the vision, immediately we sought to go to Macedonia, concluding that the Lord had called us to preach the gospel to them (Acts 16:9–10 NKJV).

rather than a "reverse mission." The reason being that the ministry efforts of these African Christian ministers in this case appear to be more of a global extension of their Christian faith than a new expression of faith in their host country.

Yet if these Christian ministers realize the need to live and work in their host country with a missional intention, they can use their platform (in their local churches) for a more effective cross-cultural ministry endeavour. They must, therefore, regard collaborating with the African immigrant churches as another stage in their mission endeavours to the United Kingdom as they reach out with an expanded vision of God's whole heart. For example, they can serve as a link between their denominations and the emerging churches to bring about meaningful Christ centred partnership. This process will in a way re-define their present ministry efforts as local church ministers to mission-minded ministers involved in cross-cultural missions and eventually result in what is termed as "reverse mission."

It is worth noting that I do not limit the impact of African Christians' efforts in Christianity in Britain. It is not my intention to diminish their important ministry contributions to British Christianity. For example, they have enabled their members (African migrants) to find refuge from discrimination and discover a sense of identity, respect and belonging; they have created spiritual awakening in their host country and a tremendous awareness of spirituality is spreading through their mission endeavours. However, they need to work harder and in more creative ways in partnership with the white majority churches in the UK to create a society that models the values of the kingdom of God. But at this stage in their missionary effort to the UK, the African Christians have not been able successfully to reach out to the wider community as their adherents are predominantly black Africans. Hence the term "reverse mission" remains a concept, a work in progress and not a reality at this stage. Nonetheless, one thing is clear, and it is that African Christians in Britain are filled with hope and aspiration and are providentially working for the kingdom expansion in their host country.

However, at this stage of the mission endeavours to Britain, it will be premature for the African immigrant churches to assume that they have accomplished their mission to Britain. For them to be successful in cross-cultural missions, they would need to develop a theological framework of their mission endeavours. In this case, there will be a need for them to develop a strong biblical grounding and theological understanding of their mission. They would need the divine principles of the Scriptures, which would give them a thorough biblical understanding and a missiological basis as well as the theological framework for their mission. This will eventually pave the way for them to do cross-cultural ministries and subsequently, lead to the accomplishment of what they term as "reverse mission."

Overall, it is God's sovereignty[23] that establishes the framework of missionary expansion of the gospel in any context as revealed in the Bible. Hence the need for Christ's people on a mission, to seek his face in prayer for directions. The Spirit-led theological framework will pave a way for a genuine partnering between the African immigrant churches and the white majority churches, a partnership, practised in the spirit of kingdom orientation. This view is shared by Newbigin who suggested that any participating in dialogue must mean "believing and expecting that the Holy Spirit can and will use this dialogue to do his own sovereign work, to bring about the desired result."[24]

5.2.2. Embracing Both Divine and Human Activities Across Cultures

The previous chapters have revealed that the emphases the African immigrant churches place on the spirit and power of the Holy Spirit is different from the white majority churches. Certainly, the emphases of the spirit and power of the Holy Spirit have been missing in many white majority churches and this is concerning. There is, therefore, the need for the white majority churches to embrace both divine and human activities and free resources to engage in discipleship across cultures. While the church (universal) is the key to God's work in the world, *missio Dei* teaches us that Christ's people need to see God on a wider canvas than just God working among Christ's people in the church. Mission as *missio Dei* makes Christ's people to understand that God

---

23. LCWE 2010 recognise this view in their statement: "Far from haphazard, this scattering is superintended by a sovereign God who determines the precise times and places in which people will live in order to accomplish his missional purposes." Frankly, God leads his people on a mission through converging circumstances. The African migrants and their host Christians must discern what God, in his providential time identity, is doing in a diverse Britain (in such a period as this). God's people have a portion of responsibility to constantly seek his face for the directions of exactly what he has called them to do. (Wan ed., *Diaspora Missiology: Theory, Methodology, and Practice*, 267).

24. Newbigin, *The Open Secret*, 186.

cannot be restricted to what has been and is happening in Western cultural context and for that matter in Britain, because God's work is universal in its impact according to Guder.[25] The notion that God is at work in a universal sense implies that white British Christians must have a proper theological understanding about the presence of the African immigrant churches in their communities. Understandably, it is clear in the Scriptures that the gospel "in its universal scope and application, demands a universal proclamation":

> For the Scripture says, "whoever believes on Him will not be put to shame." For there is no distinction between Jew and Greek, for the same Lord over all is rich to all who call upon Him. For "whoever calls on the name of the Lord shall be saved." How then shall they call on Him in whom they have not believed? And how shall they believe in Him of whom they have not heard? And how shall they hear without a preacher? And how shall they preach unless they are sent? As it is written: "How beautiful are the feet of those who preach the gospel of peace, who bring glad tidings of good things!" (Romans 10:11–15 NKJV)

It is true to say that the church (universal) has a participating function. It plays an instrumental role in what God is doing in the affairs of humankind. God is the originator or initiator of mission but his (God's) mission is conducted in and through the church as its primary locus of his dealings with humankind. This is a matter of soteriology. The Bible reveals that human beings are saved only by faith in Christ, and that this faith comes by hearing the gospel, preached in word and deed (Rom 10:13–15). In other words, Christ's people have the responsibility of making the gospel known to people from all backgrounds.

Missionaries from Britain and other Western countries have played their role in spreading the gospel to various parts of the world especially to their former colonies. This was done, among other factors, in obedience of the Great Commission (Matt 28:16–20). The call to 'go and win souls and make disciples was necessary in an age when geographical spread of Christianity was limited. When the professing church in Britain acted in missionary work, it did so out of intended obedience towards the will of God. It believed it was

---

25. Guder, *The Continuing of the Church (Gospel & Our Culture)*, 20.

spreading Christian values and furthering God's kingdom on earth. Through this action, community of believers were motivated to share the salvation that they themselves had received from God. However, the twenty-first century reality of mass migration into Britain, still awaits the evangelization response from the professing church. The demography of Britain has changed in the past few decades because of migration of people from various parts of the world. And this has created tremendous opportunities for the expansion of the gospel in Britain.

There should be the realization that the same people the church is sending missionaries to witness to abroad, are now in their streets, schools, workplaces, and communities. This happened because of mass migration into Britain in the past few decades. For example, there are migrants in the UK communities today, who come from countries, where reaching out to the people has become so difficult and complicated due to their governments policies on Christianity; countries such as Eritrea, Saudi Arabia, Libya, North Korea, and many other countries which stifle freedom of worship fall into this category. Hopefully, any Christian initiative to reach out to these newly arrived migrants in the UK communities would mean reaching out to many of the unreached people groups in the world. The reason is that the outcome of reaching out to these people in our streets and institutions could mean equipping these foreigners for the future evangelization of their countries of origin. There is the likelihood that some disciples could be emerged from this effort, and these foreigners would in turn evangelize their own people both in the UK and when they return to their own countries of origin. However, I am not advocating for the replacement of this type of Christian effort with the traditional mission endeavours of sending people from Western Europe and North America to the uttermost parts of the world. But I firmly believe that any Christian efforts to reach out to foreigners in our communities will lead to evangelization in this country as they reach out to their own kind and lead also to future evangelism in their countries of origin.

The heart of every church's mission should be to communicate the gospel of the Lord Jesus Christ's incarnation, death and resurrection (1 Cor 15:1–4). How effectively can Christians advocate this message? There are many practical ways to communicate such a message, but I believe that it must be communicated in a manner that is consistent with the character of Christ. According to Guder, Christ's incarnation demonstrates that God's mission is not dependent on any one human culture, tribe, or language.[26] Local churches must therefore see it as their responsibility to develop disciples of Jesus Christ who love God and their neighbours in an urban environment that has traditionally been underserved. Certainly, it is exceedingly difficult to understand why the white majority churches cannot discern to understand the calling of the African immigrant churches to their communities in such 'a period as this' (Esth 4:14) when the professing church is experiencing dwindling congregation and most of their local churches are already dead. However, the existing relationships between the white majority churches and the African immigrant churches have been cordial in some ways. For example, some white majority churches such as the Methodist Church, the Church of England and the Salvation Army share their places of worship with some African immigrant churches. Yet for a more effective partnering, there is the need for them to engage in cross-cultural ministries.

Any meaningful partnering should first, be determined by a sound theological underpinning for the white majority churches and the African immigrant churches. The churches involved in this partnering, must declare their theological stance, and should prove to be full gospel churches. It is unfortunate that some Bible scholars and missiologists are caught up with "everything goes syndrome." Yet the approach that sees all other religions and in some cases cults as being missions equivalent to mission given to the church (universal) does not do justice to Jesus's claims to uniqueness, nor the Trinitarian nature of God. Mission is, primarily the work of the Triune God, Creator, Redeemer, and Sanctifier, for the sake of the world according to Bosch.[27] Bosch's contention echoes what Jesus said in John 20:21. In John 20:21 NKJV, Jesus commissioned his disciples by saying: "Peace be with you! As the Father has sent me, I also send you." This commissioning affirms the sending out of Christ's people with a mission to fulfil to reach out to the entire world. The empowerment for this type of mission today comes through the spirit and power of the Holy Spirit and that explains the divine nature of the tasks of the universal church, which is specific and divinely mandated.

Therefore, responsibilities of both the white majority churches and the African immigrant churches should include sharing the gospel of Jesus Christ

---

26. Guder, *The Continuing Conversion of the Church*, 78.
27. Bosch, *Transforming Mission*, 391.

to people of all backgrounds by recognising where God is at work and discerning where they must participate and encourage. It is true to say, the incarnation of Christ lies at the heart of God's mission, and this provides the content and the inspiration for all meaningful mission endeavours (John 20:21). In Acts 1:8, the Bible shows us that Jesus Christ sent his Holy Spirit to empower his church (universal) for mission (Acts 1:8). It is vital important for them as believers to be reliant and dependant on the leadings and workings of the Holy Spirit both for their own activities in mission, their spiritual living, and for the effect of their work. There should be no place for engaging in mission endeavours that exclude the role of the Holy Spirit[28] as rightly stated by Newbigin who said:

> Mission is not something that the church does; it is something that is done by the Spirit, who is himself the witness, who changes both the world and the church, who always go before the church in its missionary journey.[29]

Both the white majority churches and the African immigrant churches have a mission to fulfil in Britain. But they must analyze their theology and get a proper understanding of their missiology, which will in turn shape their ecclesiology in the twenty-first century context of mission in the UK. What the Christian world needs today is the type of church that makes sense of both the Bible and conventional wisdom. Christ's people now need theology, culture, and the application of one to the other.[30] Chalke again, underscores the need to build Christ's church anew in Britain in order that Christ's people will bring genuinely good news to God's world. He said:

> The challenge of the ages is set before us all . . . What will be our epitaph? Will we be the generation that began to rebuild the church in the West, or will we simply preside over its further demise?[31]

---

28. Together Towards Life offers cogent advice on the Christian's dependence on the Holy Spirit for mission endeavours: "authentic Christian witness is not only in *what* we do in mission but *how* we live out our mission." (World Council of Churches, "Together Towards Life," 5.)

29. Newbigin, *The Open Secret*, 56.

30. Chalke, *Intelligent Church*, 16–17.

The church in mission can only be sustained by spiritualities deeply rooted in the Trinity's communion of love" (www.oikoumene.org/en/resources/publications/TogethertowardsLife).

31. Chalke, *Intelligent Church*, 13.

The above view was also shared by the four churches during my fieldwork interviews. They all suggested that Christ's people in the UK should seek to understand the Christian faith in a contemporary context, which has developed because of mass migration into Britain in the past few decades. They all felt that the future of the UK church will depend on the next generation, hence local churches should make it their priority to address the existential concerns of the next generation in their congregations in areas of theology and ecclesiology. The research conducted in the four churches has revealed areas where the white majority churches and the African immigrant churches can work together. One example is in evangelism. The multicultural evangelism team reaching out to a diverse community would have a good outcome. This is supported by Guder who asserts that the key of *missio Dei* is evangelism, which is the communication of the gospel.[32] Guder feels that evangelism should include meeting the material needs of the souls Christ's people have been commissioned to win. He does not think that Christ's people should turn their backs on the world and its needs. He also believes that the call to conversion is a call to be witnesses to Christ by demonstrating his love and concern for the world.[33]

Missio Dei provides a theological key for mission in a post-modern age and could also serve as an inspiration in the white British church, which struggles internally with the challenges of post-modernism, pluralism, and globalization. In part, the struggles of the white British church are due to the impact of the British government rules that make all human narratives and beliefs as being of equal value and importance. In this context, Christians become reluctant to share their views with others, because all beliefs and non-beliefs are given equal treatment in society (as there is absolute freedom of worship). *Missio Dei* aligns mission with human activities, with the understanding of mission as "participation" in something that God is already doing. There is a clear divine sanction for mission and evangelism and *missio Dei* circumscribes the biblical grand narrative by challenging popular mission theology that simply embraces the Great Commission with the Great Commandment as the basis of mission. Christ's people can equally accept that God is the originator of all mission, and he has a mission for his church,

---

32. Guder, *The Continuing Conversion of the Church*, 49.
33. Guder, 120.

or he has a church that has been given a mission. It is therefore right to say that both the African immigrant churches and the white majority churches have been given a mission by God in the multicultural context of the UK.

Chalke perceives that even though the church (universal) has been emerging for the past two thousand years, the church, he believes, is still in transition. He thinks that each generation is called to reinvent or rediscover what it is to model accessible and authentic church within its surrounding culture. However, he also thinks that of late more churches in Britain are closing than ever before hence the urgent need for a biblical response to the culture that has emerged in recent decades.[34]

5.3. *Missio Dei* as a Basis for Unity in Diversity

During the interview with the four pastors, all stated that they believed in the unity of Christ's people, but they do not think that unity should necessarily result in uniformity. What it does mean to them is that unity in the most important sense should be about matters concerning the things that really matter. They believe that the healing of broken relationships is an essential message of the kingdom of God, hence the prejudice and racism that divide Christ's people from different ethnic backgrounds has no place in their churches. Unity, as understood by the pastors, is an embodiment of the *missio Dei* that creates the church and God's works in the world. Unity, therefore, should always be the hallmark of the Christian faith. One of the defining characteristics of the theological concept of *missio Dei* is its understanding of God's mission as being Trinitarian. Verstraelen, Camps and Hoedemaker emphasized that the propagation of the gospel must be brought in accordance with the mandate of Matthew 28 based on a Trinitarian foundation of mission;[35] the righteous Christ making possible the participation of all persons in the *missio Dei*. Christ's people, therefore, participate in the *missio Dei* as those converted and transformed by God's love. Through them also love embraces and transforms the world.

---

34. Chalke, *Intelligent Church*, 13.

35. "God the Father, the Creator, has a just claim on all and uses his power to make all de facto his own. God the Son is King Christ, for whom the world must be conquered . . . God the Holy Spirit converts individuals, nations, and their cultures and guarantees the success of mission." (Verstraelen, Camps and Hoedemaker, *Missiology: An Ecumenical Introduction*, 244).

God's plan is to raise up a people from every kindred, tribe, and language of the earth for his praise. The goal of missions therefore is the glory of God.[36] The Bible tells the story of a missional God with a clear plan and intention for his creation, the redemption of humankind after the fall of man. The Bible as a grand narrative explicitly identifies Trinitarian activity and still serves as the primary source for Christians from all backgrounds. In other words, all perspectives indicate action on the part of the missional God who calls for a response from all people regardless of their background, nationality, race, or ethnicity. Christ's people in Britain must proclaim, from a Christian perspective, a mission which embraces the practice of ministry and social action in the context of how God is moving providentially in a new missional context of the United Kingdom, which has been brought about because of the mass migration of people from diverse backgrounds in the past few decades.

Verstraelen, Camps and Hoedemaker help to illustrate this point and they had this to say:

> Therefore, it is no longer possible to formulate an overall perspective on "mission" naively from one perspective, and certainly not from a Western perspective. It will only be possible to formulate such an understanding of "mission" based on theological reflection on the unity that arises in, behind, and above contextual diversity. This unity will then have to be defined "missionarily." It will have to be defined based on an understanding of the journey of Christianity in the world as a journey with a starting point (Jerusalem) and a point of reference (the Kingdom of God). And it will have to be defined in terms of the "real presence" of the starting point and focus, on the common point of reference becoming visible in all the (contextual) ramifications of the journey.[37]

In the same vein, Newbigin makes a point while writing about how the gospel can be propagated effectively in a pluralist society when he said:

> The Christian points to Jesus as the master-clue in the common search of humanity for salvation and invites others to follow. It is

---

36. Newbegin, *The Gospel in a Pluralist Society*, 180.
37. Verstaelen, Camps and Hoedemaker, *Missiology: An Ecumenical Introduction*, 120.

true that this invitation, when it is given by Christians who are in positions of power and privilege, may be radically corrupted into a kind of spiritual imperialism which is oppressive rather than liberating. Missions have been guilty of this distortion, and we must acknowledge it. But it is also worth noting that most of the vigorous evangelism in our contemporary world is being done by the churches of the Third World which have no such power or privilege.[38]

Understandably, the *missio Dei* in the contemporary world is being conducted in contexts. Therefore, it is not necessary to formulate an overall perspective from only the Western context as remarked by Verstraelen[39] and echoed by Newbigin[40] who further suggested that Western countries have cultivated a long-established attitude that is perceived as burdensome encumbrances, and this baggage, according to him stands in their way of presenting the gospel effectively. However, he acknowledges that evangelism in the contemporary world is being conducted effectively by people of the "Third World" including Christians from the sub-Saharan Africa. Migration of people from various parts of the world into Britain in the past few decades has resulted in forming African communities of faith in Britain. It is amazing to note that many of the host Christians do not come to this same place of faith as Newbigin's. It is fair to say that if these Africans can do effective evangelism as admitted by Newbigin, then they can likewise be used in reaching out to the whole British communities. However, it is sad to think of the tragedy and the cost of unbelief that keeps Christ's people from partaking in his kingdom goals, even when God has provided abundantly for his work. It seems clear that the time has come for the professing church to take advantage of this present trend of migration into Britain, seeing it as God working out his providential plan to re-evangelize Britain again. In this case, there will be a need for a meaningful partnering which will take into consideration the twenty-first century context of mission in Britain. However, any attempt of cross-cultural ministry in the multicultural Britain will prove to be a complicated context if it is going to involve all the diverse communities. The reasons

---

38. Newbigin, *The Gospel in a Pluralist Society*, 158.
39. Verstaelen, Camps and Hoedemaker, *Missiology: An Ecumenical Introduction*, 120.
40. Newbigin, *The Gospel in a Pluralist Society*, 158.

being that context can change over time and frankly, the British context has changed over the decades especially in the urban centres, yet God, as the Bible explains, is unchanging and is behind the unity in all contexts.

Therefore, for cross-cultural mission to be successful, the focus on communal responsibilities should be increased and Christ's people should do ministry based on the demographic makeup of their communities. In this case, Christians from all backgrounds in a particular community could come together to share the gospel, in both word and deed. This is very worrying as now the white majority churches and the African immigrant churches are following their own agenda and have not made many strides in coming together for any meaningful cross-cultural ministry. It will be appropriate if both sides come to self-realization that they have a God-given mandate to fulfil in the UK communities. This self-realization will then bring them together in faith, love, and submission, which will result in a powerful witness that will impact British communities. Christians in Britain must realize that the church in the UK is invited to respond to God's ongoing mission in Britain, which has come about as result of a mass migration into the UK in the past few decades. Just as the Son was obedient in being sent by the Father, so must the UK church respond with obedience and act in accordance with God's mission to the country. In this mission of God, God is both the sender and the one being sent. This accounts for the trinitarian structure of the *missio Dei*. The highest mystery of the mission out of which it grows, and lives is that God sends his Son and the Father and the Son sent the Holy Spirit.[41]

Trinity, therefore, is communion and serves as the basis for what it means for the church (universal) to be in relationship with the triune God and humankind. God collaborates best with a team, even though he works with individuals too but there is a fuller expression of his will in team working because part of what Christians communicate is that God is a relational God and that the Christian faith is, by definition, one of fellowship. Partnering therefore, will lead the African immigrant churches and the white majority churches to create a platform that will be tremendous in sharing the gospel, leading Christ's people, making disciples and modelling the love of Christ, with a greater impact in British communities. Thus, international mission teams

---

41. Vicedom, *The Mission of God. An Introduction to a Theology of Mission*, 11.

with members from diverse backgrounds, cultures and generations can speak powerfully about changes effected by God's kingdom in the UK communities.

If in the twenty-first century, Christian denominations (black, white, and others) start working together as Christ's people with a mission to reach out to UK communities, the impact would be extraordinarily powerful. Because God's people, from diverse backgrounds, working together for a common goal, reflect the unity of the Triune God and demonstrate the New Testament principle of koinonia as seen in the lives and ministries of Jesus and the first century Christians. Both the host Christians and the African Christians must work together to remove any stigma, stereotypes, discrimination, superiority complex and any perception that stands in their way of carrying the gospel to the next level. If mission is understood as originating with and done for the purpose of God, then all Christ's people, whether Africans or Whites, are part of the *missio Dei*. They must, therefore, shelve their differences in order not to hinder the work of God in a particular context. *Missio Dei* makes us understand that a theology of participation has the potential of embracing diverse communities of Christ's people. If the *missio Dei* is to reconcile, restore and renew all Christ's people into God's divine love then this is the work of the Triune God, yet Christ's people still have their portions of responsibility. The African immigrant churches and the white majority churches must identify themselves as communities of faith. Identification of the church as the community of faith participating in *missio Dei* takes the church to a new level as its very nature and activity is grounded in the nature and activity of the triune God.

The fieldwork has revealed that the teachings of John 17 is the model that seeks to disciple and educate believers about the implications of their faith. The study expounds how Jesus rejoiced in his relationship with the Father (God) by stressing the oneness he has with the Father. Jesus stressed the unity between him and his Father and prayed that his followers would mirror this relationship. The context and intensity of Jesus' prayers in John 17, therefore shows the priority Christ places on the unity of Christians as his main and repeated request in this prayer was their unity. The unity of Christ's people, therefore, is dependent on sharing the priority of seeking and doing his *missio Dei*, especially his desire to reach the unsaved and in this case the African immigrant churches and the white majority churches, mounting a programme to reach out to Britain's diverse communities.

5.4. Summary

Mission flows from the nature of God alone. The church (universal) has no mission of their own. That is to say, the mission to which Christ calls Christians is his own mission, hence the mission of the African immigrant churches in the UK is God's mission. Vicedom was right when he said that mission is work that belongs to God and that God is the one who gives the orders, and he is also the one who takes care of things. He is the one championing the cause in mission as such the church is just an instrument in his hands in that the church itself is only an outcome of his activity.[42]

What then does it mean for Christ's people to participate in the activity of God? Undoubtedly, for Christ's people to reach out, regardless of their background, there should be the need for a strong biblical grounding and theological understanding of their mission. The fundamental truths of God and the divine principles of the Bible will give them proper biblical and missiological bases and the theological framework of their mission in any context.

There is, therefore, a broad consensus that it is right to attribute all missionary initiative to God, who is triune. Others, both within or in some cases without the church (universal), may be privileged to participate in God's ongoing mission to redeem and restore the world; the church also has a unique position as a participant. In other words, the church is invited to respond to God's ongoing mission, and just as the Son was obedient in being sent by the Father, so must the church respond with obedience and act in accordance with God's mission to the world. If the purpose of mission is salvation as argued by Vicedom,[43] then the African immigrant churches must concern themselves about the wider community of Britain, which has become a mission field.

The one area in which the African immigrant churches and the white majority churches can work together is evangelism. It is true to say that both believe in the Great Commission as such they can work out a strategy for reaching out cross-culturally to the communities which have become multicultural because of mass migration to the UK in recent decades. Therefore, these churches, regardless of their background, must recognize the vital importance of mission. Their initiatives should be characterized by Christians from diverse backgrounds living and working in Spirit-led unity.

---

42. Vicedom, *The Mission of God*, 5.
43. Vicedom, 11.

The understanding that mission begins with God must inform all Christians, as they seek to share the gospel in the UK afresh for a new generation which is more globalized and diverse. When Christ's people recall that mission is God's mission and that he has called his people into it, their endeavours and efforts, at best, mirror what God has already started because all that Christ's people are doing is just responding to his calling into ministry. As Jesus attributed his work to the Father, so must all Christ's people: "Most assuredly, I say to you, the Son can do nothing of himself; but what he sees the Father do; for whatever he does, the Son also does in like manner" (John 5:19 NKJV).

It is, therefore, the task of the church (universal) to regard God's mission in the church as part of his total mission to humankind. Theologians and missiologists in Britain need to grapple with the question of a theology of mission that is open to the work of God, while at the same time confessing and proclaiming the unique *missio Dei* in which God the Father is the only source of all mission, Jesus Christ the only Lord and Saviour and the Holy Spirit the only divine life-giver and power.[44] Christ's people must realize that the church (universal) is sent into the world to call people and nations to repentance, to announce forgiveness of sin and a new beginning in relations with God and with neighbours through Jesus Christ.

The mission endeavours in which Christ's people participate in Britain should have their source in the triune God. Christ's people must cultivate the understanding of God's love for humankind, and that he (God) has sent forth his beloved Son to reconcile all things to himself that all might through the Holy Spirit, be made one in him with the Father, in that perfect love which is the very nature of God. It is this trinitarian basis of mission that forms the basis of the Christian's understanding of *missio Dei*. However, both the church and the mission of the church are tools used by God; they are the instruments through which God conducts his mission. If the church is the instrument of *missio Dei*, the African immigrant churches must understand their mission in Britain in line with the pattern of Acts 1:8.

Missio Dei is the reflection on what some Bible scholars and missiologists see as the key verse for Trinitarian mission is John 20:21NKJV. Jesus said to

---

44. Cited Engelsviken, "*Missio Dei*: The Understanding and Misunderstanding of a Theological Concept in European Churches and Missiology," 481–497.

his followers: "Peace be to you! As the Father has sent me, I also send you." This verse provides a good reference point for *missio Dei* and serves to illustrate the validity of Scripture as a starting point and a legitimate source of authority for discussions regarding *missio Dei*. The Trinitarian sending in John 20:21-22, where the mission of the followers of Christ is modelled on the mission of the Son must be taken into consideration in any meaningful partnering between the white majority churches and the African immigrant churches for the work of the ministry in Britain.

The content of *missio Dei* will be the gift of salvation, the justification of sinners, and reconciliation with God, and the new sanctified life in fellowship with Christ under his lordship. Mission confronts people with a decision to accept or reject salvation in Christ Jesus and ideally, every person should be given the opportunity to either receive or reject the Saviour. Therefore, any missional organization or a church that does not seek to integrate people into the local church would be disobedience to the *missio Dei*.

Certainly, there is a real need to discover ways in which the truths of Christianity can be explored in the twenty-first century context of mission in Britain. Britain, which once took the gospel to 'all parts of the world' has now, become a mission field. It has become a society that rejects claims of absolute truth and now sees all religious opinions as being equally valid. There is, therefore, a need for both the African immigrant churches and the white majority churches to respond to the new realities that have arisen because of the mass migration of people from diverse cultural backgrounds into Britain in recent years. Certainly, this will necessitate the development of a type of theology, which is suitable to the new emerging contexts.

CHAPTER 6

Crossing the Racial Boundary to Reach non-Africans

6.1. Introduction

The previous chapter has argued that God is the originator of missions, and for that matter, it would be right to say that the African immigrant churches are participants of his mission in Britain. This chapter seeks to look for ways in which the African immigrant churches can cross the racial boundary to reach out to the wider community and build bridges across the diverse cultures that make up the UK urban communities.

The previous chapters have revealed that the African immigrant churches have now been established in the UK, but their congregations are mainly black Africans. Yet ideally churches should not seek to be organized primarily in terms of ethnicity as this distracts from the biblical principles of unity in diversity (Gal 3:28). However, there is also the argument that for some categories of people, such as recently arrived migrants, ethnic churches are vital to aid their integration into their new communities (see chapter 1).

This study is an attempt to discover ways in which the African immigrant churches could partner with the mainline UK churches for a more effective delivery of the gospel in the UK. It was argued in chapter 1 that for the African immigrant churches to fulfil their God-given mandate in the UK there was the need for them to work with the white majority churches. However, all the four pastors in the study admitted that there existed cultural differences between the African immigrant churches and the white majority churches.

They were of the view that the first step to take to resolve these differences was for both sides to commit themselves to building the spiritual relationships of mutual love and trust, working together as people Christ has called and commissioned for kingdom goals. In two of the churches where the fieldwork was conducted, (ANC and HBC), I discovered how insensitivity to cultural realities could result in hindering ministry efforts in multi-ethnic churches. ANC and HBC (both churches are multi-ethnic churches) have discovered in their ministry practices the challenges involved in assessing the need to assimilate people from diverse backgrounds into a common theology practice in multi-ethnic churches because of the differences in the worldview of people from diverse backgrounds. They suggested that Christ's people need divine wisdom to learn how to navigate the potential tensions and misunderstandings that people from diverse cultural backgrounds bring into the fore. However, they also think that churches should be aware that their concerns to be relevant with diverse cultures should not be based on their emotions, but should be in line with Scripture.

All the participant pastors agreed that there were some important theological issues that needed to be addressed if Christians from diverse backgrounds desired to work together to impact their communities. They believed that if differing views (in the fundamental doctrines) existed in any Christian relationship, it would bring genuine divisions based on their biblical teachings. They, therefore, thought that it would be more appropriate if Christ's people from diverse backgrounds could at least agree on matters of importance, such as partnering in the areas of evangelism and nation-wide prayer crusade. These, according to them, were some of the issues that could deepen their relationship with fellow Christians and result in a healthy Christian unity.

Certainly, for any meaningful cross-cultural ministry initiative, the African immigrant churches, and the white majority churches, would first have to deal with the aspect of their cultural biases. They would have to realize that the need for working together as Christ's people, was a call of God, so achieving the highest goals of the kingdom should be their priority as people of God with a mission. The major challenges facing cross-cultural missions and for that matter all contemporary missions are the cultural and theological issues involved. This chapter therefore examines ways through which both sides could set aside their cultural biases to embrace and appreciate the good in each other's culture. It is also about how both sides could come together to formulate the type of theology (see chapter 3) which defines the current contexts that have emerged because of mass migration into Britain in the past few decades.

6.2. Causes of Disagreement among Christians

In the interview with the four pastors, all admitted that disagreement among Christians is a negative reflection on the character of God. They also believe that the Bible gives Christ's people the divine principles essential to meet the challenges of interpersonal conflicts, disagreements and misunderstandings that may arise when Christ's people working together find themselves with conflicting and diverse views. The pastors share the view that disagreement among Christ's people is more prevalent when working together as a multicultural team. The areas of disagreement, they say, are always about core values and theological differences that emerge because of the diverse cultural backgrounds of the team. The pastors understand that, apart from the social and cultural factors that have emerged in the UK because of migration of people from different ethnic backgrounds, there have also been ecclesiastical developments within Christian circles over these past few decades. It was also revealed in the fieldwork that some of the host Christians approach cross-cultural relationships, wearing their own cultural spectacles to interpret a given situation. This, in my view is ethnocentrism. Consequently, ethnocentrism has in many cases resulted in doubts, a superiority complex, and a weakening of relationship, which often results in misunderstandings and conflicts among Christ's people. Disagreement also occurs when Christ's people are working together but not necessarily as a team in a supportive framework. This denies Christ's people the ability to develop and realize their potential to fulfil their God-given vision. Ideally, it would be incumbent upon the host Christians to create an environment that welcomes the ideas and contributions that Christians from other backgrounds bring t and what they can do to advance the kingdom of God in Britain. The British churches appear to be short of ideas on how the gospel should be propagated in the current context. Hardy and Yarnell inform the author's understanding by rightly suggesting the need for Christ's people from diverse backgrounds, intentionally, to come together to share their missional challenges in the current context as part of their multicultural missional conversation.[1] This thesis reveals that ministering to people from a diverse British context will require an awareness and understanding of the culture that informs the local mission as one interviewee responded:

> It is true that we (Whites) also have our weaknesses. We are very individualistic, as such we overlook the needs of people from other cultures. We need to improve on how we relate to people who are not like us, but the problem is that we instead try to impose our ways on other people because we think that our ways are better than theirs. We need to improve upon the way we relate to others.[2]

The above comment from a respondent is genuinely concerning because it is a true reflection on some of the challenges facing the African immigrant churches in their bid to partner with the white majority churches. It seems clear that Christ's people from the minority background are always offended when the host Christians set themselves up as right, having superior power of judgement. The host Christians in most cases create an atmosphere for migrant Christians to feel as if they are only there to listen to their superiors. They make them think that being a migrant Christian in this current context means you have no ideas and worthy insights or the ability to make wise choices in your new environment. In a similar vein, Elmer feels that power, control and winning can create potential tensions between the host Christians and the migrant Christians. And when Christ's people feel offended, they respond in one of two ways. He had this to say:

> we conclude that we are average at best, or worthless at worst; our self-esteem is damaged, and we resign ourselves to tedious mediocrity and low expectations for ourselves. Or we become angry at the way our self-esteem is being challenged and questioned. The anger may turn into resentment or even

---

1. Hardy and Yarnell, *Forming Multicultural Partnerships: Church Planting in a Divided Society*, 95.
2. A respondent from the Harborne Baptist Church in a recorded interview.

open rebellion. We may rebel by adopting values and activities exactly opposite to those of the "always right" authority figure.³

Elmer understands that most Western Christians do not intentionally seek power to control because they understand the concept of empowerment, team working and relational leadership. However, despite their understanding of authentic leadership, they find it difficult to give up power when working with people from other backgrounds. Quite frequently, they slip into a controlling mode unless they consciously understand, manage, and share power that comes with their cultural baggage.

All four pastors believe that divisions and factions among Christ's people are caused at times by petty issues or what is regarded as 'secondary doctrines' which have in fact, caused many divisions to the body of Christ. These divisions and factions have caused hindrance in Christ people's efforts to evangelize the world. It is also true to say that the muddle of disunity among the many expressions of the Christian faith occurs when the authority of God's mission is infringed upon by ecclesiastical polity claiming authority for mission. However, the secondary doctrinal differences that separate Christ's people, should not bring divisions to the body of Christ at all. Adogame suggests that some African Christians perceive Western churches as dead, spiritually bankrupt and filled with carnal inclinations, while some Westerners see African churches as "too African," "mixed with African tradition and gospel," and not epistemologically viable.⁴ The pastors think that such perceptions as above and other matters make the task ahead difficult but possible. They think it is possible because they do not think that such perceptions should bring about divisions within the body of Christ. However, they also share the view that when Christ's people disagree about deeper values and essential doctrines such as those regarding the Christian's relationship with God, they assume that such differences in the fundamental doctrines will always make working together with any individual, group and more so involvement in any cross-cultural ministry initiative impossible. There is a perception in the UK that the black churches have a different theology. The African immigrant churches therefore must re-define themselves in relation to the white majority churches; they also must clarify their theology because their present

---

3. Elmer, *Cross-cultural Conflict*, 197.
4. Adogame, *The African Christian Diaspora*, 207.

environment would have an influence on their theological emphases (see chapter 3). All the pastors support the view I shared that there should be the need for a new way of theologizing among the various churches that occupy the UK Christian landscape in line with the current contexts.

Certainly, for the African immigrant churches to do any meaningful cross-cultural ministry, they would have to develop a contextual approach to ministry, which is suitable to their Western environment (see chapter 3). Both the African immigrant churches and the white majority churches would have to enter dialogue and challenge the aspects of their culture and cultural influences on theology that are not in line with biblical principles. I contend that, because of its importance, theology should be taken into consideration in any ministry efforts of Christ's people. In all mission endeavours of Christ's people, there is the need for a strong biblical grounding and theological understanding of the mission. Christ's people would need the fundamental truths of God and the divine principles of the Bible would give them a thorough biblical understanding and missiological basis, as well as the theological framework for their mission (see chapter 3). However, Verstraelen, Camps and Hoedemaker[5] warn against any attempt of Christ's people formulating an overall perspective of theology from the Western perspective (see chapter 5).

There is, therefore, the need for the African immigrant churches and the white majority churches to enter dialogue on a level playing field to arrive at what works theologically in their various contexts. There should be mutual respect between the two sides in all aspects. The white believers should welcome the African Christians as God's people with a vision and a testimony, as well as experiences to share with the body of Christ in Britain. They must see them as God's people who are in the country providentially to contribute to Christianity in Britain, which is rapidly declining. I think that theologizing can increase their dialogue and move the conversation forward to other critical issues such as their being sensitive to each other's culture and agreeing on matters that can deepen their relationships and result in unity. For example, matters such as conducting nation-wide prayer meetings and coming together as a multicultural team to build relationships of mutual trust necessary to reaching out to communities together.

---

5. Verstraelen, Camps and Hoedemaker, *Missiology: An Ecumenical Introduction* 120.

It is true to say that effectiveness in evangelism will increase with Christian initiatives such as Christ's people coming together from diverse backgrounds to reach out to diverse communities. However, Christ's people coming together in unity does not necessarily mean they are seeking uniformity. God has made available a variety of his gifts and talents in Christians. Therefore, Christ's people making the necessary efforts to come together would mean that they are coming together in fellowship with different gifts and talents as well as different ministry experiences (Rom 12; 1 Cor 12). More importantly, the goal of interdependence in any fellowship of Christ's people reflects the unity of the body of Christ amid diversity. The most exciting thing, therefore, is that the differences in personality, appearance, and gifts among the multicultural team of Christ's people will display the diverse body of Christ. It is also clear that interdependency among Christ's people is difficult to develop in individualistic societies such as Britain. Therefore, deliberate efforts must be initiated by Christ's people to learn the lessons of interdependence as illustrated by Paul in 1 Corinthians 12. There should always be the need to appreciate the uniqueness of what the other side is bringing to the fore. In 2 Corinthians 8:12–14, the reciprocity in Christian living as described by Paul is unique in Christian fellowships today because one's abundance supplies what the other lacks, leading to a mutual benefiting of each other. Therefore, the interdependency of Christ's people from diverse backgrounds will bring with it the supply of unique needs, be it spiritual gift, experiences in ministry, and many others but to mention a few and this will result in balancing the whole. Chike points out the perceived difficulty in any attempt of cross-cultural ministry initiative by both sides in the areas of ecclesiology and hermeneutics. He thinks that there are differences in the ecclesiological and hermeneutical understanding of the African Christian and the host Christian. He further states that in the African theology, the place of the Holy Spirit and his empowerment is incredibly significant.[6] As such, African Christians place much emphasis on the power encounters with demonic forces, which are confronted and overpowered by the power of God. Mbiti was making a point when he said that African Christians' understanding and use of Scripture liberates them from the "ready-made and imported Christianity" of the West as they theologize the kind of Christianity, which more fully embraces the totality

---

6. Chike, *African Christianity in Britain*, 37.

of their existence.[7] That is to say, the African theology is contextualized in their African context, and the outcome is different from Western theology, which, has problems understanding the spirit and the spirit world. Certainly, there exist differences in the theology of African Christians and their host Christians, but these differences are not in the fundamental doctrines, as such are issues which can be addressed by both sides. Therefore, the first step to take to resolve these differences is for both sides to commit themselves to building the spiritual relationships of mutual love and trust, working together as people Christ has called and commissioned for kingdom goals.

6.3. Sensitivity to Each Other's Culture

This study has revealed that any attempt at unity between Christ's people from diverse backgrounds and the host Christians would prove to be incredibly challenging. For example, when Christ's people do exactly what they think is good in their default cultures instead of learning about each other's culture, it will be impossible for them to build bridges. The study has proved that for any meaningful cross-cultural missions between the African immigrant churches and the white majority churches, both sides would have to learn to appreciate the differences of each other's culture. Also, the perceived arrogance of the host Christians which reflects in their relationship with other Christians "who are not like them" would have to be addressed. Lingenfelter echoes similar sentiments when he suggests that both the African Christian and the host Christian blame each other. He had this to say:

> The Africans see the Westerners as harsh, unbending, and uncaring; the Westerns see the Africans as undisciplined, careless about time, and having low goals regarding productivity.[8]

Certainly, Lingenfelter has explained some of the perceptions that make relationship between both sides difficult but not impossible.[9] However, he is not saying that Westerners cannot criticize the African Christians or vice versa. Rather, the issue here is the motive behind such criticism, which in his

---

7. Mbiti, *Bible and Theology in African Christianity*, 32.

8. Lingenfelter, *Leading Cross-Culturally, Covenant Relationships for Effective Christian Leadership*, 48–49.

9. Lingenfelter, 49.

own words "could be an act from positions of dominion and resistance or from positions of service." It is time therefore, for Christ's people to realize that there is no such thing as a perfect culture but there are good things in cultures that have universal values. The above contention was in line with the assertion of Newbigin when he stated that all Christ people judge some elements of culture to be good and bad. But Newbigin thinks the motive behind the judgement must be clear. Whether these judgements are in line with Scripture or from the cultural presuppositions of the one making the judgement matters a lot. Newbigin felt that history proves that Western missionaries have made judgements on other cultures, not being aware of the extent to which their judgements were not in line with Scripture but dictated by their own default cultures.[10]

It is true to say that some host Christians have little understanding of cultural values of people from diverse backgrounds other than their own default culture. Or they may be ignorant and not necessarily, biased in interpreting other people's actions. Nevertheless, the problem occurs in a situation where there is an intentional diminished view of Christ's people from diverse backgrounds by host Christians having an inflated view of themselves. This emergence of superiority will in most cases result in lack of trust in any authentic fellowship with Christ's people.[11]

Wan suggests that sacrificial relationship building is of paramount importance to any meaningful cross-cultural ministry initiative. He admonishes that a clear understanding of "word, deed and relationship" must not be done without reciprocity. Wan feels that there must be a contextualization, which he thinks is essential if Christians of the host country have a desire to effectively communicate "compassion, hospitality, and love" towards their migrant neighbours. He believes for example, that contextualization values cultural diversity and the unique gifts of each people (Eph 4:7; Rev 21:26). He had this to say:

> Contextualization promotes an integration that preserves cultural distinctiveness, not an assimilation that obscures it. In so doing it allows for host Christians to be greatly enriched by their correspondence with Christ followers from other nations

---

10. Newbigin, *The Gospel in a Pluralist Society*, 186.
11. Elmer, *Cross-cultural Conflict*, 21.

who are encouraged to bring with them their own culturally contextualized expressions of discipleship and their own "local theologies."[12]

It is worth noting that most migrant Christians crave for partnering with their host Christians on things which really matter for the kingdom of God but in most cases their approaches have been misconstrued as "people stretching out their hands to their white colleagues." Wan advises that the host Christians should encourage migrant Christians to come out with their own culturally contextualized expression of faith:

> The contextualization sees the migrant Christian as a 'hallowed person' who is not a mere recipient of charitable acts, but someone with a story, value, and gifts and experiences to share.[13]

He thinks that at its heart, contextualization is about illustration of biblical truth and becoming all things to all people to reach as many as possible (1 Cor 9:22). It is clear to say that proper understanding and expression of cultural values from both sides is necessary and would be a step towards any meaningful partnering. Understandably, diverse cultures play by different rules, yet Christ's people should not ignore cultures unless they violate Scripture. The vision essential for cross-cultural ministry, therefore, should be based on an understanding of what the Scriptures teach about the kingdom of God with a vision empowered by the Holy Spirit for the engagement in mission endeavours. Hardy and Yarnell were therefore right to suggest among other things, the vital importance of both the African Christian and the host Christian entering dialogue with those who engage in multicultural initiatives to learn from their experiences.[14] The above suggestion by Hardy and Yarnell is in line with my understanding of selecting the four case study churches in writing this study. The perspective of all the four churches is that the unity among Christ's people can become a powerful witness to the UK communities (especially the urban communities) which want to consider reaching out with the gospel to the UK's diverse communities. The pastors

---

12. Wan, *Diaspora Missiology*, 282.
13. Wan, 282.
14. Hardy and Yarnell, *Forming Multicultural Partnerships, Church planting in a divided society*, 93.

believe that the healing of broken relationships among Christ's people is an essential and urgent message of the kingdom of God. They think that the prejudice and racism that divide Christ's people from different ethnic backgrounds has no place in God's kingdom because unity among believers should always be a hallmark of the Christian faith. The above views of the participants are proof that racism has become a stigma that affects Christians from diverse backgrounds. This may explain why most African migrants choose African immigrant churches as their acceptable places of worship. Nonetheless, there are also cultural reasons that in part inform their choice because cultural norms are unique to migrants, especially the newly arrived migrants who may be very conscious of people from the wider community and are not adept in the English language.

Cultural identity serves to strengthen the solidarity of the migrant community as their coming together in the church is not only for spiritual reasons, but also for social and other reasons as well. On the face of it, cultural identity may seem positive, since it brings solidarity, but the downside is that it results in the migrants becoming glued to their own context, so that all they can do is socialize and commune with their own kind in the midst of a multicultural society. So, solidarity, if not checked will hinder any attempt of the migrants' integration into the wider community. It was also observed during a visit to the four case study churches that some of these migrants (from the British former colonies) consciously seek to integrate with the UK society, but they do it in a way that allows for the preservation of their cultural identities. The ECL, on the other hand, prefers instead intentionally to organize themselves around their own cultural allegiances and values. This is because Ethiopians, unlike migrants from the former British colonies such as Ghana, Nigeria, Kenya, and Malawi, were not colonized by the Western "powers." Migrants from the former British colonies, start their integration from their home countries before arriving on the UK shores because their lingua franca is English and their socioeconomic and political structures are also modelled on the Westminster system.

At the ECL, where the first-generation migrants mostly lack the English language skills necessary to integrate into the existing local churches, these migrants find that the host Christians' model of church does not in any way reflect their cultural expression of worship. These migrants also do not fit into other African-led churches either, because of language difficulties, as such they see the need for an independent mono-ethnic church that best suits the needs of their Ethiopian/Eritrean community as one of their pastors indicated in the interview:

> We are a first-generation migrant; we speak a different language, and so we are comfortable in our own culture and way of worship.[15]

This response reveals that the ECL was not planted out of animosity towards the white majority churches or other cultures. Instead, the Ethiopians feel that unlike migrants from the former British colonies whose lingua franca is English, most of them (Ethiopians/Eritreans) must start learning English as beginners. As such, they can best connect with God with the people who speak their language, who have the same history, culture, and the social needs. They can best use their native language in worship because of their limited English skills. They are also careful not to lose the importance of their social and cultural values. Consequently, the preservation of their culture and identity in a foreign land is of utmost importance to them. They, therefore, find it appropriate to come together for mutual support, encouragement, and protection in their newly found country. In this sense, the ECL's way of excluding outsiders in their worship is not intentional since there are cultural and language issues as motivating factors.

It was noted that though the ECL is a mono-ethnic church (and this is for cultural reasons) yet their pastors believe in Christ's people from different denominations and backgrounds working together for the advancement of the kingdom of God. For example, some of the pastors of the ECL attend cross-cultural meetings such as those organized by the *Missio* Africanus and the Centre for Missionaries for the Majority World; I have witnessed the immense contributions of the ECL pastors to these meetings which promote cross-cultural initiatives.

---

15. The Ethiopian Church, London.

6.4. Mission-Minded Leadership

During my fieldwork encounters with the case study churches, I observed that in dealing with characteristics of leadership, HBC, and the ANC[16] place emphasis on character qualities that focus on work ethic. Their emphasis is on reliability, humility, and commitments. HBC gives a higher priority to the formation of a community of believers where there is trust rather than giving priority to attaining vision and meeting goals. The COP and the ECL[17] on the other hand, emphasize spiritual, cultural, and social values. They want to work with born-again Christians who manifest the calling of God, sanctified for the work of God. They also expect their adherents to show love for fellow Christians and the unsaved and have compassion for all people. The task of creating a leadership structure that mirrors all the decision-making and leadership styles of the various ethnicities in any multi-ethnic church is a complex one. This task is so complex that only a few Christian ministries can properly organize it. In their discipleship roles, it was observed that the four pastors see a clear distinction between "leading and following." They believe that leading Christ's people is much more than having them follow you. They think that leading Christ's people is about equipping, mentoring, and encouraging them in such a way that they can be empowered and released for the work of the ministry. In other words, they can be released to do the same thing on their own that their pastors have done for them. This, to them is how effective discipleship should be conducted in any effective ministry.

The fieldwork revealed that the ANC hold diversity in remarkably high esteem. They think diversity recognizes that God gave Christians different skills, abilities, and gifts for a divine purpose and that the purpose of the church (universal) should be to train, equip and release all within the body of Christ for the work of ministry (Eph 4:11–16). However, they also recognize the complexity of leading cross-culturally as one of their pastors admonished during the interview:

> At the All Nations, we recognize how complex it is to lead our church cross-culturally. The challenge here lies in the building of a church community of faith with trust among Christians who come from different cultures, different nationalities, and a

---

16. Both the ANC and the HBC are white majority churches.
17. The ECL and the COP are both African immigrant churches.

> diverse background. These people, because of their diverse backgrounds come to us with different cultural identities, traditions, and diverse worldviews. But we believe that what the Lord is looking for is a church which is united in fellowship and diverse in ministry, a church which is multi-ethnic with a multicultural identity. So, here in the All Nations, our goal therefore, is to create a congregation with a multicultural identity and this is given all serious attention in everything we do as a church: in our worship service, teachings, preaching, discipleship ministries, and leadership structure.[18]

Lingenfelter warns that any church or Christian movement that aspires to build a multicultural team must invest time and resources to study the backgrounds of the people that comprise the new team and must also acknowledge the possible expectations of misunderstandings and differences in their opinions. Lingenfelter feels that, when Christ's people are in distress situations, they resort to finding solutions or arguing out their case by regressing to their default culture and this can happen in ministries, regardless of one's experiences in cross-cultural ministries.[19] Leaders, therefore, are advised against yielding to any short-sighted attempt to control or influence decisions. It is fair to say that Christ's people in cross-cultural ministries must listen to one another because each cultural community has its socially defined "views on how issues of resources and power should be managed including matters of accountability."[20] Gibbs notes that leaders in most churches may walk away when they face disagreements within their team, unless there is a proper structural accountability that can make them to work through their differences. The type of leaders for the twenty-first century context of mission, therefore, should be caring leaders. Leaders who are caring are the ones who are accountable for their own actions. Such leaders would not act recklessly because they always weigh the consequences of their actions before making decisions, especially decisions that affect other people's lives.[21]

---

18. The All Nations Church pastor in a recorded interview.
19. Lingenfelter, *Leading Cross-Culturally*, 26.
20. Lingenfelter, 20–24.
21. Gibbs, 128.

The model of leadership of the ANC as revealed in the research, is ideal. The ANC seek to recruit into their leadership, members that reflect the multiple backgrounds of people from different ethnicities. This model is good for cross-cultural ministries. Evidentially, natural, and gifted leaders from diverse backgrounds have emerged in the ANC and these leaders have credibility and respect from their (ethnic) community networks. For example, there are ethnic minority leaders who oversee different nationalities and ethnicities such as Zimbabweans and Punjabis. It was also revealed in the study that the Christian enterprise would have to find a balance between the unity of the gospel and how God calls Christians as people from diverse cultural backgrounds and ethnicities. Christian leaders must work hard to identify and understand the needs and aspirations of their diverse communities before seeking to engage them. This is an effective diverse mission strategy which was manifested repeatedly in a variety of forms throughout the research. For example, there is the proper understanding that Christ's people from diverse backgrounds can come together to win their communities for Christ, but this places greater responsibilities on local church pastors who are expected to be mission-minded so that they can pass this vision on to their congregations.

Ideally, pastors must shape their congregations, equip them for cross-cultural ministries and release them to work co-operatively with Christ's people from other backgrounds. The four pastors believe that the unity of believers with Christ is a gracious work of the Holy Spirit, and that the set-up of every local church should be like the triune God: The Father, the Son, and the Holy Spirit, even though different persons, yet are completely united. The Scriptures make Christians understand that God chooses to reveal his glory through the solidarity of his people, which occurs when Christ's people are united towards a common purpose, having the same aspirations and goals. And having motivations centred around the love of Christ. Local church leaders, therefore, have the responsibility of sharing the vision of their church with their congregation, with the understanding that the body of Christ is not divided and that the church is a community which seeks to serve people from diverse backgrounds and as followers of Christ, they exist as a church with a mission of service to all people. Obviously, there exists cultural differences among Christ's people from diverse backgrounds but these differences, if properly addressed would result in a new vision, a new vigour, and a new aspiration for all involved in these cross-cultural initiatives.

This study has proved that the ECL have no intention to get involved in intentional diversification of their congregation. Their place of worship is the centre of their community and cultural identity. A conducive atmosphere is created in their place of worship where they meet with people like themselves, have a give and take relationship with them. Their service, for example is conducted in the Amharic language, which is widely spoken by the Ethiopian and Eritrean ethnicities. As such, their adherents are Ethiopians/Eritreans. Nonetheless, the ECL leadership co-operates with other non-Ethiopian churches in many ways. For example, their leadership is actively involved in cross-cultural initiatives that bring Christians from diverse backgrounds together by building bridges and involving in other initiatives such as reaching out to diverse communities. It is, therefore, true to say that the ECL leadership is mission-minded but these leaders have not been able to translate this into any meaningful cross-cultural initiative among their congregation.

It is worth noting that the ECL have been intentional in making their second generation replicate their cultural heritage and maintaining their identity. For example, they have designed their ecclesiology in such a way that it would continue to maintain their cultural identity to the next generation. It is for this reason that many of the Ethiopian/Eritrean youth interviewed, expressed a strong preference for an Ethiopian/Eritrean pastor whom they thought could lead them to replicate their cultural heritage and maintain identity. They also think that having a pastor from the same background would mean the desire to empathize with their spiritual, emotional, and social needs. Because the ECL offers its members a sense of community, their youth and most of them, British citizens, still think they are Ethiopians and Eritreans, first, before being British. In other words, they identify themselves as British but retain the lifestyle of their first-generation parents. Their young people demonstrate allegiance to their cultural identity and this in part has been encouraged by their first generation.

The fieldwork has also revealed that the HBC understand the challenges in leadership and believe that the godly leader should be concerned about how power can easily be abused so it is their practice to use power Scripturally. They are of the view that Christ's people should reflect on their deeds which includes their thoughts, words, and actions in the areas of diversity especially when they are dealing with people from other ethnic backgrounds. Rather than denying that in some cases Christ's people intentionally, or in other cases ignorantly, stereotype people based on ethnicity and insidiously disassociate themselves from people of other ethnicities, Christians need to be positive to appreciate the wonderful diversity that is in the body of Christ. More than that, the HBC realizes that they cannot accomplish the work of the kingdom of God unless they are willing to work together in the fellowship of a loving community, so they welcome Christians from diverse backgrounds who seek to fellowship with them. They believe that, in the twenty-first century context of mission in Britain, this results in stronger and more creative ideas and produces more solutions to problems that are likely to result from the best efforts of just one ethnicity.

All the four case study churches have several types of leadership, but it is interesting to note that Christian leaders who build strong relationships and expand their networks are those who relate well to one another. Such leaders command respect and influence within their network. Commitments to the mission endeavours of Christ's people would be strong because of the inspiration they receive from their leadership. Robinson and Smith affirm that true leadership is primarily relational and influential and suggest that it is strategically important for Christian leaders to empower their adherents for the twenty-first century context of mission.[22] They believe that discipling, equipping, and releasing Christ's people who have been partakers of God's grace have to be the priority of the current context.[23] Understandably, mission-minded pastors should themselves be equipped to shape the culture and the identity of their congregations by reminding their adherents of God's purposes concerning them as Christ's people who engage in cross-cultural ministry initiatives. Local church pastors therefore have the responsibility to communicate to their adherents the core values of Christianity that give definition to their cross-cultural vision of their various churches and how they can work cross– culturally with others in the emerging context.

---

22. Robinson and Smith, *Invading Secular Space*, 141.
23. Robinson and Smith, *The Faith of the Unbeliever*, 121.

6.5. The Church of Pentecost's Experience in Cross-Cultural Ministry

In the 1980s, many African immigrants in London (from the COP in Ghana), upon arrival in the UK joined Christian associations such as PAUKE, GCF and ACF.[24] These immigrants with COP Ghanaian roots, found the Kensington Temple (Elim Pentecostal Church) and other Elim Pentecostal churches in London as their established places of worship. Meanwhile, the COP in Ghana and the Elim Pentecostal Church, had then entered a cross-cultural ministry understanding that the two denominations would not plant churches in the same communities. This is the reason the African members of the COP in Ghana, who migrated to Britain joined the Elim Pentecostal Church upon their arrival in the UK.

The idea of starting a COP Britain was devised through the arrangement of some of these Ghanaian migrant Christians who were members of the above-mentioned associations and were also worshipping in the local churches of the Elim Pentecostal Church. In the 1980s these Ghanaians devised a way of starting a COP despite the arrangement the COP had with the Elim Pentecostal Church. Even though, these Ghanaians were welcomed into their local Elim Pentecostal Church, they still thought that to have a unique Ghanaian/African identity in worship in the UK they would need a separate fellowship based on their Ghanaian culture. In 1986, they gathered in a home fellowship. Much progress had been made by 1989 when the fellowship, which began as an informal meeting, gained the attention of the COP headquarters in Ghana who then arranged for a minister from Ghana to migrate to the UK to take care of the newly planted church.[25]

The COP had gained a Christian landscape in Britain in the past few years, but their local assemblies conducted their services in the Ghanaian Akan language and their ecclesiastical style was modelled on the Ghanaian culture. However, the COP has been intentionally and strategically led with clear goals, objectives, and outcomes. For example, they had been aware that most of their congregations had a natural inclination of worshipping in their Ghanaian culture and had created the Akan service for them. They also realized the

---

24. See full names in the "Abbreviations page."

25. Copied from the Church of Pentecost's website: www.copuk.org/core-values. This was also mentioned in a recorded interview with one of their ministers.

needs of their second-generation adherents who would want their worship in a contemporary worship style. Recently there has been the establishment of the Pentecost International Worship (PIWCs) which run concurrently with the Akan services. The PIWCs provide a well-organized, cross-cultural church, primarily for people of non-Ghanaian cultural background and other Ghanaians who desire to worship in the English language with a contemporary worship style. This is also opened to all Christ's people, especially the second-generation Ghanaian members in the UK and elsewhere, who want to worship in the English language or in a multicultural setting. The praise and worship in the PIWCs are contemporary and designed to serve the needs of a multi-ethnic gathering.

The COP has the desire to reach out to the wider community, but they believe that their PIWCs members' ability to participate in multi-ethnic gatherings will increase as they develop confidence in their own ability to navigate the social spaces of their new host culture. They think that several factors come together to create different forms of multi-ethnic churches. For example, their claim to being a multi-ethnic church based on the premise that their congregation comprises people from diverse African backgrounds, is incredibly significant. However, they have not yet had breakthroughs in reaching out to the wider UK community. Their first-generation wants to preserve their culture and remain mono-ethnic. Subsequently, they are working a strategy to reach out to the wider community, which hopefully would be accomplished by their second-generation migrants. For example, their PIWCs service, which is conducted in the English language and has a contemporary worship style attracts people from diverse backgrounds, not necessarily from the wider community but from the various African ethnicities. Yet they are aware and convinced that the future of their diaspora church depends on the young generation catching the vision of the first-generation migrants.

Therefore, several measures have been initiated to mentor the youth to know Christ in a personal way and to know the distinctiveness of their church. They allow the youth to ask questions on issues they do not understand, and the youth are encouraged to bring forth their ideas for discussion on how to move the church forward. The leadership identifies the giftedness of the youth, train and encourage them to preach during services on weekdays as well as some Sunday services. Their local assemblies are encouraged to establish youth centres where counselling, recreation and reading facilities will be provided for the youth. These youth centres should also provide career counselling and guidance as well as mentoring. The COP has added to the other initiatives, a programme called "Welfare of Church Members" and other social obligations.[26] Under this programme, every local assembly is expected to devise special welfare schemes for the less privileged among them. The local churches are also tasked to identify the economic situation of church members and a conducive environment is created to enable members to share their economic, educational, and other social needs with the church. The COP leadership has discovered how valuable the next generation is for the future of the church. They view the second-generation migrants as valuable 'assets' for reaching out to the wider community but there are existential concerns about the youth because they naturally negotiate between their parents' cultures and the host (UK) culture so proper care should be taken to nurture them for future ministry initiatives. It is with these next generation migrants that new cross-cultural ministry initiatives can be constructed. The challenge, however, is how these second-generation immigrants can maintain their family's culture, identity, and their Christian faith, while at the same time adapting to the culture of the host country that has so much influence on them.

6.6. Summary

I am of the view that, theologizing in the emerging context, though helpful would not in itself alone bring about the desired outcome of Christ's people working together cross-culturally. However, theologizing can increase dialogue and move the conversation forward to other principal issues such as their being sensitive to each other's culture and agreeing on matters that can deepen their relationships and result in unity. It would be very appropriate if Christ's people from diverse backgrounds could at least agree on matters of the greatest importance, for example, partnering in the areas of evangelism and nation-wide prayer crusade. These, the study has revealed, are some of the issues that could deepen their relationship with fellow Christians and result in a healthy Christian unity.

---

26. This was observed during my fieldtrips to the Church of Pentecost branch in Birmingham.

Christians must unite on the fundamental doctrines, because the Christian faith is based on these doctrines. But the divisions among Christians are often over more minor issues, for example worship style. These more minor issues are secondary doctrines, hence should not bring division to the body of Christ. This study has proved that the minor doctrinal differences that separate Christ's people should not be the source of their problems.

Nonetheless, it is worth noting that when Christ's people disagree about deeper values and essential doctrines such as those regarding the Christian's relationship with God, such differences in the fundamental doctrines will always make working together with any individual, group and more so any cross-cultural ministry initiative impossible. The theology of both sides should be a type of theology that is keen to eliminate the harmful effects of an over-emphasized expression of the Christian faith. Certainly, there exist differences in the theology of African Christians and their host Christians, but these differences are not in the fundamental doctrines, rather they are issues that can be addressed by both sides. The first step to take to resolve these differences is for both sides to commit themselves to building the spiritual relationships of mutual love and trust, working together as people Christ has called and commissioned for kingdom goals.

It seems clear that Christ's people from the minority background are always offended when the host Christians do not treat them as equals. The Bible is clear that God does not show partiality. It means God expects that all people, regardless of their backgrounds, must be treated equally (Acts 10:34–35). Therefore, for any meaningful cross-cultural initiatives between the African immigrant churches and the white majority churches, both sides would have to learn to appreciate the differences of each other's culture. Having an intentional diminished view of Christ's people from diverse backgrounds by host Christians who in most cases have an inflated view of themselves will not bring about the desired unity among Christ's people. This emergence of superiority will in most cases result in lack of trust in any authentic fellowship with Christ's people.[27] So, there is the need for a proper understanding and expression of cultural values from both sides, which will be a necessary step forward in any meaningful partnering.

---

27. Elmer, *Cross-Cultural Conflict*, 21.

Understandably, diverse cultures play by different rules, yet Christ's people should not ignore cultures unless they violate Scripture. The vision essential for cross-cultural ministry, therefore, should be based on an understanding of what the Scriptures teach about the kingdom of God, and it should be a vision empowered by the Holy Spirit for the engagement in mission endeavours. Only as we are motivated by the Holy Spirit and through the living word of God can we relate to one another within the structures of human society to accomplish the purpose of God.[28]

The perceived difficulty in any attempt of such cross-cultural ministry initiative is the differences in the ecclesiological and hermeneutical understanding of the African Christian and the host Christian. In the African theology, the place of the Holy Spirit and his empowerment is incredibly significant. As such, the African believers place much emphasis on the power encounters with demonic forces, which are confronted and overpowered by the power of God.[29] But it would be fair to say that one of the most striking differences between the African immigrant churches and the white majority churches is the emphasis African immigrant churches place on the spirit and power of the Holy Spirit and their use of Scripture which have been missing in most white majority churches, even though very prominent in the Bible. In this way, it is understandable that there is indeed a difference in the way African Christians read and interpret Scripture from that of the host Christians.

It is the grace and focus on the life-changing power of the Holy Spirit and the transforming power of Jesus and the word of God that enables Christians to shift from power seeking control leadership to authentic power giving leadership. Christian leaders have the responsibility of using their power and skills in producing leaders who are also followers of Christ by creating opportunities for them to lead in cross-cultural ministries[30] Understandably, mission-minded pastors should be equipped to shape the culture and the identity of their congregations by reminding their adherents of God's purposes concerning them as Christians and communicating to them the core values of Christianity which give definition to the vision of their various churches in areas of cross-cultural ministries.

---

28. Lingenfelter, *Leading Cross-Culturally*, 110.
29. Chike, *African Christianity in Britain*, 37.
30. Lingenfelter, *Leading Cross-Culturally*, 111–122.

This chapter has discussed that the HBC leaders have a clear understanding of the challenges in leadership so they believe that the godly leader should be concerned about how power can easily be abused. It is, therefore, their practice to make sure that power is used Scripturally. They are of the view that Christ's people should reflect on their deeds, including their thoughts, words, and actions when dealing with people from diverse backgrounds. Rather than denying that in some cases, Christ's people intentionally or unintentionally stereotype people based on ethnicity, Christians need to take positive steps to appreciate the wonderful diversity that is in the body of Christ. This will in a way motivate them to include people from the diverse cultural backgrounds who are in their congregation in their leadership role.

All participants were aware of the challenges involved in creating a leadership structure that mirrors all the decision-making and leadership styles of the various ethnicities in their churches. They admitted that this is a complex task that only a few Christian ministries can manage. However, the pastors believe that leading people is much more than having people follow you. They also accept that leading Christ's people is about mentoring them in such a way that they can be empowered and released to do the same thing on their own that their leaders have done for them. This is what they mean by discipleship.

The COP has been intentionally and strategically led with clear goals, objectives, and outcomes. For example, they are aware that most of their congregations have a natural inclination for worshipping in their Ghanaian cultural style and have since created the Akan service for them. They also realized the needs of their second-generation congregations who would want their worship in a contemporary worship style. Recently there has been the establishment of PIWCs that run concurrently with the Akan services. The PIWCs provide a well-organized, cross-cultural church, primarily for people of non-Ghanaian cultural background and other Ghanaians such as the second-generation, who desire to worship in the English language with a contemporary worship style. This is also opened to all Christ's people who desire to worship in the English language or in a multicultural setting. The praise and worship style in the PIWCs is contemporary and is designed to serve the needs of a multi-ethnic gathering.

De Pree thinks that effective leadership must be authentic. This affirms the need for a relational authority instead of positional authority exercised by advocates of the hierarchical structures. De Pree thinks that the authentic leader should understand authority as more of a moral issue and pragmatic influence based on a good give and take relationship between leaders and those being led. Christ's people must therefore live within their lines of responsibilities. This will also involve showing respect to all people and accepting their differences.[31]

It has been argued in this chapter that, ideally churches in the UK should be involved in cross-cultural ministries due to Britain's urban multi-ethnic communities and that churches should not seek to be organized primarily in terms of ethnicity as this distracts from the biblical principles of unity in diversity (Gal 3:28). However, the research has shown that the ECL will remain a mono-ethnic church for the near future. The ECL is the place where the issue of identity for the Ethiopian/Eritrean believer is one in which their Christian faith and cultural loyalty is connected. Their service is conducted in the Amharic language, which is widely spoken by Ethiopian and Eritrean ethnicities. As such, they make up of the Ethiopian/Eritrean congregation. Clearly, the ECL's ecclesiology justifies McGavran's "Homogeneous Unit Principle" because in this context, the Ethiopian/Eritrean Christians in Britain prefer not to cross cultural barriers to understand and accept the gospel.[32] This supports the argument that for some categories of people, such as the recently arrived migrants and people with a high people-consciousness, the mono-ethnic church is their acceptable place of worship. The ECL leadership, on the other hand, co-operates with other non-Ethiopian/Eritrean churches in many ways. For example, their leadership participates in cross-cultural initiatives that bring Christians from diverse backgrounds together by building bridges and other initiatives such as reaching out to communities. It is, therefore, true to say that the ECL leadership is mission-minded but they have not been able to translate this into any meaningful cross-cultural initiative among their congregation.

Overall, establishing a mono-ethnic church in the multicultural context of the UK is a valid strategy for some migrants who feel best connected with God in their own culture. The vision for the multi-ethnic church, on the other hand, is to attempt to model unity amid diversity. Mission-minded pastors

---

31. De Pree, Max, *Leadership Jazz*, 140.

32. McIntosh and McMahan, *Being the Church in a Multi-ethnic Community, Why It Matters and How It Works*, 88.

who apply the vision of modelling unity amid diversity to the discipleship functions of their local churches will see their members getting involved in cross-cultural ministries. Ideally, pastors must see it as their responsibility to shape up their congregation, equip them for cross-cultural ministries and release them to work co-operatively with Christ's people from other backgrounds. The unity of believers with Christ is a gracious work of the Holy Spirit. The set-up of every local church should, therefore, be like the triune God: The Father, the Son, and the Holy Spirit, who though different persons, are completely united. The Bible makes us understand that God chooses to reveal his glory through the solidarity of his people, which occurs when Christ's people are united towards a common purpose. For example, the book of Acts serves as a model of unity in diversity among the first century Christians, the unity that was brought about because of the gospel being ministered in the power of the Holy Spirit.

CHAPTER 7

A Model of Christian Mission

7.1. Introduction

The previous chapter has attempted to find ways in which the African immigrant churches could cross-racial boundaries to impact the wider British community. The fieldwork I conducted revealed that the main programme of all four case study churches is to proclaim the salvation message of Christ and the forgiveness it offers by sharing God's own mission of love. Their aim is to bring all humanity into a communion with God through Christ in the power of the Holy Spirit. They proclaim from a Christian perspective, mission endeavours that encourage the practice of ministry and social action in the context of how God is moving providentially in the twenty-first century context of mission in the United Kingdom. They understand that there is, and always will be, only one gospel. That is to say, the definition of the gospel is the same in all backgrounds in which it is being preached. However, the demonstration of it (the gospel) will always differ from one cultural background to another. At the same time, it has become obvious that each new generation, irrespective of their backgrounds, will need to find fresh, relevant ways to communicate and celebrate their Christian faith. The church (universal) therefore needs to be born anew in each new context, culture, and generation.

It was discovered during the fieldwork in the case study churches that God celebrates diversity. The study has also revealed that the African immigrant churches are now established in the Christian landscape in the UK. They have created spiritual awakening in their host country. Evidentially, this awakening has resulted in a tremendous awareness of spirituality spreading through their mission endeavours to revive British Christianity, especially in the urban areas. Notwithstanding this, it is still not certain how these churches would reach out to the wider British community.

The research has revealed that all the case study churches have similar objectives in their mission endeavours. They have all revealed similarities in their models. They have their main components and elements in common. However, it is also interesting to note that they all have different approaches to achieving their objectives. But it is fair to say that the models identified in the research were all mission-driven models. There is clearly a healthy expression of a mission-driven model in each of the four case study churches for Christian living and evangelism, and this has something to offer Christ's people from all backgrounds. Mission was not just part of their church's reality, but it was its very essence. Even though, there are different approaches in the way they model, what is becoming increasingly clear is that healthy, growing churches can be found in all their approaches. It is worth noting that, no one ministry model will supersede the way the others model. All the perspectives of the various churches indicate action on the part of the missional God who calls for a response from all people, irrespective of their racial background, nationality, or ethnicity. This chapter will, therefore, examine a biblical foundation that shapes how the African immigrant churches can develop a model of Christian mission that inspires and transforms life irrespective of one's background.

7.2. Creating a Mission Rooted in God's Divine Initiative

Whist conducting observer-based research with COP, the ECL and the ANC it was discovered that these churches do not believe that their churches can properly accomplish their God-given task without the gifts of the Holy Spirit in operation. They have tried to model on the book of Acts. These churches understand that as the baptism in the Holy Spirit was not optional for the first century church, neither should it be optional for the twenty-first century church. They believe that the Lord wants to empower believers for ministry and the gifts of the Spirit are to empower Christ's people for the work of the ministry. They, therefore, encourage the exercise of these gifts and give their congregations the opportunity to use them. For example, these churches believe in the presence and leadings of the Holy Spirit in their worship, their daily lives and mission endeavours. They think that the new birth is the work of the Holy Spirit and that the baptism in the Holy Spirit is for power to do God's work. In addition, the gifts of the Spirit are for the building of the body of Christ and the fruits of the Spirit, to help Christians to develop Christ-like characters.

It became obvious during the fieldwork that each new generation, irrespective of their backgrounds, would need to find fresh, relevant ways to communicate and celebrate their Christian faith. The church (universal), therefore, needs to develop new perspectives in each new context, culture, and generation. Smith argues that the things that were revealed to John in the book of Revelation chapters 2 and 3, just 60 years after the church was founded, are the things that he (God) could very well say to the church (universal) today. He believes that it has over the years become difficult to look at church history and find a good model for the church (universal) today.[1] However, he thinks that the divine ideal for the church is found in the book of Acts. The church (the Jerusalem church as well as the Antioch church) in the book of Acts was a dynamic church, a church led by the Holy Spirit and empowered by the Holy Spirit. The first believers, according to him, experienced a church that was effective in bringing the gospel to the world.[2] Smith's assertion of the divine ideal of the church was right because the Bible says in Acts 2:42 that, "And they continued steadfastly in the apostles' doctrine and fellowship, and in the breaking of bread, and in prayers." These four foundations must clearly be instituted when developing a fellowship of believers. The church today, must lead people to continue steadfastly in the word of God by teaching them the apostles' doctrine, bringing them into fellowship in the body of Christ, participating in the breaking of bread, and being people of prayer (Acts 2:47). The early church (in the book of Acts) was a church led by the Holy Spirit; it was teaching the word of God and developing oneness (fellowship and koinonia). The early Christians' love, order, unity, and mission were evident to the world around them, and through this witness, the Lord added to their number daily. The book of Acts, therefore, gives Christ's people, today an insight on how the early Christians connected with the

---

1. Smith, *Calvary Chapel Distinctives*, 12.
2. Smith, 13.

world; how they gradually and eventually contextualized the gospel for each people group they encountered.

Chalke was right to suggest that local churches must see it as their God-given responsibility to present the message of Christ as a "genuinely life changing and as much as anything community and world changing." He also stated that God is love and calls his church to demonstrate the same love, else they would be robbed of their DNA.[3] Chalke argues that the church today should be a church whose Christology drives its missiology, which in turn shapes its ecclesiology. He thinks that it is time for Christ's people to do church differently. For example, he does not think that the way church services are conducted today, the liturgies and traditions, should be allowed to determine the shape and style of its mission because this will limit what communities and society can know of Christ. He made it abundantly clear when he said:

> All that we believe about God as revealed in Christ (his nature and style) must shape all that we believe about our mission (its nature and style), and the way that we do church should simply be the best way to encapsulate, express and achieve that goal.[4]

All the four pastors want their churches to reflect God's triune nature because they believe churches must strive to proclaim a type of ministry that reflects the eternal love, order, unity, and mission of the trinity. To accomplish this, they have created a healthy biblical community in their local churches. The Bible reveals that the Trinity, is the foundational reality from which all mission strategies derive. God is three distinct persons (Father, Son, and the Holy Spirit) with differing functions.[5] Concerning the inner relationship of the eternal Godhead, it is important to first point out that the divine community is a community of what the Bible describes as Agape love, which means sacrificial love. This love is evident in John 17:24 NKJV when Jesus, praying for his disciples says, "Father, I desire that they also whom you

---

3. Chalke, *Intelligent Church*, 161.

4. Chalke, 173.

5. God acts as the Father in administration; he is seen as the Son in revelation; but he moves as the Spirit in operation (Coleman, *The Great Commission Lifestyle*, 79). The Trinity is a mystery, yet a proper understanding of Scripture reveals how the Father, Son, and the Spirit function in one essence.

gave me may be with me where I am, that they may behold my glory which you have given me." In this verse, Jesus emphasizes the same oneness for his disciples that he has with the Father. The Trinity is a mystery, yet a proper understanding of Scripture reveals how the Father, Son, and the Spirit function in one essence. Clearly, he and the Father share the same purpose, plan, and power. Likewise, Christian unity is dependent on sharing the priority of seeking and doing his will. Christ must, therefore, be the centre of every congregation and all missionary efforts. Everything done in the church and all the mission endeavours of Christ's people must reflect Christ, his nature and character. God has created and redeemed humanity so that his children might participate in the loving intimacy of the Triune community for all eternity. This knowledge and participation, John says earlier in chapter 17, is the essence of all missionary initiatives that finally lead to eternal life.[6]

7.3. Servant Leadership

One of the key factors in determining whether a mission or ministry is going to be successful has to do with the issues of leadership. The fieldwork has revealed the model of leadership of all the four case study churches. For example, the leadership development of the ANC is based on the apostolic foundation, and so their appointment and calling into ministry are also based on the character and charisma, and the directions of the Holy Spirit. Clergy and lay ministries are equally encouraged. The ANC is intentional about raising leaders. They equip Christ's people to maximize their potential through practical hands-on experience, discipleship, and leadership development. They seek to recruit into their leadership, members that reflect the multiple background of people from different ethnicities and this model is good for cross-cultural ministries. In ANC, leaders have emerged from the various

---

6. Kostenberger, distinguishes between two different models of mission's ministry, an incarnational model, and a representative model. He points out that the entire missiological paradigms have been built around the scriptural interpretation of John 17:18 and John 20:21. According to him, the incarnational model is based on the continuity of the incarnate mission and ministry of Jesus Christ on earth, today. The representative model, on the other hand, is about the uniqueness of the person and work of Jesus on earth but it also includes the crucifixion, dearth, burial, and resurrection of Christ (1 Corinthians 15:1–9). Here, the primary task of his disciples is about witnessing to Jesus. The emphasis here is also about making the post-Passion gospel complete which in a sense is also the completed work of Christ. (Kostenberger, *The Missions of Jesus*, 3-4, cited in Hesselgrave, *Scripture and Strategy*, 144–150.)

ethnicities and these leaders who have proved their calling have taken responsibilities in the church by overseeing the church members from their ethnic backgrounds.

The COP believe in the five-fold ministry gifts as found in Ephesians 4:11, hence their leadership is based on the apostolic foundation, but they equally encourage lay ministries. The COP believes in communal living with members supporting one another, participating in communal work. They believe that the reason for their continued existence is their involvement in missions because missions are the heartbeat of God. Therefore, at COP, they see missions as a great responsibility of making significant contributions to global mission. They are of the view that their success in this direction will depend on their ability to rise and meet the challenges of the contemporary world. And so, at the COP, evangelism is the responsibility of every member. They believe in 'power evangelism' and think that members have a duty to share their faith after conversion. They maintain high standard of excellence in all ministries by seeking to honour God who gave humankind the Saviour.

In my fieldtrips, I discovered the simplicity of the ECL leadership. They believe that the church (universal) is a divinely ordained organism rather than a man-made organization such as a club or association as such their leadership ministry is not based solely on academic achievements but by the calling of God. They have the pastoral staff as well as deacons and elders. These people must always possess certain personal qualifications (see 1 Tim 3). They think that Christian leadership should be supernaturally chosen and ordained by God and that these people should be gifted leaders who Christ has provided for the church.

The HBC have a vision to be a community of believers who seek to use their gifts to propagate the good news. The members of HBC play a vital role in choosing their ministers, They also take active part in the day to day running of their church. It is their belief that all church members have their different spiritual gifts and talents and that these gifts can be used in worship, teaching, evangelism, social action, pastoral care, prayer and healing administration and many other areas of ministry.

At HBC when a person is baptized (through immersion), they normally become a church member. Church members are called to discern prayerfully God's will for their shared life. Final authority does not rest with the ministers, deacons or any other local, national, or international body, but with the members meeting together under God's guidance. Church members, during church meetings make significant appointments including ministers, and agree financial policy and mission endeavours. HBC is outwards focused as it is linked regionally, nationally, and internationally with other churches for support and fellowship.

There is clearly a healthy expression of a mission-driven model in each of the above four case study churches for Christian living and evangelism. This healthy expression of a mission-minded model has something to offer Christ's people from all backgrounds. Even though, there are different approaches in the way the four churches model, in spite of their different approaches, they have all been successful in their mission endeavours by creating, healthy and growing churches which are serving diverse communities. What then is God's model of mission?

The church (universal) is a divine institution rather than a man-made organization, and as such must have a "divinely-gifted" leadership as observed in the ECL. However, the church ignores the importance of the Ephesians 4 ministry functions, and this negligence limits its effectiveness. Roxburg and Romanuk are right to articulate the challenges church leadership faces in these terms:

> When we borrow from other arenas such as business or corporate governance, we form a character and identity as a leader that, though it may be successful by any number of measures, leads away from formation as God's person. It also gives the church that is involved a distorted understanding of itself and its own purposes.[7]

Roxburg and Romanuk further stated that some church leadership models derive from measuring effectiveness in terms of numerical growth. This practice, according to Roxburg and Romanuk, are not necessarily the only measures of a life with God[8] For example, growth can also be measured in terms of the spiritual maturity[9] of any given congregation. It is fair to say that

---

7. Roxburg and Romanuk, *The Missional Leader, Equipping your Church to Reach a Changing world*, 118.

8. Roxburg, and Romanuk, 118.

9. The followers of Christ grow in Christ's character, and by the same virtue, they develop in his lifestyle and ministry to the world (Coleman, *The Great Commission Lifestyle*,

today, so many Christian leadership positions are solely based on academic achievements, human calling and appointment and many churches have adopted marketing strategies to boost their growth. In many congregations all the praying, preaching, and teaching is done by only the pastors. However, this is not biblical and healthy, for God gives gifts to every Christian, and not simply those who have been ordained into leadership positions in the church and ministry. The first century church understood leadership differently from how it is understood today. For example, the congregation of the early church was a visible community of God's people. These people existed and operated together under a sense of God's love and the Holy Spirit's administration through gifted leaders in their midst. God's paradigm (or model) is in the mission endeavours of the first century Christians. For instance, this paradigm was embraced by the church at Antioch. The church at Antioch was a missionary enterprise that welcomed and involved the participation of members from all backgrounds (Acts 11:21–24). The early church was committed to equipping Christ's people for the work of the ministry, and it is clear to say that the first century church's model was that of plurality and mutuality. The early Christians acted on consensus.

The book of Acts reveals how Christ's people were committed to the whole counsel of God and to the preaching and teaching of the gospel that imparts vision, understanding and motivation for their followers. Robinson and Smith echo the concerns that many Christians feel about the traditional dispensationalist argument that the gifts of the apostle, prophet, and evangelist disappeared at the end of the apostolic period. They think that this assumption is questionable because there is evidence in recent renewal movements that these ministry gifts had been in operation in people's lives.[10] Robinson also describes the situation where the church in the West has been concentrating only on the pastoral and teaching ministries to the neglect of the apostle, prophet, and evangelist ministries. According to him, the apostle, prophet,

---

53), Coleman suggested that having the quality supply of Christian labour would lead to reproduction of live in the harvest of souls: "The key to the final harvest is found in the quality and the supply of labourers obeying the mandate of Christ. It does not matter how few their numbers are in the beginning, provided that they reproduce and teach their disciples in turn to do the same. As simple as it may seem, this is the way his church will ultimately triumph. He has no other plans." (Coleman, 64).

10. Robinson and Smith, *Invading Secular Space*, 85.

and evangelist ministry gifts stand together with those of the pastor and teacher to constitute a missionary church.[11]

The best type of church leadership is the type of leadership which emerges from being equipped by the church leaders. These emergent leaders take various responsibilities in the church. God's programme for the church (universal), as revealed in the Bible, involves equipping all Christ's people so they become ministering members. What is written in Ephesians 4:11–16, therefore opens the Christian's understanding to God's design for all ministry within the local church. This New Testament pattern provides for a supernaturally chosen and divinely equipped ministry for the church. The Bible reveals that, God has to do a work in us before he can do a work through us, and this informs his reasons for giving gifts to his people. Ephesians 4:11–16 shows a clear picture of how the local church ministry should affect the spiritual growth and maturity of church members. These gifts operating in any local church are supposed to complement one another and lead to the edification and unity in the body of Christ. If Christ's people can all find their proper calling and functions as in the ways of the early church and move according to ways of the kingdom of God, then the Holy Spirit will be able to work unhindered in the local church or mission. It is right to say that Ephesians 4:11–16 shows the way that God intended his church (universal) to be run and not by copying what someone else is doing and so following their mistakes. God's intended purpose in placing ministers in the local church is to turn sinners to saints (Matt 4:19; Acts 26:16–18), restore, mould and perfect the saints (Gal 4:19) and prepare every member for ministry and purposeful service. Local church ministers are to equip fully their congregation and make them fit to take their place in the fellowship of the local church. When Christ's people aim at reaching the measure of the stature of the fullness of Christ, they come into unity in the church. As they progress towards maturity, they avoid cunning crafty teachers of false and strange doctrines. This is what keeps the individual Christian solid in the faith and secured against all seductions. Matured believers will always speak the truth in love and serve all believers they encounter, irrespective of their backgrounds.

---

11. Robinson, *The Faith of the Unbeliever*, 147.

7.4. The African Immigrant Churches Regarding the Wider Community as Another Stage in their Mission to Britain

The African immigrant churches have done so much for people from their own backgrounds by helping them find acceptance within their community, but they need to work harder and find more creative ways to reach out to the wider UK communities. I hold the view that if the Great Commission (Matt 28:19–20), is to be fulfilled effectively in Britain, cultural and ethnic barriers would have to be crossed. Scripture reveals that the church at Jerusalem was always held in high esteem as the original centre from which the gospel came. Notwithstanding this, there was a city called Antioch which served as the city church that sponsored their pioneering tour.[12] The pattern the Lord intended Christians to follow is to establish more house churches and energetically pursue a programme of evangelism and soul winning. The church at Antioch was a multicultural church because it was a blending of races and cultures. The first century Christians, at first, preached the gospel to only the Jews. Eventually, they successfully overcame the mono-ethnic focus on Jewish people only.[13] Some of the first century Christians began to propagate the gospel of Jesus Christ to the Greek-Hellenists. By the time a church leadership nucleus was eventually formed, the congregation had clearly become a multi-ethnic church with a multicultural identity. Equipping Christ's people from diverse backgrounds leads to the development of pliable disciples, which results in the emergence of a congregation with an inclusive vision. This congregation will continue to exhibit diversity of the various ethnicities and cultures because of their foundation. For example, the leadership that emerged in Antioch included those from Cyprus in the present-day Mediterranean, Cyrene in Northern Africa, Hellenists, and the Jewish people. It is clear to say the Antioch community began by reaching out to people in their geopolitical region, so should the twenty-first century church in the UK.

---

12. Mahoney, *The Shepherd's Staff*, 234–236.

13. But as Acts progresses, the community slowly and even painfully begins to realize that something else is going on as the Spirit "drives" or "leads" it to include "half Jews" (Samaritans), individual Gentile proselytes or "God-fearers" (the Ethiopian official), worthy Gentile (Cornelius and his household) and finally, Gentiles (in Antioch) (Bevans, and Schroeder, *Constants in Context*, 10).

The Bible reveals that there were Jewish people in all the cities of the Roman Empire who were committed to the Jewish faith. Paul took the initiative to travel to many of these cities with the gospel. The pattern was that Paul would go into the synagogues and preach the good news to his fellow Jewish devout who had congregated for teachings of the Old Testament and other religious rituals (Acts 13:5). Like Jesus before him, Paul would go into the synagogues and present the gospel of Christ to the Jewish people (Matt 4:23; Acts 13:5). This usually resulted in many Jewish converts, who were already well taught in the Scriptures (the Old Testament). "From these, with a minimal amount of training and teaching, elders for the churches could be appointed."[14] Even though, the mission endeavours of the first century Christians had already expanded to the point of leaving Palestine, the main recipients of their missionary efforts were Jewish people only (Acts 11:19). However, the mission extension went further when some men from Cyprus and Cyrene went to Antioch and began to speak to Greeks also, telling them the good news about the salvation message of Christ (Acts 11:20). This mission endeavours were successful, because there was evidence that the Greeks responded in considerable numbers as they believed and turned to the Lord Jesus Christ to receive their salvation (Acts 11:20).

The African immigrant churches are now ministering to their own kind just as Paul's strategy was at first, to minister to fellow Jewish people in their synagogues. Ideally, in their missionary efforts to Britain, the African immigrant churches must work out a strategy to reach out to the wider community. Their outreach must be in line with the biblical pattern of Acts 1:8. They can also adopt Paul's strategy of first reaching out to their own kind and then expanding their outreach to the wider community. The book of Acts provides Christ's people with the understanding that the first century Christians began fulfilling the Great Commission when the disciples started reaching out in Jerusalem which was the centre of Judaism, and then Judea and Galilee, where others of their own kind lived, and in Samaria, where members of a different but familiar people lived and finally within the unreached peoples of other parts of the world.

It is clear that the gospel spread quickly from Jerusalem to other parts of the world because Jerusalem was like the modern cities of Britain that

---

14. Mahoney, *The Shepherd's Staff*, 131.

experienced migration of people from different parts of the world. It is worth noting that the Hellenized Jewish Christians, who were scattered in foreign lands, preached the gospel wherever they went. For example, the book of Acts 8:1 tells us how the first official persecution of the early church drove the Christians out of Jerusalem, and how they preached the gospel everywhere they went. Philip, on his part, went to Samaria and preached the gospel there (Acts 8:5). As a result of his preaching and miraculous signs, people listened, and many believed and were baptized (Acts 8:12). In its wider context, the persecution of Acts 8:1 and the subsequent mission endeavours of Philip in Acts 8:4 resulted in the planting of churches throughout Judea, Galilee, and Samaria. Evidentially, migrants from various parts of the world have migrated to the UK in the past few decades. Today, migration has changed the demography of Britain's urban cities, for example, London, Birmingham, Manchester, and Glasgow have now become multi-ethnic cities with multicultural identity. This migration of people from different ethnicities and nationalities presents opportunities and challenges to the society and the Christian mission. For most parts, what we are seeing today in Britain is the development of micro-melting pots in which the migrant ethnic minority populations have established a presence in the major cities of Britain (see chapter 2).

Olupona and Gemignani argue that the Western world has understood African immigrants according to a "melting pot" model of immigration (see chapter 2).[15] Mass migration to the UK cities has resulted in different races, cultures and people from diverse backgrounds coming to live together in the cities and sharing social and economic benefits together. There are problems encountered by people from diverse backgrounds trying to assimilate into a cohesive whole.[16] Despite the challenges migration poses to the UK urban communities, it could also be an amazing opportunity to present the gospel to people from unreached people groups. For example, there are people from countries like Libya, Saudi Arabia and North Korea in the UK universities and communities today. Reaching out to these people and equipping them for the work of the ministry would mean that they would in turn reach out to their own people when they return to their countries of origin.

---

15. Olupona and Gemignani, introduction to *African immigrant Religions in America*, 3.
16. Olupona and Gemignani, 3.

Clearly there is a healthy expression of a mission-driven model in each of the four case study churches for Christian living and evangelism, and this has something to offer Christ's people from all backgrounds. Even though, there are different approaches in the way the four churches model, what is becoming increasingly clear is that healthy, growing churches can be found in all their approaches. In which ways therefore, can the African immigrant churches model these churches? The reader is warned not to assume that models are a representation of what some churches do; models should be seen as just symbols of reality. Models are guides that can be applied to ministry expressions because they help to label and give description to certain practices in different contexts. It is assumed therefore, that all successful Christian models should be leading people to mission.[17] The mission of God dominated the life and teachings of Jesus; it also includes his crucifixion, death, burial, and resurrection (1 Cor 15:1–9). Therefore, Christ's people, irrespective of their backgrounds and no matter what part of the world they find themselves, are called to embrace this lifestyle modelled by Jesus Christ. His people are asked to live by the same rule that governed his time here on earth. However, adaptations to his approach to ministry must be made to suit the situational context in which they find themselves. For example, the strategy Christ adopted in the Mediterranean culture over two thousand years ago would not be the same techniques he would use today, yet the core message would remain the same. Bevans and Schroeder suggest that Christ's people must develop an understanding of the universal significance of Christ. They share this point of view:

> If to be church is to be in mission, to be in mission is to be responsive to the demands of the Gospel in particular contexts, to be continually "reinventing" itself as it struggles with the approaches of new situations, new peoples, new cultures, and new questions. The existence of Christianity seems to be linked to its expansion beyond itself, across generational and cultural boundaries.[18]

---

17. Bevans and Schroeder define mission as:" preaching, serving, and witnessing with God in the patient yet unwearied work of inviting and persuading women and men to enter relationship with the world, with one another and with Godself. Mission is a dialogue. It takes people where they are" (Bevans and Schroeder, *Constants in Context*, 285).

18. Bevans and Schroeder, *Constants in Context*, 31.

Similarly, Moltmann says,

> the historical church will ask about continuity and strive for continuity. But where the future its apostolate serves is concerned it will be open to leap forward to what is new and surprising. Here the most characteristics thing is not the old things that are preserved but the new ones that take place and come into being.[19]

Certainly, changing contexts comes with the awareness of the church which recognizes itself as missionary. Coleman understands that the urgency of mission is linked to the urgency of change and adaptation. He argues that methods are variable, conditioned by the time and circumstances, which are constantly changing. However, he also thinks that the principles, inherent in Christ's way of life would never change.[20] These principles, therefore, are the ones that can be adopted by churches trying to model other successful ministries.

In my fieldtrip to the case study churches, I observed that the ANC and the COP have been strategic in their mission endeavours. For example, the senior pastor of the ANC (the ANC is a white majority church) is a third generation Punjabi; he was born and raised in Wolverhampton near Birmingham. He was equipped to lead the youth wing of the ANC and when the senior pastor's role became vacant, he was asked to take over the responsibility of the church as a senior pastor. He has since brought changes that have been successful. The success of this third-generation Punjabi pastor in a white majority church is an indication that, if nurtured properly by the first generation, the next generation of African immigrants would be the ones to negotiate successful partnering with the host Christians and lead multi-ethnic churches. The ANC equip their church members for the work of the ministry. Leaders who emerge from their training take up responsibilities in the ministry.

In their mission endeavours to Britain, the COP mirrors the missionary efforts of the first century Christians. They understand that just as the early church's missionary effort was first to their fellow Jewish people in Jerusalem and then to Jews in Samaria and subsequently, to the Gentiles, who belonged to the ends of the earth, so the equivalent pattern would be found in their

---

19. Moltmann, *God for the Secular Society*, 360.
20. Coleman, *The Great Commission Lifestyle*, 54.

outreach to Britain. The COP has the desire to reach out to the wider community. They believe that their PIWCs[21] members' ability to participate in multi-ethnic gatherings will increase as they develop confidence in their own ability to navigate the social spaces of the new host culture. They are therefore, working out a strategy to reach out to the wider community, which they believe would be accomplished by their next generation immigrants. It is fair to say that the African immigrant churches can follow the patterns of both the ANC and the COP in their leadership development and mission endeavours to Britain. At this stage in their outreach activities, the African immigrant churches have been successful in ministering to their fellow Africans (their Jerusalem), some of them have been successful to reach out to other African ethnicities (Judea). Where the challenge is, is how they can work harder in more creative ways to reach out to the wider community (across cultural and racial barrier) and to all people.

7.5. Practical Reflection on a Model of Christian Mission

Mission is the essence of all the four case study churches. These churches have different approaches in the way they model, yet, healthy, growing churches can be found in all their approaches. In this regard, I list the following practical pointers as how this chapter could function in reality:

i. To be successful in mission endeavours, the issues of leadership should be taken seriously. The church (universal) is a divinely ordained organism rather than a man-made organization as such its leadership ministry should not be based on academic achievements alone but also by the calling of God. The church must take into consideration the importance of the Ephesians 4 ministry functions and I Timothy 3. The model of mission should be that of plurality and mutuality.

---

21. The Pentecost International Worship Centre, unlike their mother church, The Church of Pentecost, conduct services in the English language and they have also adopted a contemporary worship style to meet the needs of the second-generation migrants and the wider community.

ii. The Ephesians 4:11 and the 1 Timothy 3 type of leadership is the best Christian leadership because this type of leadership grows up amid Christians and enters ministry at some level, either as deacons, overseers, and elders for the equipping of Christ's people for the work of ministry. An example of this type of leadership in the study is the ANC senior pastor. This pastor is a third generation Punjabi, born and raised in Wolverhampton. He joined the ANC (a white majority church) and was equipped to lead their youth wing. When the senior pastor's role became vacant, he was asked to take over the responsibility of the church as a senior pastor. He has since brought changes which have been successful.

iii. The ANC realized that their type of leadership must be the one that is shared to all irrespective of one's background. They believe that leadership, if it is not shared, runs the risks of occasioning divisions. The success of the third-generation Punjabi pastor in ANC is an indication that, the second-generation migrants are properly placed in the UK society to propagate the gospel with the host Christians because they are bicultural. (They understand their parents' cultures and the host culture as well). They also speak with a perfect British accent.

iv. All the perspectives of churches must indicate action on the part of the missional God who calls for a response from all people, irrespective of their racial background, nationality, or ethnicity. The four case study churches have different approaches to achieving their objectives but what is increasingly clear is that they are all mission-driven churches. There was a healthy expression of a mission-driven model in each of these churches for Christian living and evangelism.

v. The church (universal) needs to be born anew in each new context, culture, and generation. In each new generation, the church would need to find new, relevant ways to communicate and celebrate the Christian faith. It is evident that Christ is the centre of all the four case study churches. They all believe that all their practices must reflect Christ, his nature and character. This knowledge and participation, John says in chapter 17, is the essence of all missionary initiatives which finally lead to eternal life.

vi. The ANC and HBC have learnt that liturgies and traditions of churches should not be allowed to determine the shape and style of their ecclesiology because this will limit what communities and society can know of Christ. Instead, Christ's love, order, unity, and mission should be evident to the world around them, and through this witness the Lord would add to the church.

7.6. Summary

This chapter has attempted to discover how the African immigrant churches could develop a model of Christian mission that inspires and transforms life regardless of one's background. The African immigrant churches in their bid to reach out to the wider community could model their leadership development on the ANC and their outreach initiatives on the COP. However, models are only guides that can be applied to ministry expressions because they only help to label and give a description to certain practices in different contexts. The COP is a church planting organisation. Their goal is to plant churches as was done by the first century Christians. Their mission endeavours mirror Act 1:8. They are therefore, working on a strategy to reach out to the wider community, which they believe would be accomplished by their next generation migrants. The African immigrant churches can mirror the pattern of the COP in their mission endeavours to Britain. It is scriptural to start outreach with their own kind and then end up ministering to the wider community.

The senior pastor of the ANC is a third generation Punjabi. He was appointed to lead the ANC, which is a white majority church, with the realization that his talents and spiritual gifts as well as his ministry preparation and character could best be used in a diverse community of believers. It is obvious that his leadership skill has matched his own integrity. This decision by the ANC leadership was a stroke of genius, from which the church has benefited, as it seems, it has flourished and experienced growth. It is fair to say that this can serve as a paradigm for other white majority churches preparing church members for leadership positions. In a similar vein, the African immigrant churches can mirror the ANC as they prepare their next generation migrants to reach out to the wider community.

The model in the book of Acts was the community of faith in which people became born-again and made an impact in their communities. The Lord added to the church daily as Christ's people praised and worshipped God and enjoyed the favour of the people in their communities. The early church did not only rescue souls from hell, but it also affected communities, making a difference in them, and whetting their appetite for Christ. This model is good for today's church.[22]

For a proper understanding of missions, the universal significance of Christ must be taken into consideration in mission endeavours. Mission work is linked to the urgency of change and adaptation but the principles inherent in Christ's message will not change. These principles, and not the strategy, must guide all outreach activities. The early church recognized itself as a 'missionary' church in the changing contexts as the church moved from Jerusalem to Samaria and eventually to the uttermost part of the world (Acts 1:8). It is worth noting that churches must be sensitive to the urgency of change and adaptation in their mission endeavours.

---

22. This analogy appears to oversimplify missionary efforts in today's world. As stated above, missions are linked to the urgency of change and adaptation. But Christ's people can rightly adopt the principles inherent in the message of the book of Acts.

CHAPTER 8

Conclusions and Recommendations

8.1. Conclusions

The aim of this work has been to explore how the African immigrant churches could partner with the white majority churches for a more effective sharing of the gospel in the multicultural context of the UK. The central theoretical argument was that the African immigrant churches in Britain have enabled their adherents to find a refuge from discrimination and discover a sense of identity, respect and belonging. They, however, needed to work harder and in more creative ways in partnership with the white majority churches in the UK to create a society that models the values of the kingdom of God.

The research has posed the questions: How may the African immigrant churches effectively partner with white majority churches for a more effective sharing of the gospel in the UK? Why is it that, despite, the fact that African immigrant churches profess and desire to be truly international and integrationist in their vision they do not have many non-Africans among their congregations? How can the African immigrant churches, on a small scale, give hope to the wider population in the United Kingdom through offering a model of a transformed, fulfilled, and purposeful approach to living, in an increasingly secular social context?

The study has attempted to answer these questions in the following ways:

In chapter 1, I stated the main reasons why I chose the topic. Thus, having observed situations in the African immigrant churches in the UK that raised questions in relation to the relevance of these churches in the UK landscape, I initially carried out a literature review into these areas by reviewing the works of previous scholars and key thinkers that support and provide a context of this study. I believed that the African migrant churches' inability to reach out to the wider community was partly due to their lack of vision in realizing the need of working in more creative ways in partnership with the UK white majority churches to create a society that models the values of the kingdom of God. I therefore, felt that there was a strong case for research into areas in which the African immigrant churches could partner with the white majority churches. I hold the view that a meaningful partnering between the two sides could lead into creating a platform that would be tremendous in sharing the gospel, leading Christ's people, making disciples and modelling the love of Christ, with a greater impact in the British communities.

Having learned more about what was already known of the subject matter and what gaps needed to be filled, I started the primary process by choosing to investigate four churches (from four different denominations), using a participant observation in qualitative methodology; I believed in the advantages of an in-depth study of four churches rather than much wider sampling of denominations or churches. I based the foundation of the methodology on the main research question: "How may the African immigrant churches effectively work with the white majority churches for a more effective sharing of the gospel?" This research question provided the general methodological framework for the study.

Chapter 2 has focused on the effect human migration has had on the historical development of the African immigrant churches in Britain. The past few decades experienced a big increase in the cross-border migration of people from all over the world because of globalization and other factors such as wars. This recent trend of increased migration has particularly affected Britain, even though migration of people is a reality that has been part of British experience over the centuries. The past few decades, however, have witnessed the unprecedented movement of people from the global South to destinations often associated with former colonial links, for example, migrants from Ghana or Nigeria coming to the United Kingdom. It has revealed how upon arrival on the UK shores, the African migrants first tried to join the UK mainline and evangelical churches but most of the churches the migrants encountered were churches whose practices and ecclesiastical style were different from those practised in most churches in sub-Saharan Africa. Most of them left the mainline and evangelical churches and started or joined new ones that they thought would serve their spiritual and emotional needs. Racial exclusion also was part of the reasons why the migrants left the mainline and evangelical churches to form their own. Although, it must be mentioned that this was not the experience in all UK churches as some, such as the ones associated with the Baptist Union of Great Britain, were very welcoming.

In chapter 3, I undertook a theological analysis of the African immigrant churches to find out their theological relevance and epistemological validity. I was aware that in Britain, there was the perception that the black churches have a different theology. I therefore, saw the necessity of the African immigrant churches re-defining themselves in relation to the professing church by clarifying their theology. An attempt was made to construct a theological praxis model. The key elements of the theology of the African immigrant churches were explored in a broader framework of biblical theology. My argument was that, for the African immigrant churches to become relevant in the UK Christian landscape, there was the need for them to change their theology in line with Scripture, to suit the British context. In my theological construction on what could generally be accepted as a biblical theological basis, I used the tools of biblical criticism and hermeneutics to consider texts particularly favoured by Bible scholars, for example, David Hesselgrave. This, I thought would result in at least, a tentative conclusion concerning theology while constructing a model for a theological praxis for the African immigrant churches in the UK.

I carried out an empirical study in chapter 4. The fieldwork was to investigate the four case study churches to find ways in which the African immigrant churches and the white majority churches could work together to advance the gospel in Britain. The fieldwork revealed among many other things, how the African immigrant church, though a Christian community, has become a place of refuge for Africans, especially the newly arrived immigrants. Most of them have been faced with difficulties related to immigration together with discrimination when seeking to engage with the wider society. It was also noted that Africans have the tendency to congregate because the social, spiritual, and other factors motivating them to come together have cultural significance. Also, these migrant churches operate in a non-threatening and conducive environment that meets the migrants' aspirations. There was also a clear indication that the African Christians have been struggling to re-define themselves in their newly chosen country, create a distinct identity and express their cultural values. In this case, their African Christian tiers serve as a way of developing a voice and a presence.

Chapters 5 to 7 presented a systematic analysis of the result of the findings and discussed how the results were related to the research questions. The study has revealed that the disagreements among the African Christians and the host Christians are not disagreements about deeper values and essential doctrines such as those regarding the Christian's relationship with God. Such differences would otherwise have made working together with any individual, group and more so any cross-cultural ministry initiative, impossible. Rather the disagreements were over petty issues of what is regarded as secondary doctrines which have in fact, caused many divisions to the body of Christ. However, the minor doctrinal differences that separate Christ's people should not be the source of their problems. There are also cultural differences that can be resolved with a proper approach. This gives the hope that both the African immigrant churches and the white majority churches can shelve their differences and work together for kingdom goals.

For example, through partnering with African immigrant churches, the white majority churches can help to alleviate some of the misunderstandings in British communities about the migrant Christians. In this case, the British communities would accept the African Christians with ease. The host Christians can also help to reduce the isolation of the African Christians and help in their integration.

Both sides could explore equality and respect, differences, and commonalities. They could promote an understanding of the different cultures and can promote greater participation and inclusiveness. They could also enter a dialogue to arrive at a proper understanding of the different cultures of the diverse communities within the UK urban communities. By so doing, they could identify barriers, divisions and other negative matters and issues that stop people from getting more involved in their communities. They could aim to become more active participants in community initiatives by looking for better ways of working together, which should be a continuous process. Overall, they could find ways of becoming churches that can strategize to be the vanguard of spiritual, emotional, economic, and social liberation in the United Kingdom by consistently addressing the crucial areas of people's lives and focusing their time and resources to transforming lives.

The study has revealed the necessity of both sides theologizing in the emerging context; theologizing could increase their dialogue and move the conversation forward to other important issues such as their being sensitive to each other's culture and agreeing on matters that can deepen their relationships and result in unity. For example, matters such as conducting nation-wide prayer meetings and coming together as a multicultural team to build relationships of mutual trust necessary to reaching out to communities together. It is clear to say that effectiveness in evangelism would increase with Christian initiatives such as Christ's people coming together from diverse backgrounds to reach out to diverse communities. However, Christ's people coming together in unity does not necessarily mean they are seeking uniformity. God has made available a variety of gifts and talents in his children, so coming together would mean God's people coming together with different gifts and talents as well as different ministry experiences (1 Cor 12, Eph 4:11–16) for the advancement of God's kingdom.

The understanding that mission begins with God must inform both the migrant Christian and the host Christian, as they seek to share the gospel in the UK afresh for a new generation which is more globalized and diverse. When Christ's people recall that mission is God's mission and that he has called his people into it, their endeavours and efforts, at best, mirror what God has already started because all that Christ's people are doing is just responding to his calling into ministry. As Jesus attributed his work to the Father, so must all Christ's people: "Most assuredly, I say to you, the Son can do nothing of himself; but what he sees the Father do; for whatever he does, the Son also does in like manner" (John 5:19 NKJV).

It has been argued in this study that, ideally, churches in the UK should be involved in cross-cultural ministries due to Britain's urban multi-ethnic communities. British urban communities are diverse, but churches should only model their demography and not their practices, which is divided by factors such as race and class. It is right to say that churches should not seek to be organized primarily in terms of ethnicity as this distracts from the biblical principles of unity in diversity (Gal 3:28). However, the study has revealed that the ECL for example, would remain a mono-ethnic church for the foreseeable future. The place of worship of ECL is one in which their Christian faith and cultural loyalty is connected. That is to say, the ECL prefer intentionally to organize themselves around their own cultural allegiances and values. However, the ECL was not planted out of animosity towards the white majority churches or other cultures. Instead, the Ethiopians feel that unlike migrants from the former British colonies whose lingua franca is English, most of them (Ethiopians/Eritreans) have to start learning English as beginners, as such they can best connect with God with the people from their background, people who speak their language, who have the same history, culture, worship style and the social needs. They can best use their native language in worship because of their limited English skills so they go back to their default culture as the necessary reference point for their Christian values in worship.

Clearly, the ECL's ecclesiology justifies McGavran's Homogeneous Unit Principle because in this context, the Ethiopian/Eritrean Christians in Britain prefer not to cross cultural barriers to understand and accept the gospel.[1] This supports the argument that for some categories of people, such as the recently arrived migrants and people with a high people-consciousness, the mono-ethnic church is their acceptable place of worship. Many African immigrant churches will be in this category for the foreseeable future due to language problems and cultural issues.

The study has revealed how important it is for local church pastors to equip their youth for cross-cultural ministries and release them to work cooperatively with Christ's people from other backgrounds. The model of mission in HBC is to help young people to grow to a strong and mature faith so that they would take responsibilities not just in their local church and communities but also worldwide. They commission and guide their young people in adventurous, outgoing, and pioneering ministries. For example, during an observation, the Sunday worship service was devoted to some of the youth (18–23 years) who had just returned from their missionary trip to Uganda. In their message to the congregation, they shared their missional experiences and the motivations they had received from their mission endeavours in Africa. Local church leaders have responsibilities to share the vision of their church with their congregation, with the understanding that the body of Christ is not divided and that the church is a community which seeks to serve people from diverse backgrounds. As followers of Christ, they exist as a church with a mission of service to all people.

---

1. McIntosh and McMahan, *Being the Church*, 88.

In their mission endeavours to Britain, the COP mirror the missionary efforts of the first century Christians. They understand that just as the early church's missionary effort was first, to their fellow Jewish people in Jerusalem and then to Jews in Samaria and subsequently, to the Gentiles, who belonged to the ends of the earth so the pattern would be in their outreach to Britain. Clearly, the COP has the desire to reach out to the wider community. But they believe that their PIWCs[2] members' ability to participate in multi-ethnic gatherings will increase as they develop confidence in their own ability to navigate the social spaces of the new host culture. They are therefore, working out a strategy to reach out to the wider community, which they believe would be accomplished by their next generation migrants.

The research has revealed that the first generation of African migrants, worship God in their own ecclesiastical style but the influence of the wider society has caused many migrants, especially children[3] born in Britain to their African immigrant parents, to lose faith in God, which has been the source of strength for black people over the years. The African immigrant churches are faced with an existential concern with respect to their next generation who, in many cases are experiencing a process termed acculturation. These young people acknowledge their ethnic heritage but place a greater premium on adapting their lives and values to the culture and values of the wider community, which is living in an increasingly secular social context. This is concerning because the survival of the African immigrant churches hinges on the success of raising and equipping the next generation of children born to the African migrants who are better placed to reach out to the wider community.

Nonetheless, these second-generation young Africans' ability to adapt to the lifestyle of the culture of the wider community and communicate clearly with the accent of the host country should not be underestimated. If nurtured properly, these traits of the second-generation migrants can be useful in ministering to their fellow young people in the wider community. One such

---

2. The Pentecost International Worship Centre, unlike their mother church, The Church of Pentecost, conduct services in the English language and they have also adopted a contemporary worship style to meet the needs of the second generation -migrants and the wider community.

3. The next generation of children born in the UK to African migrant parents are going through *acculturation*. These African children in the UK acknowledge their ethnic heritage but place a great premium on adapting their lives to the culture and values of the majority of the population. This is a serious problem when an increasing proportion of the wider society does not adhere to the Christian faith.

example is the senior pastor of the ANC[4] who runs a multi-ethnic church with a multicultural identity. Pastor Steve Uppal is a third generation Punjabi who speaks the English language with a British accent and understands the host culture. He has no problem relating to and communicating with his congregation who are mainly from the wider community, and other backgrounds.

It is worth noting that the ANC have raised successful leaders from their congregation. These leaders have played a vital role in taking responsibilities in the various departments of their church. They have also realized the importance of the bicultural people in the congregation.[5] The success of this third-generation Punjabi pastor in a white majority church is an indication that, if nurtured properly by the first generation, the next generation of African migrants would be the ones to negotiate successful partnering with the host Christians and lead multi-ethnic churches in the process. Any meaningful cross-cultural initiative between the African Christians and the host Christians, would hinge on how well the next generation migrants are equipped and how they respond to the gospel. A biblical example is the Apostle Paul (Acts 9:15) who understood both the Jewish and Greek cultures and therefore was better positioned to preach the gospel to the Jewish world as well as the Gentile world.

8.2. Recommendations

It is my view that my recommendations should lead to further research in diasporic studies. The twenty-first century demographic trend of Britain requires a new missiological paradigm from which new mission strategies can emerge. The white majority churches and the African immigrant churches must seek to understand the Christian faith in a contemporary context, which has developed because of mass migration. There are two areas that I think need to be addressed:

First, the research has revealed that if nurtured properly by the first generation, the next generation of African migrants would be the ones to

---

4. The All Nations Church was a white majority church when Pastor Steve Uppal took over as a senior pastor in 2001. It has now become a multi-ethnic church with a multicultural identity.

5. The next generation migrants are mainly bicultural because they lay premium with the culture of their first-generation migrant parents and at the same time understand the culture of the host country. They have the inherent nature of traversing with cultural gaps.

negotiate successful partnering with the host Christians. Therefore, any meaningful cross-cultural initiative between the African Christians and the host Christians would depend on how well the next generation migrants are equipped. Therefore, the emphasis of the African immigrant churches should be on equipping their next generation for the work of the ministry in Britain.[6]

Secondly, the past few decades of migration of people into the UK cities has created an opportunity to present the gospel to people from unreached people groups. For example, there are people from countries like Libya, Saudi Arabia and North Korea in the UK universities and communities today; reaching out to these people means they would in turn reach out to their people when they return to their countries of origin.

It is my suggestion that, because of its importance, theology should be taken into consideration in any ministry efforts of Christ's people. There should be a new missiological paradigm for the above recent phenomena. Both the migrant Christian and the host Christian should come together with a strong biblical grounding and theological understanding of their mission in this emerging context. They need the fundamental truths of God and the divine principles of the Bible to give them a thorough biblical understanding and missiological basis to develop a theological framework for the twenty-first century context of mission in the UK.

---

6. Local church pastors are expected to be mission-minded so that they can pass the vision on to their congregations. The One People Commission (a body of the Evangelical Alliance), Centre for Missionaries from the Majority World and Missio Africanus are already involved in cross-cultural ministry initiatives but they will need a new framework which prioritizes the running of cross-cultural training workshops mainly for local church pastors. These pastors will in turn shape-up their congregations, equip them for cross-cultural ministries and release them to work co-operatively with Christ's people from other backgrounds. The training should be done on regular basis so that actions can be adjusted in the light of experience.

Bibliography

Abraham, K. C. *Third World Theologies: Commonalities and Divergences.* Maryknoll: Orbis Books, 1990.

Adedibu, B. "The Urban Explosion of Black Majority Churches: Their Origin, Growth, Distinctiveness and Contribution to British Christianity and Society." PhD diss. North-West University, 2011.

———. *The Origin, Growth, Distinctiveness, and Contributions of Black Majority Churches to British Christianity.* London: Wisdom Summit, 2012.

Adogame, A. *The African Christian Diaspora: New Currents and Emerging Trends in World Christianity.* New York: Bloomsbury Publishing Academic, 2013.

Adogame, Afe. 2007. "The Rhetoric of Reverse Mission: African Christianity and the Changing Dynamics of Religious Expansion in Europe." Paper presented at the South Moving North: Reverse Mission and its Implications. Utrecht Protestants Landelijk Dienstencentrum, 26 September 2007.

Aldred, Joe., and Ogbo, Keno, eds. *The Black Church in the 21st Century.* London: Darton, Longman & Todd Ltd, 2001.

Aldred, Joe. *Respect.* Peterborough: Epworth Press, 2005.

———. "The Experience of Black Churches in the United Kingdom, Change and Diversity-Impact of Migration in Church and Society." EEA3 Conference Forum Migration. Budapest, Hungary, 2007.

Alexander, V. "'Breaking Every Fetter': To What Extent Has the Black Led Church in Britain Developed a Theology of Liberation?" PhD diss. University of Warwick, 1996.

Asamoah-Gyadu, J. K., and Ludwig F., eds. *African Christian Presence in the West.* Trenton: African World Press, 2011.

Banks, S. *Ethics and Values in Social Work.* 3rd ed. Basingstoke: Macmillan, 2006

Beckford, R. *Dread and Pentecostal: A Political Theology for Black Church in Britain.* London: SPCK Publishing, 2000.

Bediako, K. *Theology and Identity: The Impact of Culture upon Christian Thought in the Second Century and in Modern Africa.* Oxford: Regnum Books, 1992.

Bevans, S. B., and R. Schroeder. *Constants in Context: A Theology of Mission for Today*. New York: Orbis Books, 2004.

Bevans, S. B. *Models of Contextual Theology*. New York: Orbis Books, 2014.

Biney, M. *From Africa to America: Relation to Adaptation Among Ghanaian Immigrants in New York*. New York: New York University Press, 2011.

Boesak, A. A. *Farewell to Innocence: A Socio-ethical Study on Black Theology and Power*. Maryknoll: Orbis, 1997.

Boff, L. and C. Boff. *Introducing Liberation Theology*. Maryknoll: Orbis Books, 1987.

Booth, S. "Delivering Theological Education for Church Planting in Canada." *Global Missiology*, 10 April 2011. http://www.ojs.GlobalMissiology.org.

Bosch, D. J. *Transforming Mission, Paradigm Shifts in Theology of Mission*. New York: Orbis Books, 2014.

Brodersen, B. *Essentials in Ministry*. Costa Mesa: Calvary Chapel Publishing, 2007.

Brown, R. "Racism and Immigration in Britain." *International Socialism Journal*, RM 1990.

———. *Gustavo Gutierrez: An Introduction to Liberation Theology*. Maryknoll: Orbis Books, 1990.

Casciani, D. "Why Immigration Is Changing Almost Everything." 6 March 2015. http://www.bbc.co.uk/news/uk-31748423.

Chalke, S. *Intelligent Church: A Journey Towards Christ-Centred Community*. Grand Rapids: Zondervan, 2006.

Chike, C. *African Christianity in Britain: Diaspora, Doctrine and Dialogue*. Bloomington: Author House, 2007.

Coleman, R. *The Great Commission Lifestyle*. Grand Rapids: Baker House, 1992.

Davis, J. J., ed. *The Necessity of Systematic Theology, 2nd ed*. Grand Rapids: Baker House, 1978.

De Munck, V., and E. L. Sobo, eds. *Using Methods in the Field: A Practical Introduction and Casebook*. Walnut Creek: Alta Mira Press, 1998.

De Pree, M. *Leadership Jazz: The Essential Elements of a Great Leader*. New York: Dell Publishing, 2008.

DeWalt, B. and K. DeWalt. *Participant Observation for Fieldworkers*. Walnut Creek: Alta Mira Press, 2002.

Dixon, M. "The Black Church Must Respond to Disaffected Youth." *Voice*. 2011. http://www.voice-online.co.uk/article/black-church-must-respond-disaffected-youth.

Driscoll, D. "Introduction to Primary Research: Observations, Surveys, and Interviews" In *Writing Spaces: Readings on Writing*, Volume 2. Colorado, USA: WAC Clearinghouse, 2011.

Dubow, S. *Apartheid, 1948–1994*. Oxford: Oxford University Press, 2014.

Edwards, J., and D. Killingray. *Black Voices*. Nottingham: Inter-Varsity Press, 2007.

Edwards, J. Lord, *Make Us One: But Not All the Same*. London: Hodder & Stoughton, 1999.

Elmer, D. *Cross-Cultural Conflict: Building Relationships for Effective Ministry*. Westmont: InterVarsity Press, 1993.

Engelsviken, T. "*Missio Dei*: The Understanding of a Theological Concept in European Churches and Missiology." *International Review of Mission* 92, (2009): 367; 481–497.

Fryer, P. *Staying Power: The History of Black People in Britain*. London: Pluto Press, 1984.

Geertz, C. *The Interpretation of Cultures*. London: Fontana Press, 1993.

George, J. "Intercultual Theology: An Approach to Theologizing in the Context of Pluralism and Globalization" MA diss. University of Toronto, 2012.

Gibbs, G. *Leadership Next: Changing in a Changing Culture*. Leicester: Inter-Varsity Press, 2005.

Gibbs, G., and M. Coffey. *Church Next, Quantum Changes in Christian Ministry*. Leicester: Inter-Varsity Press, 2001.

Guder, D. L. *The Continuing Conversion of the Church*. Grand Rapids: Eerdmans Seventh Impression Edition, 2000.

Gutierrez, G. *A Theology of Liberation: History, Politics, and Salvation*. Maryknoll: Orbis Books, 1988.

Hall, D. W. "'But God Meant It for Good': Inter-personal Conflict in an African Caribbean Pentecostal Congregation – A Pastoral Study" PhD diss. University of Birmingham, 2013.

Hammett, J. S. *Biblical Foundations for Baptist Churches: A Contemporary Ecclesiology*. Grand Rapids: Kregel, 2005.

Hanciles, J. *Beyond Christendom: Globalization, African Migration, and the Transformation of the West*. Maryknoll: Orbis Books, 2008.

Hardy, A., and D. Yarnell. *Forming Multicultural Partnerships: Church Planting in a Divided Society*. Watford: Instant Apostle, 2015.

Hesselgrave, D. J. 1994. *Scripture and Strategy: The Use of the Bible in Postmodern Church and Mission*. Pasadena: William Carey Library, 1994.

———. *Paradigms in Conflicts: 10 Key Questions in Christian Missions Today*. Grand Rapids: Kregel, Inc, 2005.

Hiebert, P. G. *The Gospel in Human Context: Anthropological Explorations for Contemporary Missions*. Grand Rapids: Baker Academic, 2009.

Hiro, D. *Black British, White British: A History of Race Relations in Britain*. Boulder: Paladin Press, 1992.

Hitchcock, G., and D. Hughes. *Research and the Teacher: A Qualitative Introduction to School-Based Research*. London: Routledge, 1989.

Homes, C. *John Bull's Island: Immigration and British Society 1871–1971*. Basingstoke: Macmillan Press, 1988.

Jongneel, J. B., ed. *Pentecost, Mission, and Ecumenism: Essays on Intercultural Theology-Festchrift in Honour of Professor Walter J. Hollenweger*. Studies in the Intercultural History of Christianity. Switzerland: Peter Lang, 1992.

Jorgensen, D. *Participant Observation: A Methodology for Human Studies*. London: SAGE, 1989.

Kee, A. *Domination or Liberation: The Place of Religion in Social Conflict*. London: SCM Press, 1986.

Kvale, S. *Interviews: Introduction to Qualitative Research Interviewing*. London: SAGE, 1996.

Kwiyani, H. *Sent Forth: African Missionary Work in the West*. New York: Orbis Press, 2014.

Larkin, W. J. Jr. *Culture and Biblical Hermeneutics*. Grand Rapids: Baker Book House, 1988.

Latorre, M., W. Somerville, and D. Sriskandarajah. "United Kingdom: A Reluctant Country of Immigration." *Migration Information Source*. 19 Feb 2015. http://www.migrationpolicy.org.html.

Lingenfelter, S. *Leading Cross-Culturally: Covenant Relationships for Effective Christian Leadership*. Grand Rapids: Baker Academic, 2008.

Magessa, L. *Anatomy of Inculturation: Transforming The Church in Africa*. Maryknoll: Orbis, 2004.

Mahoney, R., ed. *The Shepherd's Staff*. Burbank, CA: World [Map], 1993.

Manson, J. *Qualitative Researching, 2nd Ed*. London: Sage 2002.

Maykut, S. P., and R. E. Morehouse. *Beginning Qualitative Research: A Philosophic and Practical Guide*. London: Falmer Press, 1994.

Mbali, Z. *The Churches and Racism: A Black South African Perspective*. London: SCM Press, 1987.

Mbiti, J. S. "The Biblical Basis for Present Trends in African Theology." *International Bulletin of Mission Research* 4 no. 3 (1980): 119–24. doi.org/10.1177/239693938000400305.

———. *Bible and Theology in African Christianity*. Oxford: Oxford University Press, 1986.

McIntosh, G. L., and A. McMahan. *Being the Church in a Multi-ethnic Community*. Indianapolis: Wesleyan Publishing House, 2012.

McMillan, K., and J. Weyers. *How to Write Dissertations and Projects*. Essex: Pearson Education Limited, 2007.

Moltmann, J. *God for the Secular Society. The Public Relevance of Theology*. Minneapoli: Fortress, 1999.

Mwambazambi, K. "A Missiological Glance at South African Black Theology." *Verbum & Ecclesia* 31, no. 1 (2010): 1–7. https://doi.org/10.4102/ve.v31i1.53.

Newbigin, L. *The Gospel in a Pluralist Society*. London: SPCK, 1989.

———. *The Open Secret, an Introduction to the Theology of Mission*. Grand Rapids: Eerdmans Publishing, 1995.

Niemandt, N. Developing Missional Congregations: paper delivered at the Council for World Mission African Assembly, 2012. https://www.academia.edu/8028751.

Office of National Statistics. United Kingdom. *Immigration patterns of non-UK born populations in England and Wales*. Office of National Statistics. England: 2011

Olofinjana, I. *Reverse in Ministry and Mission: Africans in the Dark Continent of Europe*. Milton Keynes: Author House, 2010.

Olofinjana, I. ed. *Turning the Tables on Mission: Stories of Christians from the Global South in the UK*. Watford: Instant Apostle, 2013.

Olupona, Jacob. K., and Regina. Gemignani. Introduction to *African Immigrant Religions in America*, 1-26. Edited by Jacob K Olupona and Regina Gemignani. New York: New York University Press, 2007.

Owen, D. "African Migration to the UK." *A Workshop Brought to You by University of Warwick*. 2008. http://www2.warwick.ac.uk/fac/soc/crer/events/African/confp_david_owen.ppt.

Patel, R., and P. Grant. *A Time to Speak: Perspectives of Black Christians in Britain, Racial Justice and Black Theology*. Working Group, 1990.

Patton, M. Q. *How to Use Qualitative Methods in Evaluation*. Thousand Oaks, CA: SAGE, Inc, 1987.

Payne, J. D. *Strangers Next Door: Immigration, Migration and Mission*. Westmont: InterVarsity Press, 2012.

Pearson, D. G. "Race, Religiosity and Political Activism: Some Observations on West Indian Participation in Britain." *British Journal of Sociology* 29, no.3 (1978): 342. https://doi.org/10.2307/590105.

Perriman, A. "'Missio Dei' in historical perspectives, part 1," Postost (blog) January 2011. https://www.postost.net/2011/01/missio-dei-historical-perspectives-part-1.

Phillips, M., and T. *Windrush: The Irresistible Rise of Multiracial Britain*. London: HarperCollins, 1991.

Ransford, O. *Great Trek*. London, UK: John Murray Publishers Ltd, 1972.

Reddie, A. *Working Against the Grain: Reimaging Black Theology in the 21st Century*. London: Equinex, 2008.

Richebacher, W. "Missio Dei: At the Basis of Mission Theology or Wrong Path?" *International Review of Mission* 92, no. 367 (2003): 588-605.

Robinson, M., and D. Smith. *Invading Secular Space: Strategies for Tomorrow's Church*. Grand Rapids, MI: Monarch Books, 2005.

Robinson, M. *The Faith of the Unbeliever*. Grand Rapids, MI: Monarch Books, 2001.

Rooms, N. *The Faith of the English: Integrating Christ and Culture*. London: SPCK, 2011.
Roxburgh, A., and F. Romanuk. *The Missional Leader: Equipping Your Church to Reach a Changing World*. San Francisco, CA: Jossey-Bass, 2006.
Rozko, J. R., and D. Paul, eds. "The Missiological Future of Theological Education." 2011. http://The_missiological_Future_of_Theological_Education.pdf.
Schreiter, R. J. *Constructing Local Theologies*. London: SCM Press, 1985.
Shenk, W. R. *Changing Frontier Mission*. Maryknoll: Orbis Press, 2001.
Smith, C. *Calvary Chapel Distinctives*. Costa Mesa: The Word for Today Publishers, 2001.
Solomos, J. *Race and Racism in Britain*. 3rd ed. Palgrave Macmillan, 2003.
Somerville, W., Sriskandara, D and Latorre, M. "United Kingdom: A Reluctant Country of Immigration." July 2009. https://www.migrationpolicy.org/article/united-kingdom-reluctant-country-immigration.
Spencer, L. *Building a Multi-ethnic Church*. London: SPCK, 2007.
Spradley, P. *Participant Observation*. New York, NY: Holt, Rinehart & Winston, 1980.
Starkloff, C. F. "Inculturation and Cultural Systems." *Theological Studies* 55, no. 1 (1994): 66–81. https://doi.org/10.1177/004056399405500105.
Sturge, M. *Look What the Lord Has Done: An Exploration of Black Christian Faith in Britain*. Milton Keynes, England: Scripture Union, 2005.
Swinton, J., and H. Mowat. *Practical Theology and Qualitative Research*. London: SCM Press, 2006.
Tanner, K. *Theories of Culture: A New Agenda for Theology (Guides to Theological Inquiry)*. Minneapolis: Augsburg Fortress, 1997.
Taylor, S., and R. Bogdan. *Introduction to Qualitative Research Methods*. Hoboken: Wiley Press, 1984.
Taylor, J. "Rush to Judgement on UK African-Derived Churches 'Inexcusable.'" May 2006. http://www.fulcrum-anglican.org.uk/?124.
Thomas, N., ed. "*What Is Contextualisation?*" In *Readings in World Mission*. London: SPCK, 1995.
Thompson, A., and T. Keller. *Redeemer Church Planting: Redeemer City to City*, 2002.
Ukpong, J. "Towards a Holistic Approach to Inculturation Theology." *Mission Studies* 14, no. 2 (1999): 103–23.
Verstraelen, F. J., A. Camps, L. Hoedemaker, and M. Spindler. *Missiology: An Ecumenical Introduction: Texts and Contexts of Global Christianity*, Grand Rapids: Eerdmans Publishing, Co, 1995.
Vicedom, F. G. *The Mission of God: An Introduction to a Theology of Mission*. St. Louis: Concordia Publishing House, 1965.

Wan, E., ed. *Diaspora Missiology: Theory, Methodology, and Practice*. Portland: IDS, 2011.

Wijsen, F., and P. J. A. Nissen, eds. *Mission Is a Must: Intercultural Theology and the Mission of the Church*. Amsterdam: Editions Rodopi B. V. Publisher, 2002.

Wilkinson, J. L. *Church in Black and White: Black Christian Tradition in Mainstream Churches in England – A White Response and Testimony*. Wells, UK: St. Andrews Press, 1993.

Williams, L. *Caribbean Theology, Research in Religion and Family: Black Perspectives*. Bern, Switzerland: Peter Lang Publishing Group, 1994.

Winter, R. ed. *Vision for the Nations*. US Centre for World Mission. Pasadena: William Carey Library, 1995.

Yin, R. *Case Study Research: Design and Methods*. Thousand Oak. Sage Publications, 1994.

Langham Literature, with its publishing work, is a ministry of Langham Partnership.

Langham Partnership is a global fellowship working in pursuit of the vision God entrusted to its founder John Stott –

> *to facilitate the growth of the church in maturity and Christ-likeness through raising the standards of biblical preaching and teaching.*

Our vision is to see churches in the Majority World equipped for mission and growing to maturity in Christ through the ministry of pastors and leaders who believe, teach and live by the word of God.

Our mission is to strengthen the ministry of the word of God through:
- nurturing national movements for biblical preaching
- fostering the creation and distribution of evangelical literature
- enhancing evangelical theological education

especially in countries where churches are under-resourced.

Our ministry

Langham Preaching partners with national leaders to nurture indigenous biblical preaching movements for pastors and lay preachers all around the world. With the support of a team of trainers from many countries, a multi-level programme of seminars provides practical training, and is followed by a programme for training local facilitators. Local preachers' groups and national and regional networks ensure continuity and ongoing development, seeking to build vigorous movements committed to Bible exposition.

Langham Literature provides Majority World preachers, scholars and seminary libraries with evangelical books and electronic resources through publishing and distribution, grants and discounts. The programme also fosters the creation of indigenous evangelical books in many languages, through writer's grants, strengthening local evangelical publishing houses, and investment in major regional literature projects, such as one volume Bible commentaries like the *Africa Bible Commentary* and the *South Asia Bible Commentary*.

Langham Scholars provides financial support for evangelical doctoral students from the Majority World so that, when they return home, they may train pastors and other Christian leaders with sound, biblical and theological teaching. This programme equips those who equip others. Langham Scholars also works in partnership with Majority World seminaries in strengthening evangelical theological education. A growing number of Langham Scholars study in high quality doctoral programmes in the Majority World itself. As well as teaching the next generation of pastors, graduated Langham Scholars exercise significant influence through their writing and leadership.

To learn more about Langham Partnership and the work we do visit **langham.org**

www.ingramcontent.com/pod-product-compliance
Lightning Source LLC
Chambersburg PA
CBHW051541230426
43669CB00015B/2675